H. M. McGARRELL

GRAMMAR
IN THE
COMPOSITION
CLASSROOM

GRAMMAR IN THE COMPOSITION CLASSROOM

Joy M. Reid
University of Wyoming

Patricia Byrd
Georgia State University

HEINLE & HEINLE PUBLISHERS
I(T)P® *An International Thomson Publishing Company*

New York • London • Bonn • Boston • Detroit • Madrid • Melbourne • Mexico City • Paris • Singapore • Tokyo • Toronto • Washington • Albany, NY • Belmont, CA • Cincinnati, OH

The publication of *Grammar in the Composition Classroom* was directed by the members of the Newbury House ESL/EFL Publishing Team at Heinle & Heinle:

Erik Gundersen, Editorial Director
Bruno R. Paul, Market Development Director
Kristin Thalheimer, Production Services Coordinator
Ken Pratt, Associate Editor
Stanley J. Galek, Vice President and Publisher/ESL

Also participating in the publication of this program were:

Project Manager: Melissa Evans
Associate Market Development Director: Mary Sutton
Assistant Editor: Heide Kaldenbach-Montemayor
Manufacturing Coordinator: Mary Beth Hennebury
Compositor, Artist, and Editorial Production Consultant: Rosalie Herion Freese
Cover Artist: Kathleen Stuart
Cover Designer: Ha D. Nguyen

Heinle & Heinle Publishers
An International Thomson Publishing Company
Boston, Massachusetts 02116 U.S.A.

Manufactured in the United States of America

ISBN: 0-8384-7210-9

10   9   8   7   6   5   4   3   2   1

TABLE OF CONTENTS

PREFACE

As a collection of essays written by two authors, *Grammar in the Composition Classroom* covers a range of topics that we have pursued individually and jointly for a number of years. While the book was designed to allow us to write essays on selected topics, we think that the ultimate result provides readers with a combination of theoretical and practical information that can be used to motivate and guide curriculum and materials design projects. The nine essays in *Grammar in the Composition Classroom* are united by the following core ideas:

- ☐ ESL composition teachers are responsible for the growth of grammatical accuracy as well as written fluency in their students' writing.
- ☐ However, the approach to grammar taken in ESL materials, curricula, and lessons has failed teachers and their students by its focus on a decontexualized list of grammatical structures. "Grammar" and "composition/grammar" classes have all too often been simply about form without any acknowledgment of the students' cultural and linguistic backgrounds, their learning styles, and their ultimate purposes for learning to write in English. Too many textbooks and curricula present a fragmented and distorted picture of the English language and ignore how "grammar" changes when we use it for different purposes in different settings.
- ☐ We need a new approach to grammar in the composition class that builds on our current knowledge about students, culture, language learning, language teaching, and English grammar as it is used in various contexts for various communicative purposes.

The organization of *Grammar in the Composition Classroom* is based on the following leading questions:

Student-focused topics:

- ☐ What are the students like in ESL programs in the U.S.?
- ☐ How are their knowledge and skills with English like and different from those of the "international" students who have been the traditional students in English-for-Academic Purposes (EAP) ESL programs?
- ☐ How do different students approach learning and using grammar?

Grammar-in-context topics:

- ☐ What is the grammar of academic reading and writing like?
- ☐ What are the problems with the current design of the grammar elements in ESL programs for college-bound students in the U.S.?

Teaching-related topics:

□ How can teachers respond to the errors in their students' writing?

□ What can teachers learn from contrastive analysis and contrastive rhetoric to help understand their students' achievements as well as their problems?

□ How can technology help?

□ What suggestions can we make about teaching issues that haven't already been thoroughly explored by other writers?

We believe that the information in *Grammar in the Composition Class-room* will allow all ESL/EFL writing teachers and teachers-in-training to assess student needs and learning styles, to use the grammar "clusters" approach regardless of the textbook materials they use, to harness the power of technologies in the presentation of materials, and to respond to student writing, and in particular to second-language writing errors, in effective ways. *Grammar in the Composition Classroom* offers powerful and exciting answers to long-term problems in instructional design for ESL writing courses and materials; we hope that many other teachers and writers will join us in seeking to apply these ideas to the ESL writing curriculum, and we encourage you to communicate your ideas and suggestions to us as we work together to help our students become effective communicators.

JOY M. REID
University of Wyoming

PATRICIA BYRD
Georgia State University

ACKNOWLEDGMENTS

We gratefully acknowledge our reviewers, whose careful reading and sound suggestions led to a more accessible coherent text: Dana Ferris (Sacramento State University), Barbara Kroll (California State University/Northridge), and Denise Murray (San Jose State University). In particular, we appreciate the ongoing review of our manuscript by Susan Conrad (Iowa State University). We also thank the many students and authors whose work appears in this text; the student samples and professional writing samples helped us attain our objectives. We are also grateful for the input from our colleagues who have used our materials to write the *Looking Ahead* textbooks: Liz Byleen (the University of Kansas), Sharon Cavusgil (Georgia State University), Linda Robinson Fellag (Community College of Philadelphia), Christine Holten (UCLA), and Judy Marasco (Santa Monica College and UCLA). Finally, we thank our editors at Heinle & Heinle Publishers—Erik Gundersen, Ken Pratt, and Nancy Jordan—for their continued support and advice.

D1445033

GRAMMAR IN THE COMPOSITION CLASSROOM

Section I
Knowing the
the Student

Based on our experience, our discussions with teachers, and our reading in the research on second-language learning and teaching, we feel strongly that planning for the grammar in ESL curricula needs to begin not with structures but with students. Indeed, much of what has gone wrong in the teaching of grammar results from an initial focus during the planning process on forms and abstractions about forms rather than on learning, the learners, and the ultimate purposes of the learners for studying writing and the grammar of written English. Thus, we begin our discussion not with grammatical structure and systems but with ideas about students.

Chapter 1

"Eye" Learners and "Ear" Learners

IDENTIFYING THE LANGUAGE NEEDS OF INTERNATIONAL STUDENT AND U.S. RESIDENT WRITERS[1]

Joy Reid

Students differ, and the educational background differences among second-language students in ESL writing classrooms can be especially diverse. Student writing by nonnative speakers of English often contains unusual, and sometimes puzzling, language structures, and the rhetorical needs of those ESL students may also demonstrate a wide range of needs. Fortunately, many teacher resources have focused on teaching ESL writing (cf. Belcher & Braine, 1995; Brock & Walters, 1993; Fox, 1994; Leki, 1992; Kroll, 1990; Reid, 1993; Swales & Feak, 1994). The context for this discussion, however, is the differences between writing by (1) U.S. resident students for whom English is a second (or third or fourth) language and (2) students who have come from non-English-speaking countries to study at postsecondary institutions in the U.S. Generally speaking, these two groups of ESL students have learned their English differently, and so their language problems have different sources and different solutions.

Before beginning this discussion, I believe it is necessary to emphasize that just because this chapter concentrates on writing *problems* by ESL students, that need not be the most important focus of the ESL writing teacher. With structured practice, teacher intervention, and revision, student fluency and confidence in their writing skills often increase; language errors decrease, and rhetorical frameworks develop accordingly (cf. Cohen & Cavalcanti, 1990; Ferris, 1997; Jacoby et al., 1995; Li, 1996). Therefore, the concentration on ESL student error in this chapter does not rest in my belief that error is the overriding consideration for the teacher or the student, but rather that it is frequently a source of puzzlement and frustration for both.

U.S. RESIDENT ESL WRITERS

At one end of the continuum of nonnative English speakers is the refugee student whose parents have fled political upheaval for the U.S. or sent the children ahead to live with relatives or even strangers. Such students are usually orally fluent in their first language, but due to limited or interrupted schooling, they may not be fully literate in that language. These students have learned English by being suddenly immersed in the language and culture of the U.S. Specifically, they have acquired English principally through their **ears**: They listened, took in oral language (from teachers, TV, grocery clerks, friends, peers), and subconsciously began to form vocabulary, grammar, and syntax rules, learning English principally through oral trial and error.

Usually, these students have graduated from U.S. high schools, have had some tutoring—often fragmented—in ESL "pullout" programs when they first entered school, and have been accumulating U.S. culture for a number of years. They have relatively developed English oral fluency and listening skills, and they understand the slang, the pop music, the behaviors, and the "cool" clothes of the schools they attend. Their background knowledge of life in the U.S. is, in many cases, both broad and deep: Their personal experiences have made them familiar with class structures and expectations; they have opinions on current controversies and issues; and they recognize cultural references to, for instance, television programs, cartoon humor, and advertising. However, their reading skills may be hampered by limited understanding of the structures of the English language, and/or a lack of literacy, and/or lack of reading experience. Their writing displays the conversational, phonetic qualities of their "ear-based" language learning, as well as the use of their self-developed language "rules" that may, upon examination, prove to be overgeneralized or false. Below is a writing sample from a Vietnamese student that is typical of the writing done by many U.S. resident students. The in-class essay was written in response to a written text (about students having jobs while in college) during her first day in a first-year university composition course.

> The main ideas of the Article is saying that *because of* working while going to School reduces the G.P.A. of students. Some of the Reasons *while* students gettings jobs is because of Advertisements and personnal luxuries that the students needed during School.
>
> What the Article is saying is true about students getting lower grade in school, while working. But if we try to put strict rules on College curriculas and stopping Television advertising, it wouldn't help *much*. Because almost all students know *what they're doing to themselves*. Students are awared of the lower grades they're getting but *there are more to it, then* just *because* of Work. I agree, that when you get a job, your hour of studying *reduces*. After coming home from work you felt tired and only wanted to put School *words* aside. I have this experiences in the past myself. It does reduced my G.P.A., but I'm not blaming it on T.V. advertising or *anything else*.

Three general areas of error bear examination here. First, there are numerous mistakes in inflection (e.g., verb endings, plurals: note the underlined words).[2] Some of these errors might occur because the student's first language is not highly inflected, as English is, and Vietnamese does not have auxiliary verbs (*to be, to have, did/does*). Consequently, the student might question whether to add a plural *-s* to *grade* or *work*, and might not suspect that *are* is needed before *getting* in the second sentence. In addition, even if the student had been tutored in English, it's quite possible that subject-verb agreement in English may not be a fully developed concept, nor agreement between demonstrative pronouns (*this/that*) and nouns. These errors may therefore be "development" (i.e., with practice, the student will learn and produce the correct usage) or "fossilized" (i.e., the student will have to unlearn the deeply acquired and practiced error, then relearn the correct form, a more difficult and time-consuming process).

It is probable, however, that many of the verb tense errors occur more from "ear-learning" than from first-language transference. That is, because the English verb tense system is complex—a single sentence, and certainly a single paragraph, may contain several verb tenses—and because these students have listened to the language rather than studied it, they may not even recognize the mistakes. Moreover, because the mistakes they make may not have interfered with their ability to communicate orally, they may have structured rules for verb use that will seem idiosyncratic to the teacher. Think, for example, of a sentence a student in my class wrote recently: *The students are taken their time.* Then try reading the Vietnamese student's paragraph (p. 4) aloud, attending to the possibility of slurring or unstressed final syllables that are not articulated, and thinking about how this student may have learned her verbs.

Second, the student has made some vocabulary mistakes and has used some idiomatic expressions (correctly or incorrectly) that indicate her immersion in U.S. culture (see the italicized words and phrases). During a conference, this student indicated that she had never noticed the word *why*; instead, she thought that *why* and *while* were the same word (*while*) with different meanings—because the *l* in *while* is not pronounced. "Like lot of English words," she said. Idiomatic language used by this student, which might be unknown to international students who have studied English as a foreign language, include *it wouldn't help much, what they're doing to themselves*, and *anything else* (although an international student might write *any other reason*). The use of *Because of* is an oral insertion that would probably not be noticed in a conversation. Following are are some other authentic examples of U.S. resident ESL writers mixing informal idioms into their writing because, like many native English writers, they do not understand levels of formality in English writing.

□ Young **folks** usually get a better **kick out of** trips than older people.

□ which is imparative **to hang around** a large number of friends

□ they will want **to take off ASAP.**

- □ **Guys** like Neil Bush are destroying the American future.
- □ when you spend time with **a couple** of your close friends.

Finally, the seemingly arbitrary capitalization needs analysis. When I asked the student why she capitalized *Article* and *School*, she told me that she had learned that all nouns had to be capitalized. Of course, she did not know very much about nouns, but she did her best. She had later added the (correct) rule about capitalizing "I," though she found that English rule peculiar and intimidating because capitalizing "I" made her "stand out too much" in her writing.

INTERNATIONAL STUDENT WRITERS

At the opposite end of the continuum from U.S. resident ESL students are international students who have chosen to attend postsecondary schools in the U.S., in much the same way that U.S. college students spend a semester or a year "abroad." Many of these nonimmigrant, visa-holding students come from relatively privileged and well-educated backgrounds. They are literate and fluent in their first language, and they have learned English in foreign language classes. That is, they have learned English principally through their **eyes**, studying vocabulary, verb forms, and language rules.

These students know, understand, and can explain English grammar; they have usually learned grammar through methodologies that focus on rule learning. Often their reading skills are substantial. Usually, however, their listening and oral skills are hampered by lack of experience, nonnative English-speaking teachers, and the culture shock that comes from being immersed in a foreign culture, the language of which sounds like so much "noise," so different from their studied English language. Their writing skills are often also limited because their prior English education has not provided opportunities for composed writing, preferring instead exercises in written grammar or answering reading questions in single sentences (Leki, 1992). Below is an e-mail from a native Spanish speaker who has spent some time in the past studying in the U.S., but who is now in his native country, Chile.

Dear Rolf Turner:
Thanks you in asking my question.
   In memorian I am study models of regression and multivariate**s** data for my **tessis academic** deductive in productivity and quality *"just and time"* in **management industrial**, (my carrer) in complexity with n variables **incidents operationals** and costs, this new study is cassual, and important help for our country chile and United States of America in potential**s** **management strategic**. Before studied T.U. industrial control my investigation in data standars in **control of qualyty final** in cocesa (cobre cerrillos s.a. chile) associate with Phelps Dodge in EEUU. I am not expert in statisticals but know ideas in mejority **methods productivity multivariates** in industries.

We might investigate three major areas of language error in this sample. First, interference from this writer's first language is visible in the false cognates: words that are close (but not exact) in meaning and used in both Spanish and English (underlined in the paragraph). For example, *en memorian* means *to remind you* in Spanish. In addition, the boldfaced phrases indicate the use of Spanish word order, in which (1) the adjective follows the noun (*qualyty final* instead of *final quality*), and (2) adjectives in Spanish are appropriately inflected (*operationals incidents*, a plural adjective for the plural noun).

Next, the structure "*Before studied . . .*" also demonstrates the transference of Spanish rules into English. Spanish allows a subject not to be named in a sentence if that subject is understood. Finally, the writer gives three examples of English use that demonstrate a lack of understanding about U.S. idioms and culture. He uses *asking* for *answering*; instead of writing *Thank you for* or *Thanks to you*, he writes *Thanks you*; and he attempts an idiom (*just in time*)—which may well be an "ear error" gained during his earlier U.S. studies.

CAVEATS: BETWEEN THE EXTREMES

Between the two ends of the continuum are immigrant students whose families have chosen to come to the U.S., and/or whose education in their first language has been substantial, and/or whose first language may not have a written language, and/or who may have studied English as a foreign language for a relatively limited period of time before they arrived in the U.S. Also along the continuum are international students who have come to the U.S. to study because they have not been successful in their own educational systems, and/or whose study of both their first language and English has been limited.

There are also differences within the differences: parental attitudes toward education that include the belief that women should not attend college; a prior education system that values rote memorization and/or teacher-centered classrooms in which students do not participate orally; a culture that values reflective thought or cooperation above the analysis and competition valued in many U.S. classrooms. And there are individual student differences in personality, learning styles, learning strategies, and motivation (Reid, 1993, 1995).

Finally, more caveats about this chapter. First, I need to point out that although this chapter focuses on linguistic and rhetorical writing problems, some ESL student writing will equal and surpass writing by native English speakers (NES). Many ESL writers will have little need of English language development; their writing problems may differ from NES writing problems in type, but the quality or sophistication of the writing may well be comparable.

I also need to distinguish between generalization and stereotype. In this chapter, I discuss two general kinds of students; I write about typical problems of students from different language and cultural backgrounds. However, I am keenly aware that while many stereotypes begin with a grain of truth, individual students differ widely in their educational backgrounds, their unique approaches to learning, and their levels of proficiency. Therefore, it is essential to approach each student as an individual, and to identify each student's needs.

INITIAL IDENTIFICATION

For the teacher of an ESL writer, discovering whether that student is a U.S. resident or an international student is the first step in identifying the student's needs and formulating an assistance plan. The process is simple: Ask the student for background information so that appropriate resources and support for the student can be recommended. Sample questions that might be asked via a written survey or an oral interview (whichever is best for the student's English language proficiency and comfort level) include those listed in Table 1.1.

Table 1.1: Sample Survey/Interview Questions to Identify ESL Student Writer's Language Background

1. Is English your second (or third or fourth) language? _____
   □ What is your first language? _____
   □ List your previous schooling
      • in your first language: grade _____ through grade _____
                                 total years _____
      • in English: grade _____ through grade _____
                                 total months/years _____
2. Did you graduate from a U.S. high school? Yes _____ No _____
3. If the answer to the last question is

NO	YES
(*Usually* indicates an international student)	(*Usually* indicates a U.S. resident)
• TOEFL score _____	• high school attended _____
• TOEFL section scores:	• graduated in what year _____
listening _____	• ESL classes taken
structure/written expression _____	_____ hours each week
reading _____	in grades _____ to _____
TWE _____	• was your first language schooling
• full-time English language study:	interrupted?
Yes _____ No _____	Yes _____ No _____
If yes, where? _____	If yes, how long? _____
how long? _____	• fluency in first language (high, medium, or low)
	speaking & listening _____
	reading _____
	writing _____

Table 1.2: Sample Follow-Up Questions for ESL Student Writers				
1. How did you learn English?	a lot	some	a little	none
• studying grammar				
• listening to English speakers				
• practicing with language tapes				
• reading English literature				
• watching U.S. movies				
• watching U.S. television				
• other: _____				
2. How would you evaluate your English language proficiency?	excellent	very good	average	poor
• speaking				
• listening				
• reading				
• writing				
• grammar				

It may also be important to discover more background information about the ESL writers. Follow-up questions for resident and international students alike are included in Table 1.2.

U.S. RESIDENT ESL WRITERS

□ INVESTIGATION

Resident students may provide more complete information if the surveys are administered orally, allowing the students to use their English speaking proficiency. Results of the surveys will differ according to students' prior experiences. For example, a U.S. resident who has studied several years in U.S. public schools, and who has had constant language support through an excellent ESL program, will probably have the necessary skills to succeed in college or university work with minimal external support. In contrast, the writing of a student who has attended only the last year or two of U.S. high school, along with some classroom study of English prior to arrival, may have a combination of international and resident errors that make solutions to writing problems more complex.

Moreover, resident ESL writers who are fluent and literate in their first languages will acquire written English more easily than students who are not fully literate in their first languages. And students whose educations have been interrupted (by war, flight, refugee camps, and the like) may also be older and may have problems external to language learning that impact their ability to learn more English. Finally, students who have attended U.S. schools for a significant period of time but whose formal ESL education has been spotty are often doubly disadvantaged. Orally fluent, they have developed (perhaps unconsciously) language "rules," some of which must be identified, unlearned, and relearned if they are to become successful academic writers (see Chapter 8 in this text for more specific information). In the meantime, they are saddled with prior experiences of failure, and their reading as well as their writing skills may be limited.

□ ASSISTANCE

U.S. resident students have many resources for assistance on college or university campuses. First, they have direct access to federally funded student programs on the campus for help and tutoring (and perhaps test accommodation) in writing, reading, and math. The student (or the teacher) can contact those offices for short- and long-term assistance, and the teacher can require that the students seek this assistance. Often the support offered by these offices provides the necessary scaffolding and encouragement that resident students need to achieve successful learning experiences.

It is possible that the campus personnel are not adequately trained to help ESL writers, but that training is available through the college or university intensive English language program, the English Department, or through written materials. The books and articles in Table 1.3 will prove helpful resources for teachers and tutors. In addition, teachers or tutors who need information about the rules of English grammar might consult the resources in Table 1.4.

INTERNATIONAL STUDENTS

□ INVESTIGATION

In contrast to U.S. residents, many international students can provide the teacher with actual data that will help analyze their writing problems. Most will have taken the TOEFL (Test of English as a Foreign Language), an examination that is required for admission at most U.S. colleges and universities. At present the test is a multiple-choice examination designed and administered world-wide each month by the Educational Testing Service (ETS), the same educational corporation that administers the SAT, GMAT, and LSAT. An overall TOEFL score of 550 or above often indicates that the student is ready for full-time postsecondary work; a score below 500 usually indicates that the student should be taking intensive English language courses.

Table 1.3: Resources for Teachers and Tutors

□ Bates, Linda; Lane, Janet; and Lange, Ellen. 1993. *Writing Clearly: Responding to ESL Compositions*. Boston: Heinle & Heinle.

□ Carson, Joan, and Leki, Ilona. (Eds.). 1993. *Reading in the Composition Classroom*. Boston: Heinle & Heinle.

□ Connor, Ulla, and Kaplan, Robert B. 1987. *Writing Across Languages: Analysis of L2 Text*. Reading, MA: Addison-Wesley.

□ Fox, Helen. 1994. *Listening to the World: Cultural Issues in Academic Writing*. Urbana, IL: National Council of Teachers of English.

□ Johnson, Donna, and Roen, Duane. 1989. *Richness in Writing: Empowering ESL Students*. New York: Longman.

□ Kroll, Barbara. 1990. The rhetoric/syntax split: Designing curriculum for ESL students. *Journal of Basic Writing 9* (1), 40–55.

□ Kroll, Barbara. 1991. Teaching writing in the ESL context. In *Teaching English as a Second or Foreign Language* (2nd Ed.) (Marianne Celce-Murcia, Ed.), pp. 245–263. Boston: Heinle & Heinle.

□ Leki, Ilona. 1992. *Understanding ESL Writers. A Reference for Teachers*. New York: St. Martin's Press.

□ Li, Xiao-Ming. 1996. *"Good Writing" in Cross-Cultural Context*. Albany: State University of New York.

□ Reid, Joy. 1993. *Teaching ESL Writing*. Englewood Cliffs, NJ: Prentice Hall-Regents.

□ Scarcella, Robin. 1990. *Teaching Language Minority Students in the Multicultural Classroom*. Englewood Cliffs, NJ: Prentice Hall.

Table 1.4: English Grammar Resources

□ Byrd, Patricia, and Benson, Beverly. 1989. *Improving the Grammar of Written English: The Editing Process*. Belmont, CA: Wadsworth.

□ Byrd, Patricia, and Benson, Beverly. 1992. *Applied English Grammar*. Boston: Heinle & Heinle.

□ Celce-Murcia, M., and Larsen-Freeman, D. 1983. *The Grammar Book: An ESL/EFL Teacher's Course*. Rowley, MA: Newbury House.[a]

□ Frodesen, Jan, and Eyring, Janet. 1993. *Grammar Dimensions: Form, Meaning, and Use* (Book Four). (Diane Larsen-Freeman, Series Ed.) Boston: Heinle and Heinle.

□ Master, P. 1996. *Systems in English Grammar: An Introduction for Language Teachers*. Englewood Cliffs, NJ: Prentice-Hall Regents.

[a]A second edition of *The Grammar Book* is scheduled for 1998.

TOEFL section scores can also be quite revealing. The three section scores on the TOEFL indicate general proficiency in listening, grammar, and reading skills; those scores are reported in double digits, but by adding a zero to a section score, you can compare it with the overall TOEFL score. For example, a section score of 55 → 550 indicates that a student has adequate language proficiency in that language skill. However, while students from different language backgrounds may have similar overall TOEFL scores, their section scores may differ, indicating potential problems in U.S. classes. For instance, often Asian students will score well on grammar and reading (e.g., 58 → 580), but less well on listening skills (e.g., 45 → 450). These students may be able to keep up with university reading assignments, but they may have problems understanding lectures or working with other students. In contrast, Arabic students may score higher on the listening section and lower in the reading section; these students may seem fluent during class discussions, but they may have substantial problems completing reading assignments. Table 1.5 summarizes TOEFL examination scores.

Several times a year, the Test of Written English (TWE) is added to the TOEFL exam; the TWE is a direct test of student writing and is evaluated holistically by experienced writing teachers at large scoring sessions held in California. The maximum score is 6; a score of 4.5 or better usually means that the student can do post-secondary written work.[3] Scores lower than 4 suggest that those students may need intensive work in U.S. academic writing. Unfortunately, many international students will not have a TWE score, either because it is not offered on every TOEFL

Table 1.5: TOEFL Examination Scores

Typical Admission Scores at U.S. Colleges and Universities[a]

	Undergraduate Students	Graduate Students
Unconditional Admission	525	550
Provisional Admission	500	525

Sample TOEFL Section Scores

Listening	55 → 550	(Add a zero to com-
Grammar	50 → 500	pare with overall
Reading	45 → 450	TOEFL score)
Overall TOEFL Score (average of three section scores) → **500**		

Test of Written English (TWE)

☐ administered with the TOEFL exam several times a year

☐ scored from 1 to 6 (including 1.5, 2.5, etc.)

☐ typical admission TWE score: 4 to 4.5

[a]The Educational Testing Service does not provide recommended admission scores for the TOEFL. Rather, it encourages admissions officers and department faculty to set those scores at individual campuses.

examination or because they chose not to take it. And many postsecondary institutions still do not require the TWE as a viable admissions tool.

Another variable in international students' preparation may be attendance in an intensive English language program, either prior to their arrival in the U.S. or in a U.S.-based program. If students have studied ESL in the U.S., they may have encountered the rhetoric of academic English writing and so may be relatively proficient in presenting written ideas; the concepts of topic sentence, supporting detail, and essay structure may be familiar to them. For students who have studied English prior to their arrival, even intensively, the rhetorical principles of academic writing may not be information that they have encountered, much less practiced (Leki, 1992).

□ ASSISTANCE

Generally speaking, international students are not eligible for federal assistance although some colleges and universities do not discriminate (or simply do not know the differences between the two types of students). However, international students who have had prior experience with an intensive English language program on or near the campus have access to previous teachers in that program, and those teachers have knowledge of other campus options. In addition, because of their prior English language study, international students are usually capable of using a handbook or a dictionary to check their errors and to expand their knowledge of English grammar and mechanics. However, because handbooks for native speakers of English do not address ESL problems effectively, I suggest the resources in Table 1.6.

Table 1.6: ESL Handbooks[a]

□ Asher, Allen. 1993. *Think about Editing: A Grammar Editing Guide for ESL Writers.* Boston: Heinle & Heinle.

□ Byrd, Patricia, and Benson, Beverly. 1994. *Problem/Solution: A Reference for ESL Writers.* Boston: Heinle & Heinle.

□ Fox, Len. 1992. *Focus on Editing: A Grammar Workbook for Advanced Writers.* New York: Longman.

□ Heinle & Heinle. 1996. *The Newbury House Dictionary of American English.*

□ Lane, Janet, and Lange, Ellen. 1993. *Writing Clearly: An Editing Guide.* Boston: Heinle & Heinle.

□ Raimes, Ann. 1992. *Troublespots: An Editing Guide for Students* (2nd ed.) Englewood Cliffs, NJ: Prentice-Hall Regents.

---

[a]Of course, the resources for teachers and students listed in Tables 1.3 and 1.4 are also relevant for teachers of international students and those students themselves, and the handbooks listed here (Table 1.6) may be used with success by some U.S. resident students.

ALL ESL STUDENT WRITERS

Other campus resources that are available to all ESL student writers (and usually assist students free of charge) include the campus writing center (or writing laboratory). The writing center is a valuable resource that will support ESL writers throughout their postsecondary careers, so students should be encouraged to investigate and use this resource. Moreover, paid tutors, often accessible through the international student services/education office, the intensive English language program, or the MA TESL/TEFL program, can provide necessary support for ESL writers.

NES friends can also serve as editors and language informants (Healy and Bosher, 1992). I advise my ESL students about appropriate approaches to such assistance:

☐ Never expect a friend to write, revise, or rewrite your paper.
☐ Sit with your NES friend and learn from him/her.
  • Identify specific problems.
  • Ask specific questions.
  • Draw conclusions and learn!
☐ Ask politely for assistance; don't demand.
☐ Offer a friendly trade, such as
  • pizza for proofreading, or
  • sharing language and cultural information.
☐ Give thanks with a smile.

It is, of course, possible for ESL students to abuse the help from friends; teachers may question how much of the draft actually "belongs" to the student. While the issue is real, the pedagogical aim is valid, and safeguards can be instituted to check for ESL student involvement:

☐ briefly conference with both the ESL student and the NES friend near the beginning of the semester to ensure that both fully understand the process;
☐ assign frequent in-class writing (formal and informal) to discern whether the ESL student is actually learning;
☐ the student can be required to write regular memos to the teacher describing the friendly tutoring sessions, identifying and evaluating the changes made, and
☐ journal/learning log entries analyzing what was learned during the tutoring sessions;
☐ the student should write a memo on the final draft that describes the changes made from previous drafts.

Table 1.7: ESL Writing Textbooks

☐ Leki, Ilona. 1995. *Academic Writing: Exploring Processes and Strategies* (2nd Ed.). New York: St. Martin's Press.

☐ Mlynarczyk, Rebecca, and Haber, Steven. 1996. *In Our Own Words: A Guide with Readings for Student Writers*. New York: St. Martin's Press.

☐ Reid, Joy. 1988. *The Process of Composition* (2nd Ed.). Englewood Cliffs, NJ: Prentice Hall-Regents.

☐ Spack, Ruth. 1996. *Guidelines: A Cross-Cultural Reading/Writing Text* (2nd Ed.). New York: St. Martin's Press.

☐ Swales, J,. and Feak, C. (1994). *Academic Writing for Graduate Students: A course for Nonnative Speakers of English*. Ann Arbor: University of Michigan Press.

☐ Weissberg, Robert, and Buker, Suzanne. 1990. *Writing Up Research: Experimental Research Report Writing for Students of English*. Englewood Cliffs, NJ: Prentice Hall-Regents.

Finally, for the many resident and international student writers whose rhetorical background is limited, the resources cited in Table 1.7 can help. First-year composition textbooks for NES writers may not address the differences in rhetorical presentation of materials between ESL students' cultural/educational backgrounds and U.S. academic prose. However, there are materials written for ESL writers that explain U.S. academic rhetoric and provide adequate practice for the students.

CONCLUSION

The discussion in this chapter does not mean to suggest that ESL student writers are any less capable cognitively than other postsecondary students. Indeed, learning and using a second language, attending and participating in classes in another language, and writing for an audience with different linguistic, rhetorical, and cultural expectations are extremely challenging tasks. Moreover, ESL students are not typical "basic writers"; for example, many international students' educational backgrounds have provided them with substantial grammar and reading skills, and they are often successful students who have fine coping skills. They need information and practice in specific areas of academic prose such as content and organization. Many U.S. residents have only limited (and often incorrect) ideas about English grammar and written communication. Yet they may have significant cultural background from their prior school experiences, and their bicultural, bilingual lives make them unique.

For both of these groups, growth and experience in their academic writing should not include banishment to workbook exercises or denigration by teachers who are irritated by missing articles. Instead, ESL writers—immigrant and international students—need specific linguistic and rhetorical information, careful analysis of their writing weaknesses by professionals in the field of teaching ESL, and consistent support and resources to improve their skills.

One suggestion, supported by Barbara Kroll (1990), Faye Peitzman and George Gadda (1994), and Linda Hirsch (1996), is that these two general groups of students be separated not only for "remediation" but also in the college or university classrooms. Hirsch's students themselves discuss the problems involved in mainstreaming ESL students with native-English speakers: content instructors who have had minimal exposure to second-language learners, the limited opportunity for student discussion (and thereby peer support) in a teacher-centered lecture course, lack of familiarity with the discourse community, and, often, substantial reading problems. Hirsch recommends collaborative learning models, adjunct teaching courses, and support groups for ESL students who have been mainstreamed. Peitzman and Gadda go further: They firmly support the need for "sheltered" first-year English classes—and courses across the disciplines—for language minority students, in which ESL students are taught by instructors who are experienced and empathetic with the needs and problems of ESL students. Kroll faces the "ear learner"/"eye learner" dichotomy squarely: She recommends sheltered first-year composition classes that are divided into "+ syntax / – rhetoric" students (often international students) and "– syntax / + rhetoric" students (often U.S. residents).

Finally, teachers and students must expect that improvement in ESL writing will be neither quick nor easy. Writing in a second language is an even more complex set of cognitive tasks than writing as a native speaker. Incorrect grammar "rules" that have been habituated must be unlearned; rhetorical expectations of a lifetime must be changed, at least for the time the student presents ideas in written English; audience expectations (cultural, rhetorical, contextual, and linguistic) must be identified and fulfilled. In short, time, effort, understanding, energy, patience, trust . . . without these qualities, both teachers and ESL student writers will be frustrated.

NOTES

1. This chapter is a developed and extended version of a previously published article for postsecondary non-English faculty across the curriculum: "Which Nonnative Speaker? Differences Between International Students and U.S. Resident (Language Minority) Students," in *What's This Language in My Classroom? ESL Across the Curriculum* (David Sigsbee, Bruce Speck, & Bruce Mylath, Eds.). San Francisco: Jossey-Bass, Inc., in press.

2. Many researchers differentiate between the terms "error" and "mistake": The first is the result of lack of understanding or misunderstanding of the grammar structure, while the latter is a "performance error" that students may well be able to correct if they monitor for errors. In this chapter, I use the two interchangeably because (1) it is often difficult to judge the intention or source of an error and (2) when a teacher focuses on students' reasons for their mistakes/errors, the result is revision of those errors, whether or not they were originally understood by the student.

3. For more information about the TOEFL and the TWE, ask the admissions office at your college or university, or write to the TOEFL Program, Educational Testing Service, Princeton, NJ 08541.

Chapter 2

Learning Styles and Grammar Teaching in the Composition Classroom

Joy Reid

The field of learning styles is complex: so many classifications, so many issues, so many instruments. Yet the basic concepts are simple:

- □ students learn in different ways
- □ teachers often teach as they learned best
- □ learning about learning styles helps both teachers and students.

Generally, learning styles are defined as "an individual's natural, habitual, and preferred way(s) of absorbing, processing, and retaining new information and skills" (Reid, 1995, p. viii). They are a combination of nature (e.g., age, gender, dominant brain hemisphere) and nurture (e.g., prior experiences, cultures, educational systems, social values). Moreover, each learning style exists on a continuum: A student may be, for example, more or less tactile, more or less group oriented, more or less reflective. Learners often have several styles that they prefer, and usually there are some styles that do not "work" for them at all.

For students, a broad understanding of learning environments and learning styles can allow them to take control of their learning; for teachers, this understanding provides the knowledge necessary to modify grammar lessons in small ways that will accommodate basic differences in their students' learning styles. Specifically, after providing some background information, I have listed various types of grammar exercises and analyzed the learning style strengths they appeal to.[1]

BACKGROUND

Whenever I see broad generalizations about teaching, I am suspicious. Whereas some classroom activities can be used to build student skills and fluency regardless of individual learning styles, and to assist students in extending their learning styles, often activities are designed without student learning styles in mind. In Table 2.1 are several generalizations (italicized) taken from one of the best

---

**Table 2.1: Quotations from Teacher-Trainers
About Teaching Grammar and Writing**

□ *If the purpose of any activity is simply development of fluency and confidence, an **overt** focus on grammatical form is **not** called for.*
What about field-independent, analytic students who learn best by analyzing discrete patterns sequentially?

□ *The first steps in teaching reading and writing skills in a foreign or second-language learning classroom center around the **mechanics** of those two skills.*
What about global, holistic, inductive students who learn most effectively by taking in the "forest," not the "trees"?

□ *. . . interaction with native speakers provided input that sometimes leads to language learning, but **interaction** guaranteed neither grammaticality nor idiomaticity.*
What about active, auditory learners, who choose to learn by trial-and-error, and who can develop both grammaticality and idiomaticity by interacting with native speakers?

□ *. . . have students work in **pairs**, with each student reading aloud his/her partner's paper; the writer can ask the reader to stop at any time to make corrections. The rationale for this technique is that some students are better able to **hear** their errors than to see them.*
What about individual, visual learners for whom reading aloud publicly is a painful experience?

□ *Second-language acquisition occurs when the learner receives comprehensible input, not when the learner is **memorizing** vocabulary or completing **grammar exercises**.*
What about the abstract, analytic student who was successful in her/his prior educational experiences that focused on memorization and grammar exercises?

□ *There appears to be a real danger of leading the students too rapidly into the "creative aspects of language use," in that if successful communication is encouraged and rewarded for its own sake, the effect seems to be one of rewarding about the same time the **incorrect communication** strategies seized upon . . .*
What about the global, risk-taking students who learn best, and perhaps most accurately, when they behave "creatively"?

□ *Learners should be encouraged to **tolerate uncertainty**, to venture informed guesses [about grammar rules].*
What about left–brained, reflective students who prefer to consider options and not to guess?

teacher-preparation books on the market (and since they are taken out of context, they are perhaps not so "baldly" intentioned), and I have boldfaced words in each quotation. My comments about learning styles are indented.[2] Please note that I have observed similar generalizations in much of the literature designed to train ESL teachers.

Currently, the move in U.S. elementary schools to more cooperative, whole-language, learning-centered classrooms has begun to change the face of teaching and learning. However, U.S. college and university systems still value the visual, analytic, field-independent student who prefers sequential, linear lessons and individual learning. In addition, students who "participate" in class (especially by asking and answering questions and by entering into verbal class discussions), and who give, and support, individual opinions, are considered successful students.

However, other cultures value different learning characteristics. Many Asian classroom teachers, for example, find such "participation" rude and insulting; both teachers and students value reflection (and perhaps accuracy) over impulsive comments (and perhaps fluency). The individualism (sometimes called "creativity") so prized in the U.S. educational system prevents the harmony and collective wisdom so highly valued by Asian educators (see Oxford, 1997). In contrast, many Hispanic educators may value cooperation far more than competition in the classroom, and collaboration far more than individualism. Predominantly Hispanic classes in the U.S. often function most successfully for the students if they are able to communicate continually with one another (noisily at times) and collaborate on all work (perhaps even tests) (see Dunn & Griggs, 1995).

Because of U.S. cultural diversity, it is important for teachers in U.S. colleges and universities to understand that within any class of students, and particularly within the diverse classroom of native English speakers and ESL students, many preferred learning styles exist. Consequently, in order to provide an atmosphere that allows all students to perform at their highest potential, teachers must become sensitive to those differences and plan lessons that accommodate those preferences. In addition, students must learn to identify their learning style preferences, analyze their learning strengths and weaknesses, and experiment with expanding their learning repertoires so that they can benefit from a variety of teaching styles without having to depend on their teachers to change or adjust their teaching styles. At the most basic level, teachers might consider the learning styles and possible modifications of their lesson plans as seen in Table 2.2.

Most students will learn better and be more comfortable if they are exposed to the learner-centered, learner-responsible philosophy that is fundamental to the application of learning style information to teaching. Therefore, teachers should spend valuable classroom time early in the course to (1) discuss learning styles with their students and (2) provide opportunities for students to identify their individual learning styles. Second, students should understand the reasons for the differences in activities their teachers plan. Of course, if teachers initially provide students the opportunity to learn about their individual learning styles, referring to ways the activities and lesson objectives appeal to a variety of learning

**Table 2.2: Learning Styles and
Lesson Plan Modifications**

LEARNING STYLE OPPOSITES	LESSON PLANNING
☐ **group** (collaborative, field dependent) learners who prefer to learn by interacting with others *versus* **individual** (goal-setting, independent) learners who learn best alone	☐ some group/cooperative work and some individual work during the same class; or let some students work alone during group work
☐ **auditory** (often field dependent, global) learners who prefer to learn with their ears *versus* **visual** (often field independent, analytic) learners who learn best through their eyes	☐ *writing* assignments and directions as well as *speaking* them; coupling class or small-group discussion with note-taking and reading/writing activities; using handouts/overheads with key terms for visual learners
☐ **concrete** learners who prefer working with others in practical, hands-on activities *versus* **abstract** learners who learn best alone, through theory and planning	☐ coupling physical activities like role playing and model building with puzzles and problem-solving activities
☐ **reflective** learners who prefer to systematically examine options and think about solutions before presenting them *versus* **active** learners who learn best by risk taking and immediate, practical trial-and-error	☐ coupling activities that require time (e.g., "read, summarize, and be prepared to talk about . . .") with activities that provide opportunities for immediate student feedback and experimentation

styles is easy. Later in the course, asking students to (1) identify the way(s) an activity "works" in terms of various learning styles, (2) suggest modifications of activities for different learning styles, and (3) discuss learner strategies they use fosters student reflection upon and implementation of their learning strengths and furthers student autonomy in learning.

In addition, students should assume the responsibility of evaluating class activities and assignments in light of their learning styles (e.g., at the simplest level, *interesting/not interesting, useful/not useful, easy/not easy*). In this way, the teacher receives consistent feedback on lessons and tasks, the classroom becomes more learner-centered, and students become more responsible for their own learning. Finally, if teachers give students choices for presentation of their assignments (e.g., writing a book report for the teacher or reporting orally to the class or preparing a poster for the class), students become more aware of their learning strengths and more independent, autonomous learners.

Of course, in reality, students must learn to cope with a variety of learning (and teaching) styles if they are to be effective learners. Many U.S. college and university instructors do not give their students choices, and most are not sensitive to individual learning styles. In fact, students with the greatest style flexibility (i.e., the ability to adapt to a variety of learning styles) are often the most successful learners. As a consequence, teachers should, in addition to becoming sensitive to their students' styles, encourage students to experiment with styles that they are less comfortable with, to "flex" their styles in order to become more adaptable learners.

LEARNING STYLES AND GRAMMAR IN THE COMPOSITION CLASSROOM

During the last decade, interest in learning styles in the ESL/EFL writing classroom has increased. Teachers may, for example, use learning styles as the content for a chapter or a module in the ESL composition course, asking students to complete a learning styles survey, then to summarize, analyze, and evaluate the results of the survey in writing (Reid, 1996). Students are also encouraged to experiment with different composing strategies that do not parallel their preferred styles: Analytic learners may, for instance, try brainstorming or freewriting with a group; global, field-dependent learners may try individual outlining as they plan their writing. Activities in the learning-styles-sensitive writing classroom may accommodate many styles: some group discussion, some role playing, some individual "desk work."

Not as much attention has been focused on using a learning-styles approach when grammar is integrated into the composition classroom. Yet students still have unique sets of learning styles. When making decisions about teaching grammar as part of a composition class, teachers need to think about

- □ the students' current stage of second-language acquisition
- □ the grammatical characteristics of the discourse being studied
- □ the item(s) of grammar to be focused on in a particular lesson, and
- □ the learning styles employed by the students.

To illustrate how such a process could occur, I have selected passages to represent three important discourse types that students are certain to encounter in their academic reading and writing. For each passage, I have chosen one major grammatical feature from the cluster that is characteristic of that discourse type,[3] and I have provided a set of grammar activities, along with an analysis of the learning styles that are most clearly accommodated by the exercises.

In a composition textbook, the grammar exercises might be found in several different places: two or three that immediately follow each authentic reading sample, and others in summary exercises at the end of the chapter. In addition, exercises in later chapters in the composition textbook may refer to the original reading sample (i.e., spiraling and reviewing), and the textbook may have a "grammar appendix," in which the actual rules for use and additional exercises may be found.

In the following three reading samples, specific grammar structures are underlined and/or boldfaced for discussion in the composition classroom.[4] Each sample is categorized according to its discourse function (see Byrd's explanation of these functions in Chapters 3 and 4 of this text), and each underlined/boldfaced language function is common to that discourse type. (Note that the act of reading itself and the underlined/boldfaced grammar structures appeal most to text-visual, analytic learners.)

Following each sample is a table with exercises that focus on the underlined/boldfaced grammar structure. To the right of the first exercise, I have labeled the learning style(s) most clearly accommodated by the exercise. Table 2.3 gives the learning styles considered and the abbreviations I use.

Table 2.3: Learning Style Category Abbreviations			
Field Dependent	**FD**	Picture Visual	**pV**[a]
Field Independent	**FI**	Text Visual	**tV**
Reflective	**R**	Auditory	**Au**
Active	**Ac**	Kinesthetic	**K**
		Tactile	**T**
Concrete	**C**		
Abstract	**Ab**	Group	**G**
		Individual	**I**

[a]Although no validated research has distinguished between ESL/EFL students' preferential differences between picture-visual (visual-verbal) and text-visual (visual-nonverbal), I have included both in this list because I have found in my teaching experience that they do indeed differ.

■ ■ ■ SAMPLE 1

Looking Ahead, **Low-Intermediate Level, "Describing" Chapter**

College Catalog Description

The Early Childhood Education program upgrades the knowledge and skills **of students** interested in working **in a variety of programs for preschool children**. Such workers need a sound theoretical foundation **in principles of human growth** and development **from prenatal to school-age children**, as well as a functional understanding **of programs** appropriate **to the young child**. Students have practical field experience in diagnosing settings, such as parent cooperatives, day care settings, family day care, kindergartens, and nursery schools, and **in agencies** providing special services **for preschool children**.

Table 2.4:
Prepositions and Prepositional Phrase Exercises

EXERCISES	LEARNING STYLES
A. *Discussion Assignment*	
Share information that you have about education for preschool children with your class. For example, what do you remember learning before you began formal school? How do day-care facilities help with preschool education?	Au, G, FD, C
As other students share their information, listen for their use of prepositions and prepositional phrases. Write at least three that you hear in your Learner's Notebook.	Au, T, FI, I, C
B. *Grammar Analysis of Student Writing*	
Read the last paragraph you wrote. Make a list of any errors with prepositions that were marked by your instructor. Did you find the same mistake more than once? What kinds of mistakes did you make: word choice? spelling? What will you do about these errors?	tV, T, F, I, C
	R, Ab, I, tV
C. *Small-Group Work*	
With a small group of classmates, look over the front page of today's newspaper. Make a list of all the prepositional phrases that you find in (a) the headlines and (b) two articles. Which prepositions were used most often?	G, Au, Ac, T, C
With your small group, draw a picture that demonstrates the way(s) in which the two most "popular" prepositions were used.	G, pV, K, FD, Ab
D. *Pair Work*	
With a partner, use a good English-English dictionary to look up the meaning of *of*.	Au, tV, C, G
□ Read the dictionary definition(s) of *of* out loud to your partner and ask your partner to give one example of each definition out loud, OR	Au, tV, C, FD, G
□ With your partner, write the definition(s) of *of* and write one example for each definition.	T, Au, tV, G, C
Then, talk with your partner about ways you might use that dictionary information: How can that information get out of the dictionary and into your own writing?	R, Ab, Au, G

Sample 1, a passage from a college catalog description of an education program, has many of the features expected in informational prose:

- □ present tense verbs
- □ complex noun phrase structures
- □ complex sentences
- □ frequent prepositional phrases

Because of the importance of prepositional phrases in this type of discourse—especially as adverbials and post-modifiers of nouns—I selected them as the focus of the series of exercises in Table 2.4.

■ ■ ■ *SAMPLE 2*

Looking Ahead, High-Intermediate Level, "Explaining" Chapter

Newspaper Article, "New Malady Hits Computer Users: 'Webaholism'"

COLLEGE PARK, MD — Lisa Bowes **had** a wonderful life as a student at Humboldt State University in California.

Every day she **chatted** with her pal Johan from Sweden. She**'d discuss** movies and her favorite hobby, quilting, with girlfriends from California. And, for about a year, she **flirted** with her special friend Jason from Pennsylvania.

There **was** only one problem. Bowes **had** hardly a friend on campus.

Instead, she **spent** long hours alone each day **typing** at a keyboard to ghostly "on-line" buddies. "I'd **spend** hours and hours . . . and hours on the computer," she **recalls**.

The short narrative in sample 2 is used to introduce a newspaper article on excessive use of the Internet, termed "webaholism" in the article. Like other such discourse, this little story uses

- □ past tense verbs
- □ time words
- □ proper nouns
- □ time phrases
- □ personal pronouns

Students need to learn about this use of narrative—giving examples that serve both to provide concrete illustration of a more abstract idea and to provide a "hook" of interesting material to draw readers into an article. In order to be able to read and write such material, students have to be able to handle verbs that show up regularly in personal experience and narrative examples:

- □ simple past tense
- □ past version of modal auxiliaries
- □ past perfect
- □ past progressive

The exercises in Table 2.5 give students with different learning styles the opportunity to practice their knowledge of these verb tenses.

Table 2.5:
Verb Tenses in Narrative Prose

EXERCISES	LEARNING STYLES
A. *Multiple-Choice Exercise (Pairs)*	**tv, G, T, R, FD**

With a partner, circle the best answer to complete each of the following statements:

1. When communicating a past experience, which verb form would you expect to use most frequently?
   - a. the simple past tense
   - b. the past progressive form
   - c. the past perfect form
   - d. the present perfect form

2. Which verb form(s) involve(s) subject-verb agreement?
   - a. the simple past tense
   - b. the past progressive form
   - c. the past perfect form
   - d. the present perfect form

3. Which verb form(s) usually need(s) two actions to express the appropriate meaning?
   - a. the simple past tense
   - b. the past progressive form
   - c. the past perfect form
   - d. the present perfect form

4. When communicating about two things that happened in the past, which verb form do you use to show the action that happened first?
   - a. the simple past tense
   - b. the past progressive form
   - c. the past perfect form
   - d. the present perfect form

5. Which verb form is frequently used with *while*?
   - a. the simple past tense
   - b. the past progressive form
   - c. the past perfect form
   - d. the present perfect form

6. Which verb form is frequently used with *since*?
   - a. the simple past tense
   - b. the past progressive form
   - c. the past perfect form
   - d. the present perfect form

B. *Multiple-Choice Exercise (Individual)*
Circle the time expression in each sentence.
Then, write the letter of the best answer in the
blank at the beginning of each sentence.   **tV, I, FI, R, T**

_____ 1. Bowes _____ since recovered from her on-line addiction.

a. had	c. has
b. have	d. has been

(continued on next page)

26

Table 2.5 (continued)

_____ 2. To get better, she _____ to give her computer away last month.
   a. had   c. has
   b. have   d. has been

_____ 3. But the curious "virtual" life she _____ before that is not unique.
   a. live   c. lived
   b. had lived   d. living

_____ 4. Other schools now _____ students who spend too much time on-line.
   a. banning   c. banned
   b. are banning   d. had banned

_____ 5. A recent study _____ that 24 million people use the Internet.
   a. finds   c. find
   b. had found   d. found

C. *Verb Analysis*

(SMALL GROUPS)

With a small group of classmates, read the following   **Au, G, tV, T, C**
paragraph out loud. Underline each verb, and then
discuss with your partner the questions that follow.

> Now 26 and a graduate student at the University of Maryland, Bowes says
> she likes her off-line life better. She's set on getting her master's in library
> science and spends her free time engaged in such activities as going out with
> her roommates or watching television with friends. "I have more of a real
> life," she says. "I'm not relying on the computer to make me happy."

☐ Look at the simple present tense verb forms.
   Why are they used?   **R, Ab, Fl, Au**

(INDIVIDUAL WORK)

Using a highlighter, mark every verb phrase in the paragraph above (verb + any helping words). Then, for each verb you marked, identify the verb tense (simple present,
simple past, or past perfect), and be prepared to discuss with your classmates why the
verb tense is appropriate in each case. (You may assume that all the verbs are used
correctly.) The first sentence is completed for you.

Verb Phrase	Tense	Explanation
says	present	Present tense is used to report what an author says in a text.

D. *Class Discussion*

Share experiences that you have had with computers   **Au, G, FD, C**
with your class. For example, do you spend hours on
the Internet? Do you consider yourself a "webaholic"?
Do you think that Internet "friends" are really friends?

   As other students share their information, listen   **Au, T, Fl, I, C**
for their use of verb tenses. Write six verbs that you
hear in your Learning Log. Then discuss the different
verb tenses with a partner.   **Au, G, R, Ac**

■ ■ ■ *SAMPLE 3*

Looking Ahead, **Advanced Level, "Reporting" Chapter**
Abstract, Academic Journal Article

We studied predation by approximately 70 domestic cats in the Bedfordshire village of Felmersham over a one-year period. All the prey items brought home by virtually all the cats in the village **were recorded** and, where possible, **were identified**. A total of 1090 prey items (535 mammals, 297 birds, and 258 unidentified animals) **were taken**, an average of about 14 per cat per year. Twenty-two species of birds and 15 species of mammals **were identified**. The most important items were woodmice (17%), house sparrows (16%), and bank voles (14%).

Academic journal writing, like the abstract given in Sample 3, is characterized by the use of:

☐ a restricted set of verbs (*be,* and various verbs for studying, observing, and reporting information)
☐ complex noun phrases
☐ prepositional phrases
☐ the presentation of numerical data
☐ passive voice

To prepare students to read and write such prose, the focus on passive sentences in the exercises in Table 2.6 include the form of the passive verb phrase, the organization of a passive sentence, and the appropriate, meaningful use of passive sentences.

Table 2.6: Passive Voice Sentences in Academic Writing	
EXERCISES	**LEARNING STYLES**
A. *Fill-in-the-Blank (Individual)*	
Complete the following paragraph by choosing the appropriate passive verbs. Only the simple form of each verb is given [in brackets]; use the complete correct verb in each of the blanks.	**FI, I, T, R, tV**
All of the cat owners in the village _____ and details of the cats [trace]	
_____ on index cards. Cats _____ and sexed, and [record] [age]	
	(continued on next page)

Table 2.6 (continued)

they _____ a letter code for identification purposes. (Neutered
     [allot]

cats _____ to their original sex.) Those people who were willing
     [assign]

to take part in the survey (only 1, with 2 cats, refused to do so), _____
                                                                    [give]

a number of polythene bags which _____ with the cat's code
                                          [mark]

letter and _____ consecutively so that it would be easier to
            [number]

establish the order in which any one cat caught its prey.

B. *Verb Analysis (Pairs)*

With a partner, list the verbs from the paragraph   **G, Au, R, Ac, T**
above that are not passive structures. Then

   ☐ identify the verb tense of each

   ☐ discuss why a nonpassive verb was used

C. *Small-Group Work*

With a small group of classmates, write a dialog   **G, T, Au, Ac, FD**
about cats. For example,

   ☐ have the authors of this research article about cats
      introduce their work to a member of the village

   ☐ have a veterinarian talk with a television reporter
      about the "murdered" mammals in this project

   ☐ have three village members who own cats talk about
      the research project

In this dialogue, use as many *active voice verbs* as you can.   **K, Au, FD, G**
Then perform this dialogue for another group. Exchange
your dialogue with the other group. Using the new
paragraph, change all of the passive voice to active voice.
Then perform the "new" dialogue for the other group.
Finally, discuss the differences in the dialogues.   **Au, G, R, Ab**
What sounded "strange"? Why?

D. *Written Assignment (Collaborative/Group)*

With a group of your classmates, pretend that you are   **G, FD, T, R, tV**
a graduate student who is interested in performing a similar
project. Write a letter to the researchers in this project.
Explain the ways in which you would like to extend or change
the original research. Ask the researchers for their advice
about your project. Use a formal style, and choose some
passive voice sentences.

CONCLUSION

Some say that the audio-lingual approach to teaching ESL/EFL is dead, and others say that communicative competence (or the Silent Way or multimedia) is the best way for students to learn. Instead, I would argue that in a single, small class of 15 students (or in a large university course of 60 or 100 students), some students will learn X (e.g., relative clauses, essay organization, listening strategies) by theory, rote, and practice, while others will learn X by experiential activities. In contrast, the same two subsets of students may learn Y (e.g., skimming, revising, pronunciation of a sound) most effectively with a different group of learning styles. Therefore, it is in the best interests of both teachers and students to:

☐ learn about learning styles

☐ incorporate that information into lesson planning and learning strategies

☐ work to expand learning and teaching styles in the classroom.

NOTES

1. For more information about student learning styles, including information about cultural differences and lesson plan development, as well as several learning styles instruments, see *Learning Styles in the ESL/EFL Classroom* (Ed., J. Reid, 1995). Boston: Heinle & Heinle.

2. Each of these comments has been taken from *Teaching English as a Second or Foreign Language* (Ed., M. Celce-Murcia, 1991, 2nd Ed.). Boston: Newbury/Heinle & Heinle.

3. See the following three chapters in this volume for a thorough discussion of grammar clusters in U.S. academic writing.

4. Each of these samples is taken from one of the four textbooks in the *Looking Ahead* series (Eds., Patricia Byrd and Joy Reid, forthcoming). Boston: Heinle & Heinle. The explanations and grammar exercises have been taken from *Applied English Grammar* (Patricia Byrd and Beverly Benson, 1992). Boston: Heinle & Heinle.

Section II
Selecting and Organizing the Grammar

ISSUES INVOLVED IN THE TEACHING OF WRITING have been dealt with extensively in other publications—for example, Joy's *Teaching ESL Writing* and Joan Carson and Ilona Leki's *Reading in the Composition Classroom*. In this section of *Grammar in the Composition Classroom,* we turn to the next major topic that must be considered when planning for teaching grammar in the context of teaching writing. Once we know about the students who will be in our programs and classes and about their purposes in learning English, we can start to make decisions about what grammar to teach.

Chapter 3

Grammar in
the Composition Syllabus

Patricia Byrd

PREPARING ESL STUDENTS FOR ACADEMIC READING AND WRITING

The central responsibility of ESL programs that prepare students for academic study in U.S. colleges and universities, often termed English for Academic Purpose or EAP programs, is to develop the language skills required for success in academic study. Certainly EAP programs are also concerned with the development of study skills along with knowledge about and skill at living in U.S. general and academic cultures. However, the primary rationale for such programs has to do with the development of "academic literacy"—which includes the ability to take written notes while listening to a lecture as well as the ability to read textbooks and to use textbook language (and lecture notes) for required writing tasks (such as tests). While computer technology and the Internet are starting to have some impact on the materials that students are required to read in their academic courses, the printed textbook remains a basic tool of U.S. undergraduate education. Students must read such textbooks, understand lectures based on them, write in response to them, and write using the information and the language in them.[1] Thus, teachers and curriculum coordinators in EAP programs need to understand more about these textbooks and the language used in them. By basing our materials and courses on the materials required in degree courses, we can more accurately prepare our students for their academic study.

Working from an understanding of the communicative requirements of the degree courses taken by our students does not mean that ESL programs are

33

responsible for preparing students with the content of those courses; we are not, and are not expected to be, teachers of psychology, political science, biology, and so forth. Working seriously with content does not mean that ESL writing courses are attempting to supplant disciplinary courses, but rather that students learn to deal with content in their writing. Leki and Carson (1997) argue for EAP writing courses that teach "text-responsible" writing in which the students are held responsible for accuracy of content as well as for accuracy and fluency in language.

We can help students learn to recognize how language is used differently in the different courses that they are required to take, developing not just their "English" but also their ability to think about how to use their English language skills to meet different academic demands. A special issue of the journal *English for Specific Purposes* (volume 16, number 1, 1997) provides articles on various aspects of EAP curriculum development. In addition to providing such valuable discussions as that on extensive and intensive reading in EAP programs (Carrell & Carson, 1997), the reference lists with the articles are a wonderful resource for teachers, curriculum coordinators, and materials designers who want to read in the literature on EAP curriculum design and development.

As shown in Chapter 4, the studies by Biber and other researchers interested in discourse analysis provide a guide for the development of the grammatical component of EAP curricula and materials. In Biber's work, he characterizes the texts in his corpus in terms of six factors for what he terms a "multidimensional" description (Biber 1988). Because his first two dimensions (involved vs. informational and narrative vs. nonnarrative) are so central to communication in English, we have chosen to focus primarily on the intersections of these grammatical clusters. In addition, putting these core dimensions on a matrix allows for the combination of informational grammar with narrative grammar—a combination that helps to explain many passages of textbook writing with their case studies and narrative examples. Biber's use of a two-dimensional analysis in the early section of *Variation Across Speech and Writing* (pp. 9–24) demonstrates the usefulness and power of combining these two core dimensions. Conrad (1996) illustrates another use of the two first dimensions (involved-informational and narrative-nonnarrative) in her analysis of textbook and professional writing in biology.

The matrix approach used here (Figure 3.1) also acknowledges the close relationship between features of informational discourse and of the discourse that Biber terms "abstract" with its past participle clauses and passive sentences (with and without *by*-clauses). Thus, the dimension that he labels "abstract vs. nonabstract" is folded into the matrix. In sum, a matrix built with three of the dimensions that are often of major importance in academic writing gives us an overview of the grammatical features of the academic language found in college and university courses.

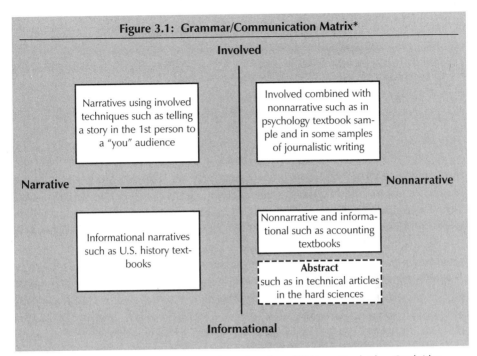

Figure 3.1: Grammar/Communication Matrix*

Involved

Narratives using involved techniques such as telling a story in the 1st person to a "you" audience

Involved combined with nonnarrative such as in psychology textbook sample and in some samples of journalistic writing

Narrative — **Nonnarrative**

Informational narratives such as U.S. history textbooks

Nonnarrative and informational such as accounting textbooks

Abstract such as in technical articles in the hard sciences

Informational

*Adapted from D. Biber (1988), *Variation Across Speech and Writing*. Cambridge: Cambridge University Press.

GRAMMAR IN ACADEMIC TEXTBOOKS

Samples from academic textbooks are given here to demonstrate the ways in which grammatical features cluster in particular discourses. Samples were selected to show the major discourse types: History textbooks generally make extensive use of the grammar of past time narrative; textbooks in the laboratory sciences and social sciences tend to rely on the grammar of informational writing (with presentation of theory and definitions for basic terminology); and textbooks and journal articles in many different disciplines include repeated use of the grammar of reporting other people's information and writing in both direct and indirect quotations.

☐ GRAMMAR OF U.S. HISTORY TEXTBOOKS

In the U.S., undergraduates are often required to take courses in U.S. history (and sometimes in the history of a state) as part of the core curriculum.[2] The language used to present this information combines features of past time narrative with the more compressed language used in academic settings to present information (participle phrases and long, complex noun phrases, for example). Consider sample 1, from a popular introductory textbook used in U.S. history courses.

■ ■ ■ *SAMPLE 1*

A Sample of U.S. History Textbook Discourse

The American Past: A Survey of American History (4th Edition)
J.R. Conlin
The Harcourt Press (Harcourt Brace Jovanovich College Publishers), 1993

The English King Henry VII passed up a chance to have Christopher Columbus plant his flag on an American beach. Henry failed to act when Columbus, momentarily discouraged in Spain, wrote to him proposing that he sail westward to the Indies in Henry's employ. Nevertheless, England's claim to a piece of the Americas was almost as old as Spain's. In 1497, Henry VII sent another Italian sailor, John Cabot, across the North Atlantic in search of a route to Asia. Cabot discovered Newfoundland and Nova Scotia, which he claimed for England. Cabot actually touched on continental America a year earlier than Columbus did.

The French showed little interest in overseas exploration until 1523, when a French privateer captured a Spanish ship bringing Aztec gold home. His curiosity aroused by so pretty a cargo, King Francis I sent his Italian navigator, Giovanni Verrazano, across the ocean. Verrazano claimed much of what is now the east coast of North America for France. When the pope scolded Francis, reminding him that all the world's non-Christian lands had already been divided between Portugal and Spain, the king dipped his pen in sarcasm. He asked to examine the section of Adam's will that gave the pope the right to bestow so pretty a gift.

ENGLAND'S PROBLEMS

Adam's will or no, Cabot and Verrazano not withstanding, Spain enjoyed a near monopoly in the Americas for a century. It was not that England, France, and other European nations were indifferent to American riches. It was, simply, that through most of the 1500s—Spain's *siglo de oro or* —"golden century"—no European nation was quite up to challenging Spanish might. During the second half of the 1500s, France was convulsed by vicious civil wars to determine which great duke would be king. Henry VII resolved a similar dispute in England in 1485. But the Tudor dynasty he founded was vexed by the miscarriages of a queen, a royal divorce, short reigns, and religious tensions. Only toward the end of the sixteenth century under Elizabeth I, the last of the Tudor monarchs, did the English challenge Spain in America.

The Protestant Reformation

The sixteenth century was a time of religious turmoil in much of Europe. It was the era of the Protestant Reformation. During the same years that Cortez was shattering Aztec civilization, the German monk Luther was shattering the unity of

European Christendom. While Francisco Coronado was exploring the deserts of western North America, and Hernan DeSoto the Mississippi Valley, a French lawyer named John Calvin was laying the foundations of a dynamic religious faith that would profoundly influence American as well as European history.

The language here is that used in other storytelling: past tense verbs, proper nouns, personal pronouns to refer to those proper nouns, and time words to indicate the flow of the story. On the other hand, history in textbooks is also like other informational writing with complex sentences that often have reduced relative clauses, in the form of present and past participle phrases. Writers with lots of time to revise their work, and writing in a tradition that values sentences packed with information, can provide sentences such as these from the history sample:

> When the pope scolded Francis, **reminding him that all the world's non-Christian lands had already been divided between Portugal and Spain**, the king dipped his pen in sarcasm.
>
> Henry failed to act when Columbus, **momentarily discouraged in Spain**, wrote to him proposing that he sail westward to the Indies in Henry's employ.

As a language teacher and materials writer, I find this sample of history textbook writing suggestive of how much work needs to be done with naming traditions in academic textbook prose. This sample also provides a condemnation of how little work ESL/EFL has traditionally done with naming—at least with the use of proper nouns in academic discourse. For example, students need to understand that first reference will be to *Christopher Columbus* and many subsequent references will be to *Columbus*—but that names of royalty are handled in a different pattern, with *Henry VII* often referred to as *Henry*. Little work is ever done in ESL/EFL classes with the forms—and variations on those forms—of proper names, especially as those names are used in academic writing. This use of proper names is not just a "reading" problem, for the students in U.S. history courses will be expected to use those names in their own writing on tests and in project work. Jordan (1997) and Hamp-Lyons (1997) discuss another aspect of the use of names in academic writing—the ways that names and initials are used in by-lines and references. For example, I am at various points *Pat Byrd; Patricia Byrd; H. Patricia Byrd; P. Byrd; Byrd, P.;* and even *Byrd, H.P.* Hamp-Lyons points out the difficulty for women academics (and their readers) in dealing with name changes in societies that expect married women to adopt the names of their husbands and divorced women to drop the same and revert to their "maiden" names. For students who come from other naming traditions, learning about the various uses of names in the materials that they read and write on is not a trivial task.

Another major characteristic of this material is the huge amount of new vocabulary that is thrown at the reader—every page is a new setting with new people entering the story. For example, confusingly for those not accustomed to the story, *Henry* on one page is *Henry VII* and on a nearby page becomes *Henry VIII*.

Also characteristic of sentence structure in history materials is the use of appositives for two important functions—to provide additional information about the people, places, and events being discussed and to provide definitions of terminology (Currie & Beaubien, 1996). This last function is in contrast to the presentation of definitions in other types of textbook writing. Compare the definition given below from the accounting textbook materials to the definition from the history textbook. The first definition is from Smith and Skousen's *Intermediate Accounting* (p. 108). The term being defined is given in boldface type and is part of a bulleted list of terms. The definition is clearly a definition and an important one. The second sentence is from Conlin's *American Past* (p. 38) and appears to be a definition first of "Calvinism" and then also of "original sin," but the style used in this text does not highlight terminology or separate definitions from the rest of the text.

- **Revenues** are inflows or other enhancements of assets of an entity or settlements of its liabilities (or a combination of both) from delivering or producing goods, rendering services, or other activities that constitute the entity's ongoing major or central operations.

They were disciples of the French lawyer and Protestant theologian John Calvin, who believed that human nature was inherently depraved, that men and women bore the guilt and burden of Adam and Eve's original sin within their breasts.

In sum, the language that students taking a history course need to handle include at least the following:

- □ How to use proper names
- □ How to keep up with the pronouns that are needed to refer to those people
- □ How to re-tell and summarize a story using past time narrative
- □ How to recognize definitions presented through appositives and how to use that abbreviated language when asked to define terms on an examination
- □ How to comment on the story's meaning—how to generalize about the past and how to compare and contrast past events, people, and ways of life
- □ How to recognize definitions of terminology when they are not highlighted in the text but are presented as part of the flow of the discussion.

GRAMMAR OF ACCOUNTING TEXTBOOKS

Sample 2, from an accounting textbook, was selected because so many ESL students eventually major in business and because of the dramatic contrast between the language of a history textbook and the language of a textbook written in a style more like that of the social sciences and laboratory sciences. The writing used in the sample from an accounting textbook is dominated by the characteristics that Biber (1988) called informational and abstract. The writer's basic purpose is to present theory and definitions that are fundamental to this academic discipline. Sample 2 illustrates the grammar of definitions in such discourse—definitions that students will be expected to learn, to repeat, to interpret, and to apply.

■ ■ ■ *SAMPLE 2*

Sample of Definitions of Terminology
Intermediate Accounting (11th Edition)
J.M. Smith and K.F. Skousen
Cincinnati, OH: South-Western Publishing Co., 1992

THE 10 ELEMENTS OF FINANCIAL STATEMENTS

Assets are probable future economic benefits obtained or controlled by a particular entity as a result of past transactions or events.

Liabilities are probable future sacrifices of economic benefits arising from present obligations of a particular entity to transfer assets or provide services to other entities in the future as a result of past transactions or events.

Equity or net assets is the residual interest in the assets of an entity that remains after deducting its liabilities.

Investments by owners are increases in equity of a particular business enterprise resulting from transfers to it from other entities of something valuable to obtain or increase ownership interests (or equity) in it. Assets are most commonly received as investments by owners, but that which is received may also include services or satisfaction or conversion of liabilities of the enterprise.

Distributions to owners are decreases in equity of a particular business enterprise resulting from transferring assets, rendering services, or incurring liabilities by the enterprise to owners. Distributions to owners decrease ownership interests (or equity) in an enterprise.

Comprehensive income is the change in equity of a business enterprise during a period from transactions and other events and circumstances from nonowner sources. It includes all changes in equity during a period except those resulting from investments by owners and distributions to owners.

Revenues are inflows or other enhancements of assets of an entity or settlement of its liabilities (or a combination of both) from delivering or producing goods, rendering services, or other activities that constitute the entity's ongoing major or central operations.

Expenses are outflows or other using-up of assets or incurrences of liabilities (or a combination of both) from delivering or producing goods, rendering services, or carrying out other activities that constitute the entity's ongoing major or central operations.

Gains are increases in equity (net assets) from peripheral or incidental transactions of an entity and from all other transactions and other events and circumstances affecting the entity except those that result from revenues or investments by owners.

Losses are decreases in equity (net assets) from peripheral or incidental transactions of an entity and from all other transactions and other events and circumstances affecting the entity except those that result from expenses or distributions to owners.

These definitions have the following grammar: (1) present tense verbs; (2) generic noun phrases[3] used to name concepts or professional terminology; (3) sentences that are of the definitional type—a term in the subject position, a form of *be* as the verb, and a complex and highly compressed noun phrase as the complement of the verb; (4) numerous prepositional phrases attached to nouns, and (5) use of logical rather than chronological connections among pieces of the text. It needs to be emphasized that this kind of writing is noun-phrase oriented, with relatively little variation in the verbs and a heavy use of simple-present-tense verb phrases. As with most textbook writing, the student is faced with handling large numbers of new terms and ideas as each chapter brings on new concepts and terminology. However, in contrast to the history sample, the accounting sample has fewer new words because some basic terminology is recycled throughout the book (Byrd, 1995). Notice in this sample of definitions of terminology how many noun phrases are used—and how few pronouns.

□ TEXTBOOK WRITING THAT EMPLOYS FEATURES OF "ORAL" GRAMMAR

Sample 3, from a psychology textbook, shows how some of the features of "oral" communication can be used by writers in an attempt to "involve" the audience with the content.

■ ■ ■ *SAMPLE 3*

Sample to Show "Oral" Grammar in Writing

Psychology (3rd edition)

David G. Myers

NY: Worth Publishers, 1992

Or consider the vividness of your memories of unique and highly emotional moments in your past—perhaps a car accident, your first romantic kiss, your first day as an immigrant in a new country, or where you were when you heard some tragic news. One such memory of mine is of my only hit in an entire season of Little League baseball. Most Americans over 45 feel sure of exactly what they were doing when they heard the news of President Kennedy's assassination (Brown & Kulik, 1982). Few San Francisco Bay area residents will hesitate in recalling exactly where they were when the 1989 earthquake struck. You perhaps remember where you were when you learned that the space shuttle *Challenger* had exploded. This clarity for our memories of surprising, significant events leads some psychologists to call them **flashbulb memories**, because it's as if the brain commands, "Print this!"

How do we accomplish such memory feats? How can we remember things we have not thought about for years, yet forget the name of someone we met a minute ago? How are memories stored in our brains? Why can even our flash-bulb memories sometimes prove dead wrong? (People who hours after the *Challenger* explosion recalled where they heard the news were sometimes wildly inaccurate when again recalling their whereabouts 1 to 3 years later.) Does what we know about memory give us clues to how we can improve our memories? These will be among our questions as we review insights gleaned from a century of research on memory.

Here questions are asked and answered, and the reader is addressed as *you* and tied to the writer with *we*. What to do with this type of grammar and writing in an ESL/EFL writing class is a bit of a puzzle. Many of our students need to learn to separate out the differences between formal written communication and the language that they use in conversation. Often these students (discussed as "ear learners" in Chapter 1) use vocabulary that is considered too informal for academic writing. (There is, of course, a possibility that the students who use these words do not know the formal versions of them yet and so are using the only vocabulary that they have, rather than making an inappropriate choice.) Thus, it could be argued that learning about using an "oral" style in formal writing might be confusing for these students. On the other hand, they are likely to encounter such writing in their classes. Certainly they will see questions used in their textbooks on a regular basis. Thus, it is also possible to argue that learning about the use of questions in formal writing would be a useful skill for ESL/EFL writers.

□ TEXTBOOK WRITING THAT COMBINES SEVERAL DISCOURSE TYPES

The samples of textbook writing seen so far in this chapter were selected because they clearly represent single types of grammar clusters. Textbook materials, however, often combine different types in a single passage. One of the basic patterns of academic writing is the combination of a generalization (in informational language) with an extended example (Kaplan & Shaw, 1984). Another is a general narrative pattern punctuated with general truth statements (using present tense verbs) to explain the meaning of the historical events being recounted.

Two samples are given to show how this combination of different grammatical clusters in one text can occur. Sample 2, the introduction to the second chapter in the accounting textbook quoted from on page 39, begins with a brief example that is told using past time narrative; the explanation that follows (sample 4) has the characteristics of informational grammar.

■ ■ ■ *SAMPLE 4*

Sample to Show Example Narrative Tied to a Generalization as Part of an Attempt to Persuade

Intermediate Accounting (11th edition)

J.M. Smith and K.F. Skousen

Cincinnati, OH: College Division South-Western Publishing Co., 1992

In 1987, General Motors elected to change the estimated useful life of its tools and dies. The change resulted in an increase in income from operations of over $1.2 billion, accounting for approximately 25% of earnings for that year. If accounting rules allow such flexibility and judgment in the reporting of revenues and expenses, is accounting more of an art or a science? Should accounting standards allow management such discretion in reporting financial information?

Contrary to the preceding example, the general public often views accounting as a scientific discipline based on a fixed set of rules and procedures. This is a natural perception since the public's exposure to accounting generally relates to financial statements, tax returns, and other reports showing dollar amounts that give an impression of exactness. Those within the profession, however, recognize that accounting is more an art than a science and that the operating results and other accounting measurements are based on estimates and judgments relative to the measurement and communication of business activity.

Sample 5 shows combinations of discourse types being used for different communicative purposes. This passage from a psychology textbook connects Maslow's theories to a disturbing experiment done during World War II. The passage starts with informational generalizations, moves to a past time narrative to recount the experiment, and closes with an interpretative sentence that hedges on that interpretation by using modal auxiliaries to tone down the statement and make it more acceptable in this type of argumentation.

These passages show the principled ways that textbook writers move from one grammatical cluster to another. Students are sometimes told "not to shift tenses" in a passage of writing. Perhaps teachers might more accurately show students that tense shifts occur in passages when the purpose for the writing shifts. Otherwise, the writer sticks to the verb forms required by the grammar cluster being used.

■ ■ ■ *SAMPLE 5*

Sample to Show Combinations of Three Types in One Passage

"A Hierarchy of Motives"
David G. Myers, *Psychology (3rd edition)*
NY: Worth Publishers, 1992

Some theorists, such as the late Abraham Maslow of Brandeis University, believe that all motives are organized in a hierarchical manner, which can be graphically depicted as a pyramid (see Figure 3.2). At the base of the hierarchy are physiological needs, such as for food, water, and elimination. The increasingly "human" needs operate in the upper levels, such motives as compassion and creativity being near the top. According to Maslow, instigation of "higher" motives is unlikely unless "lower," more basic motives have been satisfied; a person who never has quite enough to eat is not likely to display compassion or creativity.

Evidence supporting this idea is provided by an experiment conducted with conscientious objectors during World War II; they were placed on a semistarvation diet for 24 weeks, resulting in a 25 percent average weight loss. According to observers, all voluntary activities were reduced. Humor, sociability, and courtesy all but disappeared, and surliness became common in interpersonal relationships. Personal grooming became a common obsession. When a normal diet was restored, these symptoms disappeared. It would seem that when energy is scarce, it will be channeled to the more basic needs of the body; achievement, affiliation, and other "higher" motives must wait their turn.

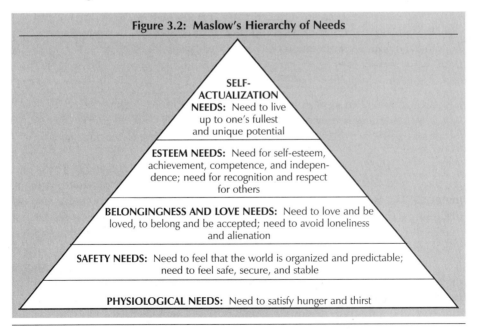

Figure 3.2: Maslow's Hierarchy of Needs

SELF-ACTUALIZATION NEEDS: Need to live up to one's fullest and unique potential

ESTEEM NEEDS: Need for self-esteem, achievement, competence, and independence; need for recognition and respect for others

BELONGINGNESS AND LOVE NEEDS: Need to love and be loved, to belong and be accepted; need to avoid loneliness and alienation

SAFETY NEEDS: Need to feel that the world is organized and predictable; need to feel safe, secure, and stable

PHYSIOLOGICAL NEEDS: Need to satisfy hunger and thirst

□ LANGUAGE OF REPORTING OTHER PEOPLE'S INFORMATION AND WRITING

A fundamental yet difficult task for students in academic programs is learning how to report information and to use language that they have found in other people's work (Carson, 1992). This task has two components—learning how to report other people's ideas and words and then learning how to reference the use of those ideas and words. Keeping these two components separate is an important instructional goal—"quoting" is not just learning about punctuation but, more importantly, about reading, selecting, and using information and language from sources. Whatever the complexities of using a referencing system, many writers new to U.S. academic culture find that learning how to select and use ideas and words and how to integrate them into their writing is a more important first step toward academic literacy than learning about punctuation.

As the basis for their own use of reporting, students will find a wide variety of techniques used in their textbooks to integrate other people's information and words into the text. Consider the following, taken from Chapter 7, "States of Consciousness," in Myer's *Psychology* (1992, pp. 189–202):

Louis Armstrong's remark about jazz could also be said of consciousness: "Unless you know what it is, I ain't never going to be able to explain it to you."

At its beginning, psychology was sometimes defined as "the description and explanation of states of consciousness" (Ladd, 1887).

"Psychology must discard all reference to consciousness." Behaviorist John B. Watson (1913). [in a sidebar on page 189—a source of quotations given in italic print with quotation marks throughout the book]

In a quiet, low voice the hypnotist suggests, "Your eyes are growing tired. . . . Your eyelids are becoming heavy. . .now heavier and heavier. . . . They are beginning to close. . . . You are becoming more deeply relaxed. . . . Your breathing is now deep and regular. . . . Your muscles are becoming more and more relaxed. Your whole body is beginning to feel like lead."

In addition to these reports of other people's words and ideas, textbooks are likely to include summaries of journal articles and books and other scholarly material. The importance of such summaries seems to vary from one academic discipline to another. For example, Myer's *Psychology* is built around such summaries along with numerous references to research reports that are given to justify generalizations, while other textbooks such as those from accounting and U.S. history make less use of this feature. Study is needed to clarify the importance of such summaries in different undergraduate textbooks and required courses. However, it seems certain that students are going to have to read summaries such as the one in sample 6 and to take language as well as information from them in order to handle writing tasks such as test taking and report writing.

■ ■ ■ *SAMPLE 6*

Reporting Other People's Ideas and Words in *Psychology* (an Introductory, Undergraduate Textbook)

I. PARAPHRASING OF PUBLICATIONS (PAGES 388–389)

All of us communicate nonverbally as well as verbally. If irritated, we may tense our bodies, press our lips together, and gesture with our eyebrows. With a gaze, an averted glance, or a stare we can communicate intimacy, submission, or dominance (Kleinke, 1986).

Most of us are good enough at reading nonverbal cues to decipher the emotions in an old silent film. We are especially good at detecting nonverbal threats. In a crowd of faces, a single angry face will "pop out" faster than a single happy one (Hansen & Hansen, 1988). Some of us are more sensitive to these cues than others. Robert Rosenthal, Judith Hall, and their colleagues (1979) discovered this by showing hundreds of people brief film clips of portions of a person's emotionally expressive face or body, sometimes with a garbled voice added. For example, after a 2-second scene revealing only the face of an upset woman, the researchers would ask whether the woman was expressing anger or discussing a divorce. Rosenthal and Hall reported that some people are much better emotions detectors than others, and that women are better at it than men.

Among couples passionately in love, eye-gazing is typically prolonged and mutual (Rubin, 1970). Would intimate gazes similarly stir feelings between strangers? To find out, Joan Kellerman, James Lewis, and James Laird (1989) asked unacquainted male-female pairs to gaze intently for 2 minutes either at one another's hands or into one another's eyes. After separating, the eye-gazers reported feeling a greater tingle of attraction and affection.

II. EXACT QUOTATION FROM *PSYCHOLOGY*

A. From a Sidebar with a Picture of Paul Ekman (page 390)

Paul Ekman (Ekman & Friesen, 1975): "Emotions are shown primarily in the face, not in the body. There is no specific body movement pattern that always signals anger or fear, but there are facial patterns specific to each motion."

B. From the Text on Page 391

Expressions not only communicate emotion, they also amplify and regulate it. In his 1872 book, *The Expression of the Emotions in Man and Animals*, Darwin contended that "the free expression by outward sign of an emotion intensifies it.´. . . He who gives way to violent gestures will increase his rage."

Was Darwin right? I was driving my car one day when the song "Put On a Happy Face" came on the radio. "How phony," I thought. But I tested Darwin's hypothesis anyway, as you can, too: Fake a big grin. Now scowl. Can you feel the difference?

In addition, students will need to learn about the ways that different academic disciplines use evidence to support generalizations: The authors of these textbooks are not just giving students information about psychology or accounting, but are also modeling the ways in which psychologists and accountants are expected to present and defend statements of fact and theory.

In sum, "quotations" in textbooks represent two major categories:

1. reports that involve the exact words of the source and use quotation marks or other special formatting, and

2. reports that summarize or paraphrase the originals.

In both cases, certain verbs are commonly used: *find, mention, say, report, summarize,* and so forth. These verbs frequently require a noun clause in their objects with the connecting word *that* frequently deleted. These quotations often use adverbials to introduce the report and to connect it to the surrounding information. Finally, the indirect quotations generally involve some type of sequencing of the verbs when the writer adapts the original to fit the indirect format. Of course, when writers use such methods for adding other people's words and information to their own writing, they must be careful to punctuate the sentences appropriately—not just to indicate the end of the complex sentence with a period (a sometimes difficult task for writers new to English) but also to use the quotation marks required by the exact quotation method. This referencing step with its particular punctuation and style of referring to the original source, as stated earlier, needs to be carefully distinguished from the task of reporting in ESL lessons and materials.

The vital point to be understood here is that the language of reporting other people's information and writing comes in a cluster of grammatical features that need to be learned together: verb types, verb tenses, noun clauses, complex sentences, adverbials, and punctuation are, all together, the grammatical signature of this cluster.

These samples indicate something, too, of the demands made on students to adjust to the writing styles used in different academic disciplines. While both psychology and accounting use the same grammatical elements and clusters of grammar, they go about presenting and using information in ways characteristic of their own discourse communities. Although it is true that ESL students do not need to become grammarians (that is, the focus of their work should be learning to use English to communicate rather than memorizing abstract information about English grammar), they do need to become linguistic anthropologists or perhaps "language-in-use detectives." Students need to understand that their textbooks are going to use various combinations of grammar (narrative, informational, interactive, persuasive) for somewhat different purposes and in often radically different formats.

□ THE LANGUAGE OF REFERENCING QUOTATIONS

Students will encounter a number of different styles for giving references in their academic textbooks—APA and MLA formats among others. For example, Smith and Skousen (1992) use footnotes to give references to sources used in that accounting textbook; D.G. Myers uses the APA journal style in his introductory psychology textbook (with a 63-page reference list at the end of the text); Conlin provides a list "For Further Reading" at the end of each chapter in his U.S. history textbook but does not refer to his sources in the text itself. In addition to these differences in referencing systems, students will find quotations handled in a variety of ways with punctuation and special formatting sometimes used to indicate exact quotation and sometimes used to indicate dialogue written by the textbook author rather than a true quotation. (Sample 6 illustrates how quotation marks can be used for various purposes within a passage of textbook prose.) Students also need realistic advice on when referencing is required rather than blanket statements about plagiarism. Few instructors are going to expect students to use references on quizzes and examinations, for example, even when the student quotes definitions and concepts in language taken as exactly as possible from the textbook. Even on examinations, however, students might be expected to connect concepts to the authority figures most associated with the concepts.

□ GRAMMAR OF TEXTBOOK ACTIVITIES AND PROBLEM SETS

In addition to information about academic textbook prose, teachers and materials writers working in EAP programs need also to understand, in detail, the grammar of the activities and exercise sets given in many textbooks.[4] Consider sample 7, questions and problems from the textbooks that were the source of the samples given earlier. We know very little about the answers that would be considered acceptable to the instructors who assign such tasks to their students. It appears from the wording of these materials that students would need to use informational language to handle the tasks from the physics textbook, to give the definitions required by the "questions" listed in the accounting text, and to respond to the accounting exercise. In contrast, the accounting case study is labeled a "discussion" and asks the student to "evaluate" an argument—a task that would require the use of at least some of the language of overt persuasion along with informational language to describe the situation being evaluated.

■ ■ ■ *SAMPLE 7*

Activities and Problems from Selected Textbooks

I. FROM *COLLEGE PHYSICS*

Questions from Chapter 11, "Thermal Physics"

1. Is it possible for two objects to be in thermal equilibrium if they are not in thermal contact with each other? Explain.

2. A piece of copper is dropped into a beaker of water. If the water's temperature rises, what happens to the temperature of the copper? When will the water and copper be in thermal equilibrium?

Problems from Chapter 11, "Thermal Physics"

1. The pressure in a constant volume gas thermometer is 0.700 atm at 100°C and 0.512 atm at 0°C. (a) What is the temperature when the pressure is 0.0400 atm? (b) What is the pressure at 450°C?

2. A constant volume gas thermometer is calibrated in dry ice (-80°C) and in boiling ethyl alcohol (78°C). The two pressures are 0.900 atm and 1.635 atm. (a) What value of absolute zero does the calibration yield? (b) What pressures would be found at the freezing and boiling points of water?

II. FROM *INTERMEDIATE ACCOUNTING*

Questions from Chapter 13, "Noncurrent Operating Assets— Utilization and Retirement"

1. Distinguish among depreciation, depletion, and amortization expenses.

2. What factors must be considered in determining the periodic depreciation charges that should be made for a company's depreciable assets?

Exercise from Chapter 13, "Noncurrent Operating Assets— Utilization and Retirement"

EXERCISE 13-1 (Computation of asset cost and depreciation expense):
A machine is purchased at the beginning of 1993 for $36,000. Its estimated life is 6 years. Freight-in on the machine is $2,000. Installation costs are $1,200. The machine is estimated to have a residual value of $2,000 and a useful life of 40,000 hours. It was used 6,000 hours in 1993.

1. What is the cost of the machine for accounting purposes?

2. Compute the depreciation charge for 1993 using (a) the straight-line method and (b) the service-hours method.

Discussion Case from Chapter 13, "Noncurrent Operating Assets—Utilization and Retirement"

Case 13-1 (We don't need depreciation!)

The managements of two different companies argue that because of specific conditions in their companies, recording depreciation expenses should be suspended for 1993. Evaluate carefully their arguments.

1. The president of Guzman Co. recommends that no depreciation be recorded for 1993 since the depreciation rate is 5% per year, and price indexes show that prices during the year have risen by more than this figure.

2. The policy of Liebnitz Co. is to recondition its building and equipment each year so that they are maintained in perfect repair. In view of the extensive periodic costs incurred in 1993, officials of the company feel that the need for recognizing depreciation is eliminated.

Many exercises and assignments like those given from the physics and accounting textbooks will require the student to repeat language from the textbook—in definitions of terminology, for example. However, test and project assignments also can involve comparisons and hypothesizing not found in the explanatory text in the textbooks. For example, students were asked on a U.S. history test to compare the status of indentured servants in seventeenth-century New England to the status of slaves in the U.S. South at the same period of time (Linda Gajdusek, personal communication, October 1995). The textbook described the two different situations but did not compare them. Thus, a student responding to this test question would have to use the language of past time narrative to describe the two situations but would also need to add comparative language (how slaves and indentured servants were alike and different) and perhaps some persuasive language to give opinions about the two situations.

APPLICATIONS TO ESL/EFL CURRICULA AND MATERIALS

By understanding the grammar in the types of materials that our students use in their degree courses, teachers and materials writers can develop lessons, materials, and curricula that are built around the language that students actually encounter and are expected to be able to use in their academic writing. This discourse-based needs analysis has been made simpler through the research reviewed in Chapter 4. We know that our students will encounter particular types of discourse, and we know much about the language of that discourse. As a result of this knowledge, we can build our classes around authentic language drawn from authentic samples but can at the same time focus on coherent clusters of grammar items. Using discourse-based needs analysis, we can make principled selections of the grammar to be focused on in our classes and our materials.

If the grammar is not divided among the different proficiency levels, then how is grammar to be approached in the curricular plan for an ESL writing program? The following principles can guide in making decisions about the organization of grammatical content in a multilevel series of composition courses.

PRINCIPLE #1. **At all levels, students work with authentic reading materials and take on authentic writing tasks.**

PRINCIPLE #2. These authentic materials require that **students learn about grammatical features characteristic of academic discourse—even** at the lowest proficiency levels.[5]

PRINCIPLE #3. **Grammar is selected based on the features of the discourse that the students need to handle.** That is, decisions about grammar are based not on the entire universe of English grammar but on the parts of that total system that are characteristic of particular discourse and that cluster together in that discourse type.

PRINCIPLE #4. **Grammar is presented in clusters of features.** Rather than having a segment of the course that is planned to teach "past tense verbs," the teacher provides lessons on reading and writing past time narratives. Students then work on learning to use past tense verbs because those are characteristic of the discourse they are studying.

PRINCIPLE #5. **The proficiency levels are distinguished not by the individual items of grammar assigned to each, but by the complexity of the reading and writing to be done by the students.** All students work on informational writing but with materials appropriate to their current skills in English. Beginners read some definitions and then do fill-in-the-blank or sentence completion exercises to practice the grammatical areas required by definitions; advanced learners work with complex definitions of terminology from an undergraduate textbook and include such definitions in their own writing. All students work with past time narrative—but beginners tell the story of their family, whereas advanced students recount a research project to support a theory presented in their essays.

PRINCIPLE #6. **The curriculum gives students multiple opportunities to encounter the language of academic reading and writing.** The overall curriculum is built around a spiraling pattern that carries the students through the same types of discourse at different levels of difficulty, giving them repeated opportunities to understand and to expand their knowledge and skills at using these fundamentally important grammatical clusters. The first level introduces the grammar; the other levels provide for more opportunities for observation, ial and error, practice in context, growth and expansion, working on both ncy and accuracy in written communication appropriate to academic study e U.S.

CONCLUSION: PLANNING THE WRITING-GRAMMAR CURRICULUM

Around the U.S., programs are reconsidering their purposes in light of two major trends—one in the U.S. and one inside our profession. First, the shift in U.S. population that has occurred in the late twentieth century means that ESL students are making up a growing segment of the students seeking to attend U.S. colleges and universities. This population change is being felt especially in community colleges in urban areas. In 1995, approximately 750,000 students were enrolled in ESL programs associated with community colleges in the U.S.—and predictions were for a 10 percent to 12 percent annual growth in that population. Second, many ESL professionals have been deeply influenced by studies such as that of Long and Crookes (1992) that call for materials, lessons, and programs designed on the basis of the "real-world tasks" that are the ultimate goals of ESL learners. As a result of these two trends, faculty and administrators in ESL programs are taking on the work of re-thinking the purposes of their programs and the curriculum design that is developed to achieve those purposes.

Studies on academic writing (e.g., Bazerman, 1988; MacDonald, 1992; Swales, 1990) are helping us to understand the ways in which the various academic disciplines go about creating written communication. With that information, we can help our students to be more effective members of the various discourse communities that they encounter in their first years at the university. In their first two years of study in a U.S. college or university, students take courses in a wide variety of academic fields as they complete their general education requirements. In a single term, they could easily be taking history, accounting, political science, and biology—and then switching to sociology, geology, physics, and music during the next term. Students talk about their problems in terms of the amounts of reading that they have to do. This problem is compounded by the very different ways in which language is used in the different disciplines. We cannot possibly prepare students for each of these fields. What can we do to prepare students in the length of time that we can reasonably expect them to take ESL courses? First, research studies have demonstrated that the language used in the disciplines involves the various clusters of grammar that we have discussed here and in Chapter 4. Second, these studies of language in context and other studies of the use of language by different disciplines (e.g., Bazerman, 1988; MacDonald, 1992; Swales, 1990) show that there are three major disciplinary types that students are likely to encounter—the sciences (biology, chemistry, physics), the social sciences (sociology, political science), and the humanities (philosophy, literature).[6]

The first answer to our "what to do?" is that we need to design programs that give students control over the features of these clusters and skill at recognizing how those clusters can be used in different settings. The second answer is that we must be sure that students have multiple opportunities to learn about how language is used in the three major disciplinary areas in U.S.

higher education. Students need to recognize that in these different areas, language is used in different ways to explain knowledge, to give evidence, and to write appropriately about knowledge and evidence. Orientation to U.S. academic study needs to include giving students knowledge about and experience with the ways that the disciplines use language—and as background to that knowledge, students need to understand the disciplinary organization of colleges and universities.

When I first started teaching ESL in 1969, I was assigned a grammar course to teach and given a syllabus that had been designed by the director of the program. We studied verbs most of the ten-week session: present tense, then past tense, then present progressive, then past progressive, and on through the various choices. Unless memory is totally distorting what we did, I seem to remember something that I thought of as "past tense week." We also worked on question formation and the modals (*will* = "future certainty," *can* = "ability," and so on). As I look at materials and curricula for teaching grammar now, I find that old design lurking right beneath the surface. There is still a tendency to start planning for a program or a set of materials with a list of grammar items (verbs, nouns, adverbs, adjectives, prepositions) and then to seek out the contexts. "Grammar **in** context" has the advantage over my first teaching experience of providing students with some contextualization of the grammar they are studying. However, the grammar is still presented in discrete pieces that do not reveal the underlying unity and the strong relationships between certain grammatical forms in certain discourse settings. As importantly, the focus is still on teaching grammar rather than on teaching reading and writing for academic communication.

The change in preposition that leads to "Grammar **from** context" has far-reaching implications for teaching grammar: First, we make initial decisions about the materials that students have to be able to use—we work from the real-world materials and real-world tasks that they will encounter. That is, the focus from the beginning is on teaching the reading and writing skills that students need for their academic study with grammar presented in support of that reading and writing. Second, we look for and then use the grammatical items that cluster together in the discourse that the students need to be able to understand and produce. "Grammar **from** context" frees us from the linear, disconnected presentation of grammar that is the weakness of the old grammatical syllabus and of many of the newer grammar-in-context designs. At the same time, we are not abandoning grammar, nor are we left making random judgments about what grammar to include in a writing program. By using this discourse-based approach, we have an orderly, systematic presentation of grammar that is truly useful for our students because it is characteristic of the types of materials that they encounter in their academic programs. And, we keep our program focused on teaching toward the content and formats that are the true educational goals of our students.

NOTES

1. In addition to their required textbooks, college and university students are sometimes required to read academic articles and use that material in their own writing (in reports and on tests). However, most reading materials are assigned from traditional textbooks. G. A. Myers (1992) discusses the importance of textbooks in the university education of scientists. Students also are usually expected to take notes from lectures based on the content of these textbooks. Carson (1992) and Ferris and Tagg (1996) provide extremely useful data and discussion about the interactions between listening and reading/writing in undergraduate courses.

2. Reading and writing about such content provides enormous challenges for students coming from other cultural (and political) backgrounds. Even students who are now legal residents of the U.S. might have been here so briefly that information that college and university instructors expect students to know before entering their courses is new to them. The proper role of the EAP program in preparing students for these courses might very well include some instruction in the content. However, such a step is fraught with difficulties, because ESL teachers might know the "facts" of the "story" of U.S. history but might very well not understand how those facts are presented in history courses or what the current interpretations of those facts might be.

3. A "generic" noun is one that is used to indicate a group or class rather than a specific individual. The following sentences illustrate the generic noun types in English:

A teacher works very hard.

Teachers work very hard.

The teacher works very hard.

Chalk is a basic tool for teachers.

These nouns are used extensively in statements of theory and definitions of terminology.

4. In addition to the tasks given in textbooks, the tasks assigned by instructors for course projects need to be examined when those differ from the ones suggested by an assigned textbook.

5. As was said earlier but needs to be repeated because it goes against the curriculum design in so many ESL programs: Jodi Crandall (1985) showed in her work on elementary school arithmetic that passive constructions are used in the very earliest lesson in grade school arithmetic. That is, programs cannot wait to introduce passive voice until students are "more advanced."

6. Of course, the system has some ambiguities. Psychology can sometimes be more of a science but in other settings more of a social science. Business administration courses are generally in the social science mode but with their own twist on what makes for good writing and good evidence. History sometimes is in the social science mode for its writing but then sometimes more in the humanities tradition—and struggles with its orientation to narrative or analysis (MacDonald, 1992). The point remains that ESL students need to encounter the three major disciplinary types and to see how language use is similar yet different in those settings.

Chapter 4

Grammar FROM Context

Patricia Byrd

FORM, MEANING, AND CONTEXT

To make decisions about the grammar to teach in composition classes and to include in composition materials to prepare ESL/EFL students to attend U.S. colleges or universities, teachers and materials writers need to know as much as possible about the grammar that is required by academic reading and writing tasks in those settings. Chapter 5, "Rethinking Grammar at Various Proficiency Levels," provides samples of written English to illustrate the principle that the same grammar is used in passages that are quite different in audience, purpose, and proficiency level: The grammar of narrative is basically the same whatever the communicative purpose for using the narration—and so on for the other grammar cluster types. However, the samples in Chapter 5 only suggest the detailed information that is now available about the grammar of discourse.

Many of us have learned to think about grammar in terms of the Larsen-Freeman pie chart. In her 1991 discussion of grammar, Larsen-Freeman recommends that grammar be approached from three angles—"form," "meaning," and "pragmatics," providing visual support for that analysis by presenting it as a pie chart (p. 280); see Figure 4.1. "Form" includes all of the issues of pronunciation, spelling, and formation that are characteristic of a particular unit of grammar. "Meaning" includes the various meanings the unit can have in different contexts. "Pragmatics" is defined as the contexts in which the grammar is used.[1] The arrows indicate that analysis of grammar can start with any one of the segments—from "form" to "meaning," from "meaning" to "pragmatics," from "pragmatics" to either "form" or "meaning." This analysis is useful for many purposes—Larsen-Freeman even recommends self-analysis through which a teacher might realize that she or he knows about the forms of an area of grammar but not about how those forms are used in particular contexts. For example, I know quite a lot about the forms of prepositions and prepo-

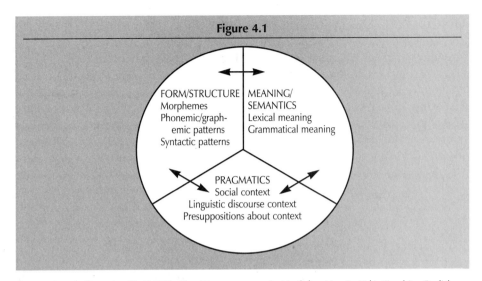

Figure 4.1

Source: Larsen-Freeman, D. (1991). Teaching grammar. In M. Celce-Murcia (Ed.), *Teaching English as a Second or Foreign Language* (pp. 279–296). NY: Newbury House.

sitional phrases and something about the meanings that they can have, but I still have much to learn about how prepositional phrases are used in particular contexts.[2]

Since the focus of *Grammar in the Composition Classroom* is on the language of academic writing, the Larsen-Freeman pie chart has been modified (see Figure 4.2) to emphasize the relationship between context and the meanings that forms have in particular contexts. The arrow points from the discourse side of the chart to indicate that **the search for grammar starts with context**; form and meaning are combined into one set because forms get their meanings when placed in contexts.

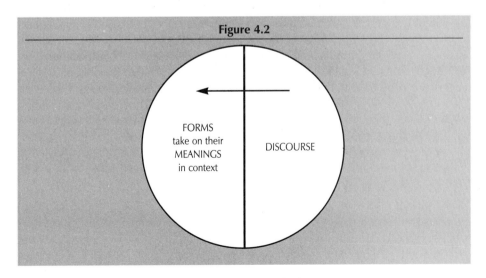

Figure 4.2

DISCOURSE ANALYSIS AND GRAMMAR

Studies of the way grammar is used in discourse suggest that rather than being equal partners, form and meaning might usefully be viewed as dependent upon context (e.g., Bardovi-Harlig, 1996; Biber, 1988; Conrad, 1996a and 1996b; McCarthy, 1991; Pica, 1983b; Schriffin, 1981; Swales, 1990a, 1990b; Zydatiss, 1986). The word *walked* does not take on its full meaning until it is placed in particular contexts. Compare these two sentences, for example:

1. *Margaret walked to school before class this morning.*
2. *If Bill walked to school, he would save lots of money and lose lots of weight.*

In the first sentence, the verb is used to refer to past time, while in the second it is used for a hypothetical statement.

Two strands in the study of discourse are of immediate usefulness for ESL/EFL teachers, materials writers, and curriculum coordinators. The first strand involves studies that focus on the ways selected items of grammar are used in particular settings. The second strand looks at the whole system and suggests ways to develop an overarching framework to give internal coherence to the grammar in ESL/EFL lessons, materials, and programs. The rest of this chapter is structured around these two strands, the practical implications of studies of grammar in discourse and then the value for ESL/EFL of Biber's work on spoken and written English.

PARTICULAR GRAMMAR IN PARTICULAR SETTINGS

To show how research about grammar in particular contexts can be used to develop ESL/EFL materials, two examples are given here.[3] The first example gives information about verbs in context along with teaching applications, while the second example considers nouns and noun phrases in context and implications for ESL/EFL lessons and materials. Both are offered to illustrate a process of application that can be used in lesson and materials design and development.

☐ APPLICATIONS OF DISCOURSE STUDIES OF THE VERB TENSE AND ASPECT

Bardovi-Harlig (1996) models the way in which discourse studies can lead to practical applications for the teaching of ESL/EFL. In the first stage, she considers the nature of verbs in a particular type of discourse, demonstrating the different uses of past tense verbs in the two major subdivisions that make up a narrative. The "foreground" of a narrative is the story that is being told; it is chronological in organization and is most often presented in simple past tense. The "background" of a narrative is the other material that is woven into a story to give additional information, descriptions of characters and settings, and information about prior events that somehow influence the story. Bardovi-Harlig shows that the background of a narrative is usually the location for the use of past perfect and past progressive—as well as simple past tense. Here is Bardovi-Harlig's explanation of the verb forms that can be found in the foreground in contrast to the background of a narrative:

> The simple past tense carries the main story line, or *foreground.* Foreground events occur in chronological order (what happened first is reported first, in other words). In contrast, other tense/aspect forms populate the *background*. The background provides information which elaborates or evaluates events in the foreground. The background is not in chronological order. The background can be used to set the scene or to make comments about events in the foreground, or to predict future events. These diverse functions result in the use of diverse tense/aspect forms. Simple past also occurs in the backgorund. The important point is that other forms generally do not occur in the foreground. (p. 10)

For example, sample 2 from Chapter 5, this volume, recounts the destruction of a Native American village by a group of Spanish adventurers in the sixteenth century. The foreground uses the past tense verbs *entered, disappeared, began, attacked, killed, rallied, set,* and *lasted* to tell this horrible story. The rest of the material is background that describes the village and gives information about the details of the carnage.

> On the morning of October 18, 1540, the entourage entered Mabila, a village located on a plain above a wide river. The town was surrounded by a palisade, and inside were eighty large houses fronting a square. Tascaluza disappeared inside a house, and the Indians began to dance and sing while the Spanish grew more suspicious and uneasy. Suddenly, the Indians attacked, shooting arrows from the houses and forcing the Spanish to flee the village, leaving some of their horses behind. The Indians promptly killed the feared animals. De Soto rallied his men for a counterattack and set fire to the village. The battle, most of it hand-to-hand combat, lasted until nightfall. In his manuscript, the Inca claimed 11,000 Indians died; Biedma reported 5,000 killed; and the more reliable Ranjel related that the Spanish found 3,000 Indian bodies without counting the dead inside the burned village. The Gentleman of Elvas reported 2,500 dead. The Indian losses were probably fewer than any of these figures, but by any count they were extensive. Whether Tascaluza died or escaped was not discovered, but his town of Mabila and his Indians were destroyed.

In the second stage of the process of applying theory to practice, Bardovi-Harlig devises teaching activities that build student knowledge of the grammar and skill at using it. Students learn about the internal structure of narrative and about the grammar associated with different parts of that structure. In this particular application, Bardovi-Harlig uses transcripts of materials from the U.S. National Public Radio to have authentic samples of English for students to work from. Students learn to analyze narratives into foreground and background and then observe how the verbs work for these two different but interrelated aspects of the total narrative. Later they can write the chronology of a story and then add the background, using authentic samples of spoken or written narratives to guide their understanding of how the grammar of narratives works. Similar activities can be done using academic content—for example, narratives from history textbooks or the narratives that recount the steps in a research process from sociology or psychology materials.

□ APPLICATIONS OF DISCOURSE STUDIES OF THE NOUN PHRASE

Studies of the English article system and noun phrase in academic and popular scientific writing (e.g., Byrd, 1995; Master, 1987 and 1990) have shown a remarkable characteristic of English: In text after text, over 50 percent of noun phrases have no article or determiner at all. Put another way, most of the noun phrases in these written materials were "nouns without articles," for example, the nouns in bold type in this definition from an accounting textbook:

> **Liabilities** are **probable future sacrifices** of **economic benefits** arising from **present obligations** of a particular entity to transfer **assets** or provide **services** to **other entities** in the future as a result of **past transactions** or **events**.

To see how these noun phrases function in different discourse types, I looked at noun phrases in a sample from a popular U.S. history textbook and a sample from a frequently used accounting textbook. While in both samples over 50 percent of the noun phrases were without articles or determiners, different kinds of noun phrases were used in the two different settings. The "nouns without articles" in the history text tended to be proper names (*Christopher Columbus, Henry VII, Catherine of Aragon*); in the accounting text, few proper nouns were used but many gerunds and plural nouns for concepts and professional terminology were given (*accounting, operations, accounting rules*). The following sentences from the longer textbook samples used in Chapter 3 illustrate this type of noun phrase. The first sample is from an accounting textbook; the second, from a U.S. history textbook.

> In 1987, **General Motors**[1] elected to change the estimated useful life[2] of its tools and dies[3]. The change[4] resulted in an increase[5] in **income**[6] from **operations**[7] of **over \$1.2 billion**[8], accounting for approximately 25% of

earnings[9] for that year[10]. If **accounting rules**[11] allow such flexibility[12] and judgment[13] in the reporting[14] of **revenues**[15] and **expenses**[16], is **accounting**[17] more of an art[18] or a science[19]? Should **accounting standards**[20] allow **management**[21] such discretion[22] in **reporting**[23] **financial information**[24]? [24 noun phrases with 13 without articles or determiners—and 14 if *judgment* is counted as technically not having its own separate determiner.]

The English King Henry VII[1] passed up a chance[2] to have **Christopher Columbus**[3] plant his flag[4] on an American beach[5]. **Henry**[6] failed to act when **Columbus**[7], momentarily discouraged in **Spain**[8], wrote to him proposing that he sail westward to the Indies[9] in Henry's employ[10]. Nevertheless, England's claim[11] to a piece[12] of the Americas[13] was almost as old as Spain's. In 1497, **Henry VII**[14] sent another Italian sailor[15], **John Cabot**[16], across the North Atlantic[17] in **search**[18] of a route[19] to **Asia**[20]. **Cabot**[21] discovered **New-foundland**[22] and **Nova Scotia**[23], which he claimed for **England**[24]. **Cabot**[25] actually touched on **continental America**[26] a year[27] earlier than **Columbus**[28] did. [28 noun phrases with 15 without determiners]

This information suggests that the obsession of ESL/EFL teachers and materials with teaching students "how to use articles" is possibly off track. Perhaps students need to learn first when they can use noun phrases with no article or determiner—something many of them tend to do naturally, if without principled purpose. Another implication is that we need to teach particular noun types in particular settings—we shouldn't teach students about nouns and noun phrases in the abstract, but should work on proper nouns in narrative settings such as history and generic nouns (for the names of concepts) in authentic materials from business administration, the social sciences, and the laboratory sciences.

□ USING DISCOURSE-BASED RESEARCH TO BUILD ESL/EFL GRAMMAR LESSONS

Many other studies are available in the growing literature on discourse, especially academic discourse (e.g., Conrad, 1996a and 1996b; Love, 1993; Myers, 1991; Pica, 1983b; Stockton, 1995; Swales, 1990a and 1990b). This process of building grammar lessons from research information and authentic examples gives a model that can be used by teachers and materials writers to move away from lessons that present forms in terms of time lines and other abstract approaches to meaning. We start the process with a needs analysis to learn what our students need to be able to do in English; then we learn about the characteristics of that particular type of communication; then we build lessons and materials to help students gain the knowledge and skills necessary for such communication. For example, our students need to be able to read and write about U.S. history because they will be required to take a course in U.S. history in their general education requirements. To be able to handle this material, students must be able to use simple past tense, past perfect, and past progressive verbs (among other grammatical features of history text). That is, in this ESL/EFL program to prepare students for U.S. undergraduate study, students learn about the past tense verbs in order to read and write history text. The program does not take teaching past tense verbs as its first priority. Teaching that verb set becomes a priority only because of the communication goals of the students. Studies of grammar in discourse become important for the ESL/EFL program because they allow us to make accurate decisions about the grammar to include in our lessons and materials.

However, these studies of grammar in discourse, as helpful as they can be, do not provide an overall framework that gives coherence to the total package of grammar to be presented in a set of materials or in the curriculum of an ESL/EFL program. To get the overview that we need, we must turn to studies that look at the functioning of the whole system.

THE CLUSTERING OF GRAMMAR IN PARTICULAR SETTINGS: SYSTEMATIC PRESENTATION OF GRAMMAR

ESL/EFL teachers have long recognized that past tense verbs show up in past time narratives and that present progressive verbs are frequently used for communication about present time events. Researchers using computers to analyze large collections of spoken and written English are developing much more sophisticated analyses that detail the grammar items that tend to cluster together in particular settings (Biber, 1988; Biber, Conrad, & Reppen 1994; Conrad, 1996a and 1996b; Grabe, 1987; Sinclair, 1987a, 1987b, & 1991). These studies offer a method for both analyzing and presenting English grammar in context that can be used in the development of a coherent approach to grammar in curriculum design and materials development.

In *Variation Across Speech and Writing* (1988), Douglas Biber reports a large-scale research project through which he analyzed the grammatical features of computerized collections of both written and spoken English.[4] The first stage of his study was to develop a list of potentially important grammatical features based on previous research studies, to collect and convert into computer format a selection of spoken and written samples, and to count the occurrence of the grammatical features in those texts. The second stage involved use of statistical procedures first to find out which of the grammatical features clustered together and then to interpret the meanings of those sets of grammatical features based on their uses in the text samples. Finally, he used the grammatical dimensions that he had developed in the second stage to analyze the texts—to see what kinds of grammar tend to show up in what kinds of texts.

Based on this study of the ways that grammar items cluster across many different types of spoken and written English, Biber demonstrates that English communication in both speaking and writing varies along six dimensions. That is, no one set of grammatical features can be used to characterize a genre or to describe the differences between spoken and written English, but rather texts differ from each other in terms of their use or lack of use of features from the six dimensions.

The first two of Biber's categories will be considered in detail in this chapter; these grammatical dimensions are

1. Involved vs. Informational grammar[5]
2. Narrative vs. Nonnarrative grammar.

(Of the four other clusters of grammar identified in Biber (1988), two will be discussed later in this chapter—Factor 4, "Overt expression of persuasion" and Factor 5, "Abstract.") Biber commented that the features that he found as characteristic of the involved-informational dimension are not an artificial result of his statistical procedures but "rather an extremely powerful factor representing a very basic dimension of variation among spoken and written texts in English" (p. 104). Likewise, the contrast between narrative and nonnarrative is a fundamental one in English communication.

It is important to realize that these clusters of grammatical features are based on empirical evidence—on what grammar occurs in the texts that Biber analyzed. He did not "decide" on these clusters but discovered them through the application of statistical procedures to a large sample of English that included both written and spoken English.

Biber's analysis is an especially powerful tool for language teachers. First, he shows that speaking and writing are not separate languages, but rather that both make use of the same basic grammatical resources. For example, a spoken conference presentation at a meeting of biologists will have many of the characteristics found in written versions of that same information. On the other hand, a newspaper feature article that uses an informal style involving a pattern of questions and answers will be very like a spoken conversation in the basic elements of grammar that are employed by the writer. Second, Biber points to a method through which we can have a discourse-first approach to language teaching and yet have a coherent and nonrandom approach to grammar.

□   INVOLVED AND INFORMATIONAL GRAMMAR

Biber's dimension #1 involves two extremes: "involved" and "informational" (Biber, 1988). "Involved" communication is what is generally thought of as informal, interactive communication: using lots of questions, talking about personal topics, and generally being less formal in style (using shorter words and repeating them more often, for example). According to Biber's research (1988), the language of "involved" communication (whether spoken or written) includes frequent use of the following grammatical elements (p. 102).[6] Biber's original list was organized by statistical frequency; the items have been reorganized in Table 4.1 in order

Table 4.1: Grammar of Involved Communication (Biber, 1988:102)

I. Verbs

1. "private verbs" (Biber takes these from Quirk, Greenbaum, Leech, & Svartvik [1985:1181–1182]: *anticipate, assume, believe, conclude, decide, demonstrate, determine, discover, doubt, estimate, fear, feel, find, forget, guess, hear, hope, imagine, imply, indicate, infer, know, learn, mean, notice, prove, realize, recognize, remember, reveal, see, show, suppose, think, understand.*)
2. present tense verbs
3. *be* used as a main verb
4. modal auxiliaries used especially for the "possibility" meanings with heavier use of *can, could, may, might* (and their contracted forms)
5. contractions

II. Pronouns

6. 1st and 2nd person pronouns
7. *it* used for wide range of references to concepts, things
8. demonstrative pronouns
9. indefinite pronouns (*anybody, anyone, anything, everybody, everyone, everything, nobody, none, nothing, nowhere, somebody, someone, something,* taken by Biber from Quirk et al. [1985:376ff])

III. Sentence-Level Grammar

10. deletion of *that* (for example, *I think she's a wonderful teacher.*)
11. sentence relatives (such as *He is always late to class, which irritates me a lot.*)
12. other relative clauses
13. questions and *do* as a pro-verb in questions (Questions *with who, what, when, where, why,* and other WH-questions are especially important.)
14. negation with *not*
15. statement final prepositions
16. *because* and other subordinators that indicate causes or reasons
17. conditional subordination
18. use of *and* to string phrases together in a relatively loose manner

IV. Vocabulary

19. "discourse particles" such as *well, now, anyway, anyhow, anyways*
20. "emphatics" such as *for sure, a lot, such a, real* + adjective, *do* + verb, *just, really, most, more*
21. general hedges such as *at about, something like, more or less, almost, maybe, sort of, kind of* (for example, *He is kind of tired,* but not *She is the kind of person who helps her neighbors*).
22. adverbs
23. amplifiers such as *absolutely, extremely, perfectly*

to pull together related grammatical items to show the categories to which the various items belong. Biber (1988) sums up the "involved" cluster as "verbal, interactional, affective, fragmented, reduced in form, and generalized in content" (p. 105).

At the other end of the continuum from "involved" communication is a type that Biber calls "informational" (pp. 102–108). In contrast to the informal

Table 4.2: Grammar of Informational Communication (Biber, 1988:102)

I. Verbs
    1. very few different verbs, the same verbs repeated often
    2. agentless passives
II. Nouns and Noun Phrases
    3. lots of different nouns
    4. longer nouns than in "involved"
    5. "attributive" adjectives—those coming in front of a noun
    6. prepositions—heavy use of prepositional phrases to modify nouns
III. Present and Past Participial Phrases (often adding additional information to nouns)
IV. Place adverbials used to indicate location in a text (For example: *It was shown here.*)

"involved" style, the informational style is characterized by the frequent use of the following grammatical features, many of which focus on the creation of complex noun phrases.[7] That is, while "involved" communication is verb-oriented, "informational" communication is noun-oriented.[8] The table of features of informational grammar in Table 4.2 is built on Biber (1988).[9] Biber's original list was organized by statistical frequency; the items have been reorganized in order to pull together related grammatical items to show the categories to which the various items belong. Biber (1988) sums up the "informational" dimension as being designed to provide a high degree of information:

> High frequencies of all these features [nouns, longer words, prepositional phrases, high number of new words in relation to the number of words in the text, and adjectives in front of the nouns] can be associated with a high informational focus and a careful integration of information in a text. (p. 104)

It is important to notice that spoken English can be "literate" in its grammar, as in scripted speeches and radio or television presentations, and that written English can be "oral" in its grammar when a writer uses the grammar of the "involved" cluster to attempt to connect with the reader in ways similar to a conversation. But these terms can be confusing since they seem to imply that we have separate languages for writing and for speaking—a misinterpretation of how English is used.

"Informational" and "involved" are opposite ends of a continuum. Thus, some communication can be highly informational with few of the features of involved communication—for example, the definitions of accounting terminology on page 39. Yet other communication can be highly involved with little use of the features of informational communication—for example, the dialogue given on page 85 between two characters in a murder mystery. Other communication can combine features from both ends of the continuum—for example, the sample from the psychology textbook on page 86 has the complex noun phrases and full sentences of informational writing but also uses questions and first- and second-person pronouns as in involved communication.

□ NARRATIVE AND NONNARRATIVE GRAMMAR

Biber's second major grammatical dimension contrasts the grammar of narrative to the grammar of nonnarrative communication. Using a narrative or a nonnarrative approach turns out to be a fundamental decision in communication in English that cuts across many different genres and communication settings. Table 4.3, features of narrative grammar, is based on Biber (1988). Biber's original list was organized by statistical frequency; the items have been reorganized in Table 4.3 in order to pull together related grammatical items to show the categories to which the various items belong. It is important to notice that narrative includes not just past tense verbs but other grammar associated with storytelling—the use of time adverbs to set the time line, for example. Narratives, of course, do not have to be fiction or folktales. Nor does the purpose of narrative have to be creation of fiction, since narratives can be based on "real-life" events, and they are certainly used for a wide variety of communicative functions.[10]

In contrast to narratives, nonnarrative communication has two major features in Biber's analysis. The connections between nonnarrative and informational communication are considered in Chapter 3. The features of nonnarrative grammar given in Table 4.4 come from Biber (1988). Biber's original list was organized by

---

Table 4.3: Grammar of Narrative Communication (Biber, 1988: 102)

I. Verbs
  1. past tense (the usual approach, although some narratives can involve present tense for particular effects)
  2. perfect aspect verbs (past perfect and present perfect to set up time relationships in the narrative)
  3. public verbs (Biber took these from Quirk et al. [1985]: *acknowledge, admit, agree, assert, complain, declare, deny, explain, hint, insist, mention, proclaim, promise, protest, remark, reply, report, say, suggest, swear, write*)
II. Sentences
  4. negation using *neither/nor* rather than just the basic *not* version
  5. present participial clauses
  6. sentence-level strategies include using present participle clauses
III. Third-Person Pronouns (to refer to the nouns used in the narrative)

Table 4.4: Grammar of Nonnarrative Communication (Biber, 1988: 102)

I. Verbs: present tense verbs
II. Nouns and Noun Phrases: longer and more elaborate noun phrases (with adjectives in front of the nouns)
III. Sentences: Past participle clauses (reduced form)
IV. Words: longer words than in narratives

statistical frequency; the items have been reorganized in Table 4.4 in order to pull together related grammatical items to show the categories to which the various items belong.

The relationship between narrative and nonnarrative is a continuum with some communication being more purely narrative and other communication more purely nonnarrative in nature. However, texts can be found that combine features of the two—for example, the sample of U.S. history textbook writing on page 36 uses narrative grammar to tell its story but also has the complex noun phrases and dense, packed sentences expected in nonnarrative communication.

□ THE GRAMMAR OF ABSTRACT COMMUNICATION

In addition to these two major dimensions, Biber found the following features that characterize the more abstract communication often found in academic settings (journal articles and conference presentations both can have these features).[11] This type of communication has heavier use of passives and relatively lower variety in vocabulary (the same technical terms are repeated rather than introducing new vocabulary). As Biber (1988) says, this type of communication is "abstract, technical, and formal" (p. 113). Some teachers look at this set of features and are inclined, as a graduate student in my grammar seminar once did, to see these as the features of "bad writing" because of the heavy use of passive voice and "technical jargon." Biber is not describing the language of literature and of beautiful writing; he uses a corpus that is built on a wide range of authentic selections of spoken and written English. While surely some abstract writing can be made less unpleasant to the English teacher's eye, we need to understand that such writing serves an important purpose within the discourse community that uses it, providing a tool that can be very exact in its meanings. And, of course, being able to write like this is a sign that a writer knows how to appeal to other members of that group and to signal to them that she/he, too, is a member of that discourse community.

□ OVERT EXPRESSION OF PERSUASION

Biber (1988) describes another type of communication that is important in academic settings in the cluster of grammatical features that he labels "overt expression of persuasion." This type of communication involves modal auxiliaries for a variety of meanings when the writer expresses an opinion or makes a claim about the meaning of information. The following statement from a psychology textbook illustrates the way that a textbook writer used modals to limit the extent of his claim about the meaning of an experiment; this type of persuasion depends on convincing the audience that exactly the right interpretation of the data has been made without overgeneralizing:[12]

It **would seem** that when energy is scarce, it **will be channeled** to the more basic needs of the body; achievement, affiliation, and other "higher" motives **must wait** their turn.

In addition, Biber found heavy use of "suasive verbs" such as *agree, arrange, ask, beg, command, decide, demand, grant, insist, instruct, ordain, pledge, pronounce, propose, recommend, request, stipulate, suggest, urge* (taken by Biber from Quirk et al. [1985:1182–3]). This cluster also includes conditional subordination with *if* or *unless*. That is, the cluster involves the expression of opinion and the overt attempt to persuade the listener/reader to a point of view. Such communication can often be found in very particular locations in academic discourse— for example, in the conclusion of an essay, article, or textbook chapter, and in statements about ethics or professional standards.

CONCLUSION

While Biber's research is complex and built around application of statistical methods to large-scale computerized databases, his results go directly to the heart of a major problem in ESL curriculum design—how to handle the grammar—and provide a straightforward answer to our difficult problem. When we know what kinds of materials our students read, write, listen to, and talk about, then we know how the grammatical resources of English are organized in those various discourse types. In the ESL writing course, we can focus on the discourse while at the same time providing lessons and materials that develop students' knowledge and skills of the grammar of different types of academic writing. Thus, we move **from** the discourse to the grammar and more effectively prepare our students to handle the language actually used in their degree courses.

NOTES

1. For example, a tripartite analysis of the modal auxiliaries would have these features:

Form: 1. Used in verb phrases as modal + verb, modal + perfect, modal + progressive, or modal + perfect + progressive

2. Not combined with *to* infinitive

3. A system of interrelated forms that come in matched sets: *will/would, shall/should, may/might, can/could. Must* is generally paired with *had to.*

Meaning: Generally used to add shades of meaning to statements based on opinions and values. Several meaning subsets can be identified: (1) asking and giving permission, (2) predicting with more or less certainty about the future, (3) explaining skills and abilities, (4) making observations and stating opinions about events.

Pragmatics (Use in Context): Used in settings where opinions and values are stated. Some of the contexts include, for example, (1) conclusions of essays, chapters, speeches, and so forth to discuss future implications of the ideas and content previously presented, (2) statements of ethics and morality, (3) New Year's Day statements and end-of-the millennium statements that predict the future (while generally also making value judgments about the present).

2. Biber (1988) demonstrates the frequent use of prepositional phrases to postmodify nouns as one of the features that characterizes informational communication with its long, complex noun phrases.

3. These are just two samples from a rich and growing literature on the nature of English in context. Studies focused on English in academic textbooks and professional writing in various disciplines are a treasure trove of information for ESL/EFL teachers, curriculum coordinators, and materials writers. Among these are studies such as Conrad (1996b), Haas (1994), Love (1993), Stockton (1995), and Swales 1990b. Moreover, every new issue of the journal *English for Specific Purposes* offers more studies—although that is certainly not the only place where such studies are published.

4. The corpora used by Biber are the Lancaster-Oslo-Bergen Corpus of British English (the LOB) and the London-Lund Corpus of Spoken English. While Conrad (1996a and 1996b) has used Biber's methodology to analyze textbooks used in teaching biology and history courses in U.S. universities and Byrd (1995) has analyzed the grammar of both U.S. history and accounting textbooks, we do not yet have a large-scale corpus based on large samples of textbook discourse.

5. Biber sometimes characterizes involved as "oral" and informational as "literate," but he is using these terms to suggest that involved communication is often if not always conversational and that informational communication is often but not always written. While Biber's use of these terms is always clear in his presentation of his work, I have avoided the words "oral" and "literate" in this chapter because of the comments of reviewers who found them potentially confusing in light of Biber's demonstration that spoken and written language do not make up a dichotomy. As Biber says and shows, conversational English uses structures that are effective in interaction with our listeners and that can be used when time is limited, and written English uses structures that would be harder to use in speaking and that are available in writing because we have more time to be exact and detailed—but we can write as we speak and speak in a manner much like our writing. The differences between speaking and writing are not simple and cannot be explained in terms of a dichotomy.

6. Samples to illustrate "involved" grammar are given on pages 85–86 in Chapter 5.

7. Samples to illustrate "informational" grammar are given on pages 87–90 in Chapter 5.

8. Unfortunately, ESL/EFL grammar and writing materials often are heavily weighted toward study of verbs with relatively little attention given to the formation and use of complex noun phrases.

9. A feature of Biber (1988) that needs further investigation and discussion is the location of present tense in the "involved" cluster—which means the exclusion of present tense from the "informational" cluster except at those points along the continuum where involved and informational features would be mixed together in substantial amounts. One explanation is that his analysis shows the importance of verbs in involved communication and the importance of complex noun phrases in informational communication. In addition, present tense shows up as characteristic of the "nonnarrative" in factor 2 (the narrative vs. nonnarrative continuum). Nonnarrative looks a great deal like informational—a characteristic that is used in the interpretation of Biber in Chapter 3, this volume. In a study using many of the same methods as Biber (1988), Grabe (1987) also has similar results, finding present tense as a fundamental characteristic in his two most powerful factor sets—both his "immediacy of context" continuum and his "orientation of discourse" continuum. This similarity confirms the importance of present tense and the difficulty of determining its exact location in a particular cluster.

Finally, present tense is the most commonly used verb throughout most samples of communication that would otherwise be characterized as "informational." Because of its usefulness in pedagogical applications, present tense as a feature of informational communication is included in the interpretation of Biber's work in Chapter 3, this volume. Perhaps study focused exclusively on the grammatical features of academic text might offer a solution for this one subset of English discourse.

10. Samples that show narrative used for a variety of purposes and at a variety of proficiency levels are given on pages 77–83 in Chapter 5, this volume.

11. This type of communication is analyzed in Chapter 3 as a subset of the "informational" category.

12. See page 43 in Chapter 3 for the full passage from which this sentence was taken.

Chapter 5

Rethinking Grammar at Various Proficiency Levels

IMPLICATIONS OF AUTHENTIC MATERIALS FOR THE EAP CURRICULUM

Patricia Byrd

PROFICIENCY LEVELS AND GRAMMAR: THE ESL/EFL TRADITION

The tradition in ESL/EFL has been to try to divide English grammar into proficiency level chunks, assigning particular items to entry-level students while other items are reserved for the next levels. Teachers are often given lists of grammar items that are supposed to be covered in each proficiency level and to be used in making decisions about promotion of students to the next higher level. (See Table 5.1 for an example of such a curriculum, taken from one used in a large U.S. community college ESL program.) Systems for dividing grammar among proficiency levels have been based on two general principles: (1) notions of linguistic interconnectedness—which things must be learned in preparation for the next higher level and (2) notions of easiness and difficulty—which structures are easier or harder for students to learn. The lack of consistency in the decisions that have been made using these standards suggests that the "interconnectedness," "ease," and "difficulty" are not stable concepts that can be defined with certainty. Indeed, some lack of clarity about the differences between "easy/hard to learn" and "easy/hard to teach" have added to problems with such systems (see Byrd, 1994, for a discussion of the ease/difficulty matrix). Unfortunately, decisions about what grammar to teach at what levels have sometimes been based on what happens to have been presented in a particular textbook: One level takes the first half of the book, and the next level takes the second half of the book.

Table 5.1: A Traditional Divide-Up-the-Grammar Curriculum Statement

LEVEL 1
- ☐ simple sentences (affirmative & negative)
- ☐ compound sentences (*and, but, or, so*)
- ☐ complex sentences (*while, before, when, because, after*) [optional for this level]
- ☐ simple questions (*yes, no*)
- ☐ information questions (*who, what, when, where*)
- ☐ nouns (singular & plural)
- ☐ pronouns (objective, demonstrative)
- ☐ possessives (noun, pronoun, adjective)
- ☐ position of adjectives (comparatives and superlatives) [optional for this level]

LEVEL 2
- ☐ 75% mastery of level 1
- ☐ simple sentences
- ☐ compound sentences
- ☐ complex sentences with time clauses
- ☐ simple questions
- ☐ information questions (*which, whose, whom, when, because*)
- ☐ noun phrases (count, noncount with articles)
- ☐ pronouns (reflexive and impersonal *you*)
- ☐ adjective clauses (restrictive) [optional at this level]
- ☐ noun modifiers

LEVEL 3
- ☐ 75% mastery of level 2
- ☐ simple sentences
- ☐ compound sentences
- ☐ complex sentences with time and cause-and-effect clauses
- ☐ simple questions
- ☐ information questions
- ☐ tag questions
- ☐ nouns (collective and abstract)
- ☐ adjective clauses (restrictive)
- ☐ adjective clauses (nonrestrictive) [optional at this level]

LEVEL 4
- ☐ 75% mastery of level 3
- ☐ simple sentences
- ☐ compound sentences
- ☐ complex sentences
- ☐ simple questions
- ☐ information questions
- ☐ embedded questions
- ☐ noun clauses (reported speech)
- ☐ adjective clauses (reduction)—participles as modifiers

PROBLEMS FOR STUDENTS AND LEARNERS CAUSED BY THIS TRADITION

The problems inherent in attempts to divide English into proficiency levels are powerfully illustrated in Crandall (1985), a study of the language used in teaching arithmetic. Crandall found that passive sentences occur in the very first levels of elementary school in statements such as "4 is divided by 2." Thus, ESL curricula that are designed to prepare young children to participate in arithmetic classes cannot delay the teaching of the passive as a "more advanced" grammar topic—as is often done in ESL/EFL materials and curricula based on the "divide up the grammar by levels" approach.

A common complaint voiced by teachers working in traditional systems such as that illustrated in Table 5.1 is "I can't cover all the material. If I don't, the students won't have another chance. But my students just can't learn all of this material in one term!" A peculiarity of the traditional design is its assumption that students can "put off" elements of grammar for later in their lives—notice how the curriculum in Table 5.1 delays the use of noun phrases and articles until level 2 and demands mastery (or 75% mastery) at that level. The frustration of teachers with such a plan is only natural—such a division is both *inauthentic* (students can't wait until level 2 to start working with noun phrases since any authentic English will have articles and noun phrases) and *unrealistic* (few students will "master" noun phrases in a single term of study).

For teachers, these subdivisions in the traditional design seem to lead repeatedly to the same practical problem—whatever grammar students need frequently seems to be taught in another level of the curriculum or textbook. Teachers find that they need to teach grammar that is supposed to be delayed to a higher level; they also find that students do not yet have "mastery" of grammar that they were supposed to have learned at a lower proficiency level. Studies of second-language acquisition, and of learning more generally, support the learning pattern that most of us have experienced for ourselves—learning usually takes place slowly, over time, with inconsistencies in performance (Larsen-Freeman, 1991; Ellis, 1994, especially chapter 9). Students cannot be expected to learn everything correctly through just one presentation during just one academic term; most learners need repeated "spiraling" of a topic and of various aspects of a topic. For example, students of Vietnamese origin will usually require long periods of study before they can become consistent in their use of features of English unknown in Vietnamese, such as use of suffixes to mark plural nouns or verb tense (Byleen,1986). Thus, it would not be wise to place study of noun plurals only in one level of a multilevel curriculum or textbook series.

Teachers have reported student frustration when the grammar that they want to learn is not available in the current textbook or the current course. Additionally, systems built on these subdivisions have created another problem for learners that results from the frequent changes that students make in moving from one program or school or institution to another over the years that they are learning English.

Because of the lack of congruence between the designs of different programs and of different sets of materials, students are unlikely to have coherent encounters with the English language.

These practical problems point to the underlying distortion with this approach to English grammar. There is no evidence at all that the English language has proficiency levels. While the grammatical and lexical resources of English can be used to create communication that is more or less difficult for particular users to understand, the language itself exists as a unified whole. Two fundamental insights derived from the unity of English grammar need to be applied to the development of lessons, curricula, and materials:

☐ The grammar of English does not exist in proficiency level chunks.

☐ As a result, proficiency levels cannot be defined in terms of separate pieces of English grammar.

"Beginner" cannot be characterized in terms of features such as simple past tense and one or two of the modal auxiliaries; nor can "Intermediate" be defined as having control over past tense plus present tense and a few more of the modal auxiliaries. Attempts to make these impossible distinctions have long distorted materials and curricula.

STUDIES OF "SIMPLIFIED" READINGS: IMPLICATIONS FOR PROFICIENCY LEVELS

Work focused on the creation of more "readable" textbook materials provides another angle on the topic of grammar and proficiency levels. In a study of techniques for making reading materials more comprehensible, Britton, Gulgoz, and Glynn (1993) show that reading passages can be made more accessible to students by improving the ways in which the content is presented.[1] They provide three principles based on the work on human learning of W. Kintsch and his colleagues to guide the revision of "expert written content" to make it more accessible in textbook presentations:

Principle 1: Make it easier for the learner to establish coherence by rewriting each sentence so that it repeats the linking word from the previous sentence.

Principle 2: Make coherence easier to establish by arranging the parts of each sentence so the learner first encounters the part of the sentence that specifies where that sentence is to be connected to the rest of the mental representation and second encounters the other part of the sentence, which tells the learner what new information to add to the previously specified location in the mental representation [that is, giving old information before new information].

Principle 3: Make coherence easier to establish by making explicit any important implicit references: For instance, when an important concept is referred to implicitly, refer to it explicitly if the reader may otherwise miss an important coherence link. (pp. 21–22)

Britton, Gulgoz, and Glynn demonstrate that these techniques of text reorganization and expansion improve readability much more than the older traditions of text simplification. Other studies of text simplification have similar results. In their review of the literature on linguistic simplification of text, Ross and Long (1993) found that the simplification process produces unnatural target language models. Young (1991) demonstrated that ESL readers use different strategies to process edited texts from authentic texts. Lotherington-Woloszyn (1993) showed that not only could students readily tell simplified from authentic versions of texts—but they were overly optimistic about their ability to comprehend the simplified texts and overly negative about their ability to comprehend the authentic texts.

In sum, the dangers of using inauthentic text that has been simplified to make it easier are (1) that the materials can remain difficult (because of the loss of connectors and other language used to guide the reader through the text) and (2) that the students learn to read unnatural text rather than developing strategies for reading authentic text. The implications for proficiency level design are clear: We cannot build our designs around lists of grammar structures that limit student access to certain items—and that require that the reading materials that they use contain only those items.

The simplification of reading materials has much in common with divide-up-the-grammar curriculum design. Yano, Long, and Ross (1994) comment about simplified reading materials:

> In addition to their limitations as valid models and variable helpfulness for comprehension, such linguistically simplified readers' input can negatively affect learner output and language acquisition. . . . Worse, removal of possibly unknown linguistic items from a text may facilitate comprehension but will simultaneously deny learners access to the items they need to learn. Linguistic simplification can be self-defeating to the extent that the purpose of a reading lesson is not the comprehension of a particular text, which learners are unlikely ever to encounter again outside the classroom, but the learning of the language in which the text is written and/or the development of transferable, non-text-specific, reading skills. (p. 191)

The same problems result from the "divide-up-the-grammar" curriculum that attempts subdivisions of English into "simplified" chunks for each proficiency level.

Research into the implications of schema theory for ESL has also demonstrated repeatedly that second-language reading comprehension improves when the content of the reading passage is familiar to the learners (Johnson, 1981; Carrell, 1987; Crandall, 1995). Thus, while some materials are more difficult (and thus in some sense "more advanced") for some readers, the difficulties are often the result of a lack of background knowledge. A research article on chemistry will be almost impossible for most nonchemists to read, but the difficulties arise from the nonchemist's complete lack of familiarity with the content of the piece of writing and with the ways that chemists use English when they write for each other—rather than from the complexity of the grammar.

The point here is that the differences between texts that can be labeled "simple" or "advanced" have to do with background knowledge that the texts demand of readers as well as with organization, vocabulary, and even formatting[2]—not the items of grammar that are found in each. Indeed, a piece of writing for young readers or for new readers that tells a story set in the past is going to be very like a university-level history textbook in the items of grammar used in both. The major differences have to do with the range of vocabulary used and with the complexity of the sentence patterns—materials at different educational levels make different conceptual demands. Both, however, will have the same general grammatical framework of past tense verbs, proper nouns and personal pronouns, and adverbs and other markers of the narrative sequence (prepositional phrases, for example, and other indicators of time and location). (Chapter 4, Grammar FROM Context, provides more discussion of the grammar clusters in academic writing.)

DIVISIONS INTO PROFICIENCY LEVELS
BASED ON LEARNERS' GRAMMAR

Certainly, learners can be classified into proficiency levels based on a plan for grouping together students with roughly the same skill at using English. It should, nevertheless, be remembered that proficiency levels are based as much on the financial realities of the ESL program as on linguistic knowledge and skills: A program or department can have as many levels as there is money to hire teachers to staff them.[3] Moreover, no teacher has ever had a class in which all of the students were perfectly matched in every aspect of their linguistic skill. In other words, proficiency levels are not absolutes; they change from program to program in the numbers of levels, the names given the levels, and the linguistic skills of the students in those levels. The only "absolute" is the true beginner who knows nothing of the language being studied.

Krashen's "Natural Order of Acquisition" (e.g., Krashen, 1982) might be pointed to as "scientific" evidence that grammar items can be used as the basis for proficiency levels. Application of this aspect of Krashen's work to program design seems impossible for several reasons.[4] First, as intuitively appealing as the concept is for teachers, few concrete details are known about the natural order of second-language acquisition, and whole programs cannot be built around, for instance, the late development of control over subject-verb agreement by many learners. Second, learners from different language backgrounds may have different "natural orders of second-language acquisition"—think of the differences between the learning of English by speakers of Spanish and by speakers of Japanese. Third, for curriculum and materials design, a major problem with current knowledge about the "natural order" of second-language acquisition is the focus on limited numbers of grammatical forms—and forms taken out of context. The point at which a learner knows how to add -s to make noun plurals is not as important a question for language teachers as the point at which a learner can use plural nouns to communicate about plural topics or generic topics. We need a natural order of acquisition focused on a richer definition of language—and language in use—than seems to lie behind many studies of the order of acquisition (Gregg, 1994). In sum, the "natural order of acquisition" does not provide a basis for organizing grammar in the ESL curriculum that solves the problems created by the current system.

AN ALTERNATIVE WAY OF ENVISIONING GRAMMAR IN THE ESL CURRICULUM

The tradition of trying to make proficiency level decisions based on dividing grammar across the levels has not worked well either for teachers or for learners. If dividing grammar into discrete sets to define proficiency levels doesn't work to the benefit of teachers and students, then how is grammar to be presented in a multi-level program? Studies of grammar in discourse provide a strategy for having appropriate work on grammar at different proficiency levels while at the same time not distorting the features of English grammar or making inappropriate and impossible demands on the learner.

In *Variation Across Speech and Writing* (1988), Douglas Biber reports on research into the grammar of both spoken and written English, showing the ways that particular features of grammar are "clustered" together in sets that are used in different types of discourse. Briefly, important grammatical clusters for working with ESL students include the linguistic features of (1) narrative communication (not just fiction but other storytelling such as that featured in case studies or examples based on past time events), (2) interactive communication (interacting with the audience by asking questions and using language that is thought of as "oral"), and (3) informational communication (stating facts, theories, definitions, generalizations, and using language thought of as "literate" to give information).[5]

What teachers and students need is an approach to grammar in the curriculum that is both more realistic and more authentic. The approach to grammar explained in this chapter and in Chapters 3 and 4 is built on a plan that gives students experience learning and using the grammar of written English in a spiral pattern that keeps returning to the same vitally important topics at all levels. At each level, a student works on the grammar topic with materials and activities appropriate to her/his language proficiency. For example, teachers know that all students at all levels need to work on:

□ writing complete sentences—rather than the fragments that they import from their spoken English,

□ various aspects of the English verb system, and

□ the meaning and use of the English noun phrase.

Moreover, students at all levels need to be working with coherent samples of authentic English.

The samples in the following section are given to show how the same features of grammar keep recurring in materials (1) at different levels of sophistication in content that are aimed at readers of (2) different ages and (3) levels of education. The first set of passages (samples 1–12) uses the grammar of past time narrative at a range of different proficiency levels and for different communicative purposes. The second section (samples 13–15) looks at writing that uses grammar often labeled "conversational," but that is frequently found in written formats. The final section (samples 16–22) illustrates the grammar of writing that is focused on giving information and making generalizations. While this survey does not cover all of the grammatical clusters that are important in written English, it provides the fundamental background of the types and functions of grammar in discourse. More detailed information about the grammar of these discourse types is given in Chapter 4.

LOOKING AT THE GRAMMAR OF PAST TIME NARRATIVE

"Narrative" includes traditional storytelling in fiction and folktales but also embraces other types of writing with similar grammatical features such as biography, autobiography, case studies, history, and examples of past time events and actions used to support statements of theory. Take a close look at the grammar of the following passages to answer the following questions:[6]

- □ What kinds of verb phrases are used?
- □ What kinds of nouns predominate—common or proper?
- □ What pronouns are required to refer to those nouns?
- □ What kinds of sentence structures are used? (Look especially for participle phrases and various clause types.)
- □ What kinds of adverbs and adverbials are used along with what types of logical connectors? How is the sample organized—chronologically? Logically? Or some combination of the two?
- □ Finally, how are the samples alike? Different?

Samples 1 and 8 are from fiction and are given to represent the kind of writing that generally is thought of when the label "narrative" is used. Samples 2–7 show how narrative (and the grammar of narrative) is used for a wide range of purposes in materials aimed at the mature reader. Samples 8–12 are from books shelved in the "juvenile nonfiction" section of a public library in Atlanta; these are given to show how the same features of grammar are used in materials aimed at a younger audience of less mature readers.

■ ■ ■ SAMPLE 1

Narrative in Fiction for Experienced (and Probably Adult) Readers

The first paragraph of *The Yearling*
Marjorie Kinnan Rawlings
NY: Charles Scribner's Sons, 1938

A column of smoke rose thin and straight from the cabin chimney. The smoke was blue where it left the red of the clay. It trailed in to the blue of the April sky and was no longer blue but gray. The boy Jody watched it, speculating. The fire on the kitchen hearth was dying down. His mother was hanging up pots and pans after the noon dinner. The day was Friday. She would sweep the floor with a broom of ti-ti and after that, if he were lucky, she would scrub it with the corn shucks scrub. If she scrubbed the floor she would not miss him until he had reached the Glen. He stood a minute, balancing the hoe on his shoulder.

■ ■ ■ SAMPLE 2

Narrative in a Historical Study of the State of Alabama for Experienced Readers

De Soto Against Tascaluza from Chapter Two "Exploration and Colonization"
Alabama: The History of a Deep South State
W. W. Rogers, R. D. Ward, L. R. Atkins, and W. Flynt
Tuscaloosa: University of Alabama Press, 1994

On the morning of October 18, 1540, the entourage entered Mabila, a village located on a plain above a wide river. The town was surrounded by a palisade, and inside were eighty large houses fronting a square. Tascaluza disappeared inside a house, and the Indians began to dance and sing while the Spanish grew more suspicious and uneasy. Suddenly, the Indians attacked, shooting arrows from the houses and forcing the Spanish to flee the village, leaving some of their horses behind. The Indians promptly killed the feared animals. De Soto rallied his men for a counterattack and set fire to the village. The battle, most of it hand-to-hand combat, lasted until nightfall. In his manuscript, the Inca claimed 11,000 Indians died; Biedma reported 5,000 killed; and the more reliable Ranjel related that the Spanish found 3,000 Indian bodies without counting the dead inside the burned village. The Gentleman of Elvas reported 2,500 dead. The Indian losses were probably fewer than any of these figures, but by any count they were extensive. Whether Tascaluza died or escaped was not discovered, but his town of Mabila and his Indians were destroyed.

■ ■ ■ *SAMPLE 3*

Narrative Used to Illustrate an Observation about Human Aging for Experienced Readers

From "Patterns of Aging: Does Everything Go Downhill?"
*The Longevity Factor: The New Reality of Long Careers
and How It Can Lead to Richer Lives*
Lydia Bronte
NY: Harper Collins, 1993

Several of the Long Careers Study participants had relatives whose lives followed this pattern. Interviewee Ollie Thompson told about his grandmother, who at 103 could thread a needle without glasses and did all her own housework. One day, for no particular reason, she called Thompson's mother and told her to bring all the grandchildren over for dinner, because she felt a bit weak. She took everyone out to a movie and then for ice cream afterward; then the group caught a bus back to her house and had dinner. After dinner she told Thompson's mother, Martha, that she was tired and thought she would turn in. Martha went upstairs to her bedroom with her, tucked her into bed, and returned to the living room. An hour later, Martha went up to check on her and found she was dead. "She wasn't sick at all," Thompson remembers. "She just slept away."

■ ■ ■ *SAMPLE 4*

Narrative Used to Present a Case Study for Further Discussion of Principles Being Discussed in a Chapter Called "Integrity in Action" for Experienced Readers, "Beyond the Blame Game"

*Adult ADD: A Reader-Friendly Guide to Identifying, Understanding,
and Treating Adult Attention Deficit Disorder*
Thomas A. Whiteman and Michele Novotni, with Randy Petersen
Colorado Springs, CO: Pinon Press, 1995

Diane had a problem. Her ADD symptoms were affecting her work and she was on the verge of being fired. Her greatest difficulty was in prioritizing her tasks; she tended to major on the minors.

Through counseling, she determined to make a last-ditch effort to communicate with her boss about her problems. She did not make demands but suggested certain ways the boss could help her be a better worker. (Her counselor helped her devise these ideas.)

First, she asked if she could meet with the boss for a few minutes at the start of each day to go over her list of things to do. The boss would identify the most important projects for her to tackle. Diane asked for "time spacing" on her monthly reports—intermediate deadlines in mid-month. Previously, she had waited until the last minute to prepare these, but now she asked her boss to hold her accountable to those earlier deadlines.

Diane also asked for a flex-time arrangement. She knew she had to be there for most of the working day, but she got her best work done when no one else was around. The boss agreed to let her come to work an hour-and-a-half late and stay an hour-and a-half late, so she could have that prime time at the end of her working day. In fact, the boss agreed to all her suggestions. He had to spend a few extra minutes with her, but he got a much more effective employee out of this arrangement.

■ ■ ■ *SAMPLE 5*

Narrative Used to Make a Point about the History Behind Current Economic Policy for Experienced Readers

From "Why Does an American Need a Swiss Bank Account?"
How to Open a Swiss Bank Account: Everything You Need to Know
to Open and Use a Swiss Bank Account, to Protect Your Money
from Inflation and Assure Complete Privacy
James Kelder
NY: Thomas Y. Crowell Company, 1976

Until 1971, the dollar was a hard currency, "as good as gold." On August 15 of that year, President Nixon decreed that, "temporarily," the United States would no longer convert dollars into gold for the central banks of other nations. Since these central banks were the only holders who could still exchange dollars for bullion, gold backing for the dollar was thus, for all practical purposes, eliminated.

Mr. Nixon, in effect, declared to the world that the United States was insolvent. We would no longer honor the claims against our national gold reserves that our dollars represented. We couldn't because there wasn't enough gold in the Treasury's vaults to redeem even the dollars held by foreigners.

■ ■ ■ *SAMPLE 6*

Narrative Used to Give Evidence
to Support a Theory:
An Example from a Psychology Textbook
Used in Introductory Undergraduate Courses

From "Thinking and Language"
Psychology (3rd edition)
David G. Myers
NY: Worth Publishers, 1992

One American prisoner of war returned home from North Vietnam 80 pounds lighter after several years in a jungle camp. One of his first desires was to play golf. To the astonishment of his fellow officers, given his time away from the game and his emaciated condition, he played superbly. They wondered how. The pilot replied that every day of his imprisonment he imagined himself playing 18 holes, carefully choosing his clubs and playing the ball under varying conditions.

■ ■ ■ *SAMPLE 7*

Narrative in Accounting Textbook
Used in Introductory Undergraduate Courses to Give Examples

From "Receivables"
Intermediate Accounting (11th edition)
J. Smith and K. Skousen
Cincinnati, OH: South-Western Publishing Co., 1992

In 1938, McKesson & Robbins, Inc., reported total assets of $87 million. Of that amount, $9 million represented fictitious accounts receivable. Certain company officials had responded to the desire to increase assets and revenue by making false entries for sales.

The most notorious accounting scandal of the 1970s was the Equity Funding case. Between 1964 and 1973, Equity Funding created $85 million of bogus revenue by falsely recording loans receivable from insurance customers. As the fraud deepened and the need for extra reported revenue increased, Equity Funding also began to create insurance policies for nonexistent customers. Overall, revenue was overstated by more than $140 million during the fraud period.

A much-publicized fraud of the 1980s involved ZZZZ Best, a carpet-cleaning concern started by young entrepreneur Barry Minkow. ZZZZ Best enhanced reported results by reporting revenue and receivable from imaginary fire-damage restoration jobs.

■ ■ ■ *SAMPLE 8*

Narrative Fiction Written for Young Readers (by an Award-Winning Author)

From *The China Year*
Emily Cheney Neville
NY: Harper Collins, 1991

Henri's life had been pretty average before she went to China—average, that is, for a New York City kid. She lived in a loft apartment with her mother, who was a painter and potter, and her father, a college professor. She was in the eighth grade at Intermediate School 104, and she had a best friend named Tillie and a summer boyfriend in the Poconos named Walt.

All that disappeared the year her father got an exchange appointment to teach English literature at Peking University, Beijing, China. Her second life began in Beijing, where they lived in a two-room apartment and she had a Chinese friend named Minyuan and no other friend at all except Caitlin, aged six. Perhaps most important, Henrietta had no school, only lesson assignments by mail from a correspondence school in Massachusetts. She had no one to talk to about school or boyfriends or anything, no telephone to talk on, no place to hang out and munch chips or pizza.

■ ■ ■ *SAMPLE 9*

Narrative in the History of Science for Young Readers

From "Gregor Joann Mendel: The Mystery of Heredity"
Break-Throughs in Science
Isaac Asimov
Boston: Houghton Mifflin Company, 1959

In 1900 three strangers met at a crossroads of research. Each, without knowledge of the other two, had worked out the rules that govern inheritance of physical characteristics by living things. The three were Hugo de Vries of Holland, Carl Correns of Germany, and Erich Tschermak of Austria-Hungary.

Each made ready to announce his discovery to the world. In preparation, each looked through previous issues of various scientific journals, to check earlier work in the field. Each, to his astonishment, found an amazing paper by someone named Gregor Johann Mendel in a 35-year-old copy of an obscure publication. Mendel, in 1865, had observed all the phenomena that the three scientists were preparing to report in 1900.

Each made the same decision. With the honesty that is one of the glories of scientific history, each abandoned his own claims and called attention to Mendel's discovery. Each man advanced his own work only as confirmation.

■ ■ ■ *SAMPLE 10*

Narrative in a History of Greeks in the U.S.
Written for Young Readers

From "West of Atlantis"
The Greeks in America
Jayne Clark Jones
Minneapolis, MN: Lerner Publications Company, 1990

The first sizable settlement of Greeks in America took place in 1767, under rather unusual circumstances. Florida had become a British colony in 1763. An enterprising Scottish doctor named Andrew Turnbull obtained permission from the governor of Florida to work 20,000 acres of uncultivated land near St. Augustine. Under the terms of his contract with the government, Turnbull was to bring only Protestants to Florida. (The Orthodox Greek Christians qualified.)

Turnbull's wife was the daughter of a Greek general from Smyrna, and Turnbull himself was familiar with the Mediterranean area. He collected, as settlers to work his land, destitute and desperate people from Greece, Italy, Corsica, and Majorca. To induce them to come with him, he described Florida as a paradise and promised to make them landowners. He agreed to supply them with passage, food, and clothing for three years—and return passage if they wanted to leave after six months' trial. In addition, he agreed to give each family 50 acres of land and an additional 25 acres for each child in the family. He brought about 1,400 men, women, and children to the settlement, which he named New Smyrna in honor of his wife's home.

The voyage was terribly hard and many of the colonists died at sea, but even worse conditions awaited them in Florida. Instead of working in vineyards and olive groves as they had been led to expect, they found themselves cultivating cotton in swampy, malaria-infested bottomlands and being harassed by hostile Native Americans. Furthermore, their work was directed by English overseers who knew none of the languages spoken by the colonists and who treated them cruelly.

■ ■ ■ *SAMPLE 11*

Narrative to Provide Multicultural Reading Materials
for Young Readers

From "Dustin Nguyen"
Contemporary American Success Stories:
Famous People of Asian Ancestry
Barbara J. Marvis
Childs, MD: Mitchell Lane Publishers, 1995

Though his father had been a television producer when he lived in Vietnam and his mother had been a dancer and an actress, neither one was happy when their son, Xuan Tri (Dustin) decided to become an actor here in the United States. They thought Dustin should be an engineer and they worked hard to pay for his college. In fact, they went on paying for his college tuition for more than a year after he had dropped out because they thought he was still in school. When they found out he had been taking acting lessons and auditioning for TV roles, they were very angry and disappointed.

■ ■ ■ *SAMPLE 12*

Narrative Grammar in a History Book
for Young Readers

From "Cotton-Picking Days"
Mary McLeod Bethune
Rinna Evelyn Wolfe
NY: Franklin Watts, 1992

Mary Jane, the fifteenth child of seventeen, was born on July 10, 1875, in Mayesville, South Carolina. Looking into her new daughter's open eyes, Patsy McLeon, an ex-slave, thought, "She will show us the way out."

Neither Patsy nor Mary's father, Samuel, had a surname until Samuel chose McLeod, his ex-master's family name.

Tall and muscular, Samuel was a kind, skillful carpenter and farmer, who also worked well with leather and tin. Patsy cooked nearby in the big McIntosh house. Small and lithe, she walked with the queenly grace of her royal African ancestors. Her smile lit Samuel's heart.

When Samuel asked McLeod for permission to marry Patsy, his master agreed. But first Samuel had to earn the money to buy her. So after doing a normal day's work, he labored for other farmers, and, in two years, the loving couple celebrated their wedding.

While all of these samples of "narrative" have differences in their "stories" and thus in much of their vocabulary, they are very similar in grammar with the following features playing major roles in each: (1) simple past tense is the most important verb, but past perfect and past progressive are used, too; (2) proper nouns for several different characters are included in most narratives—and some of those names are used in different forms within the same passage; (3) personal pronouns are used to refer back to the "characters" with *she* and *he* (and their various forms) predominant; (4) time words and phrases are used to coordinate the chronological organization of the passages.[7] Use in all of these samples of complete and often complex sentences contrasts with the grammatical features found in the "written conversations" given in the following section.

LOOKING AT THE GRAMMAR OF WRITING THAT USES FEATURES OF CONVERSATION

One of the problems of many inexperienced writers is not understanding the differences between the language used in conversation and the language used in the formal writing of the academic world. Such writers have problems writing "complete sentences" and have a tendency to use vocabulary that is considered too "slangy" for most academic writing. This topic requires careful thought because written English is not fundamentally different from spoken English—written English is not a different language from spoken English (Biber, 1988). For the most part, it is true that speaking and writing occur under different sets of constraints—speaking generally involves interaction with listeners and the pressures of occurring in "real time"; writing generally provides the freedom to revise and correct, but creates a problematic distance from readers. In some contexts, we write like we speak, and in other contexts we speak like we write. The grammar that has often been discussed as that characteristic of conversation is found in written formats, not just in the dialogue in fiction but in academic textbooks as well as in newspaper articles. Look at the following samples, and compare their grammar to that of the narratives in the first set of samples:

□ What verb phrase types are used?

□ What kinds of nouns and pronouns are found here (especially in contrast to what you saw in the narrative samples)?

□ How does the writer attempt to make the writing sound more conversational in the sentence types that are used?

□ How are these pieces organized and what language is used to signal the organization?

Sample 13 is from a mystery novel and is included to show written dialogue, the type of writing that comes most immediately to mind when thinking about other types of writing, as shown in samples 14 and 15. Fewer samples are given for this category because it occurs with much lower frequency in lengthy passages; however, writers often switch to it in passing with references to the reader as "you."[8]

■ ■ ■ *SAMPLE 13*

Dialogue from a Novel Written to Have Interaction between Two Main Characters, Written for Experienced Readers

From Colin Dexter, Chapter Six in *The Jewel That Was Ours.*
NY: Ivy Books, 1991

"You here already, Lewis?"
"Half an hour ago, sir. The Super called me. They're short-staffed at St. Aldate's—"
"Must be!"
"I've already been upstairs."
"No problems?"
"I'm—I'm not quite sure, sir."
"Well—'Lead on, Macduff!'"
"That should be 'Lay on Macduff!,' sir. So our English teacher—"
"Thank you, Lewis."
"The lift's just along here—"
"Lift? We're not climbing the Empire State Building."
"Quite a few stairs, sir," said Lewis quietly, suspecting (rightly) that his chief was going through one of his temporary get-a-little-fitter phases.

■ ■ ■ *SAMPLE 14*

Interactive Language in a Newspaper Article Written for a General Audience

From Miles Blumhardt, "City's Leash Ordinance Is Doing Wildlife a Favor."
In *Coloradoan*, 1996

What predator do you think kills the most livestock in this country after the coyote?
Black bear? Mountain lion? Bobcat? Fox? Eagle?
No, think closer to home.
Dogs accounted for more than $10 million in livestock losses in 1991, according to the National Agricultural Statistics Service. The loss was a distant second to the coyote, which was responsible for nearly $38 million, but was equal to losses by all other predators.

■ ■ ■ *SAMPLE 15*

Interactive Language in a Psychology Textbook Used in Introductory Undergraduate Courses to Speak Directly to the Reader and to Indicate a Relationship Between the Author and the Reader

From "The Developing Child"
Psychology (3rd edition)
David G. Myers

The developing person is no less a wonder after birth than in the womb. Physically, mentally, socially, we are always in the process of becoming. As we journey through life from womb to tomb, when and how do we change?

Usually we notice how we differ. To developmental psychologists our commonalities are just as important. Virtually all of us—Confucius, Queen Elizabeth, Martin Luther King, Jr., you, and I—began walking around age 1 and talking by age 2. As children we all engaged in social play in preparation for life's serious work. We all smile and cry, love and hate, and occasionally ponder the fact that someday we will die.

These three samples differ considerably in their sentence structure. Sample 13 has the short phrases (frequently termed "utterances" to give them a label that distinguishes them from "sentences," e.g., McCarthy, 1991). Sample 14 uses a combination of complete sentences and phrases. Sample 15 uses only complete and rather complicated sentences. However, all three samples show a common pattern built around question asking and answering: (1) written questions and (2) the reader addressed as "you." Thus, the writers of samples 13 and 14 use features common in conversations to pull their readers into a "conversation" about their topics.

Even though the first conversation is part of a narrative, it is not structured so much chronologically as "logically" around the presentation of background information needed by the reader to understand both the characters and the place of the dialogue in the action. The other two samples are also organized around providing answers to questions posed by the writer. Thus, time words and phrases are not important in this type of writing, while logical connectors such as *however* can be.[9]

LOOKING AT THE GRAMMAR OF INFORMATIONAL WRITING

One of the fundamental purposes of communication is the sharing of information, including data, theory, definitions, and other types of generalizations about habitual behaviors and the natural world. While such communication is the basic stuff of academic textbook writing, it is also an important part of everyday life and is used in a wide variety of communication settings and types. Holding in mind the features that you saw in the narrative samples and "oral" samples, look at the grammar of the following samples of informational writing.[10]

- □ What kinds of verb phrases predominate? What tense forms? Active or passive?
- □ What kinds of nouns are used (especially in contrast to the nouns used in narrative)? How are generic nouns[11] used?
- □ How are the noun phrases structured—what kinds of words are combined to make up the noun phrases? How long are they?
- □ How are the passages organized and what linguistic features are used to manage the organization and the connections between sentences?
- □ How are the sentences like or different from the sentences in the other sets of samples?

These samples, like those in the narrative set, were chosen to show informational writing aimed at both mature and younger readers. Samples 20–22 show the same topic for different readers—mature, young, and very young.

■ ■ ■ *SAMPLE 16*

Description of an Instrument from a Physics Textbook
Used in Introductory Undergraduate Courses

From "Electric Forces and Electric Fields: The Oscilloscope"
College Physics (3rd edition)
R. Serway and J. Faughn
Fort Worth, TX: Sanders College Publishing, 1992

The oscilloscope is an electronic instrument widely used in making electrical measurements. The main component of the oscilloscope is the cathode ray tube (CRT), shown in Figure 16.24a. This tube is commonly used to obtain a visual display of electronic information for other applications, including radar systems, television receivers, and computers. The CRT is essentially a vacuum tube in which electrons are accelerated and deflected under the influence of electric fields.

The electron beam is produced by an assembly called an electron gun, located in the neck of the tube. The assembly shown in Figure 16.24a consists of a heater (H), a cathode (C), and a positively charged anode (A). An electric current through the heater causes its temperature to rise, which in turn heats the cathode. The cathode reaches temperatures high enough to cause electrons to be "boiled off." Although they are not shown in the figure, the electron gun also includes an element that focuses the electron beam and one that controls the number of electrons reaching the anode (that is, a brightness control). The anode has a hole in its center that allows the electrons to pass thorough without striking the anode. These electrons, if left undisturbed, travel in a straight-line path until they strike the face of the CRT. The screen at the front of the tube is coated with a fluorescent material that emits visible light when bombarded with electrons. This results in a visible spot on the screen of the CRT.

■ ■ ■ *SAMPLE 17*

A Description That Provides an Extended Definition of a Tool in a Book Written for Experienced (and Probably Adult) Readers

From "Rules: Steel Rule"
Tools and How to Use Them: An Illustrated Encyclopedia
A. Jackson and D. Day
NY: Alfred A. Knopf, 1978

A good quality steel rule is a very accurate tool for measuring and laying out work. Not only are the gradations very precise, but being steel the rule can be very thin and therefore reduce errors in marking produced by parallax. A steel rule is essential for any kind of metal work and is also a useful tool in the woodwork shop.

Steel rules have metric or imperial graduations or a combination of both. The rules will usually be graduated on two edges and often on both sides with increasingly smaller divisions of the basic measure. A combined metric and imperial rule is the most useful.

■ ■ ■ *SAMPLE 18*

Definition of Terminology in a Physics Textbook Used in Introductory Undergraduate Courses

"Definitions of Conservative and Nonconservative Forces"
College Physics

In general, a force is conservative if the work it does on an object moving between two points is independent of the path the object takes between the points. The work done on an object by a conservative force depends only on the initial and final positions of the object.

A force is nonconservative if the work it does on an object moving between two points depends on the path taken.

■ ■ ■ *SAMPLE 19*

A Description of the Sun with Embedded Definitions of Terminology from a Book for Young Readers

The Solar System: Facts and Exploration
F. L. Vogt
NY: Henry Holt and Company, 1995

The sun is a bright sphere of hydrogen and helium gases. The atoms in these gases are split into subatomic particles (electrons and protons) and rearranged into ions. Ions are atoms that have fewer or greater numbers of electrons orbiting their nuclei than normal. When ions have fewer electrons orbiting their nuclei, they are positively charged. When they have more they are negatively charged. The driving force behind the rearrangement of the Sun's gas atoms is the Sun's great temperature. Deep inside its core, the temperature climbs to as high as $16,000,000°F$ ($8,900,000°C$).

■ ■ ■ *SAMPLE 20*

Information about Bird Songs from a Book Written for Experienced Readers

From "Songs and Singing"
The Audubon Society Encyclopedia of North American Birds
J. K. Terres
NY: Alfred A. Knopf, 1980

The songs and singing of birds interest many people—ornithologists because of the function of singing in communication between wild birds, and the role that singing plays in their behavior; both ornithologists and birders (see Birder), because in knowing birds' songs (and calls) they can identify birds even though the birds themselves may be hidden from view; and these people and many others, because of the beauty or simple appropriateness of a wild bird's song and its power to add to the loveliness and interest of the natural world.

Most passerines have sounds that advertise territoriality and availability as a mate. Usually delivered during a restricted period of the year, these primary songs are often complex, with elaborate patterns of notes grouped into phrases. In this way they are usually differentiated from calls. The primary song is what we commonly hear in spring and summer, and its functions are associated with the major activities at that time of year: courtship and territoriality.

■ ■ ■ *SAMPLE 21*

Description of Hummingbird Nests from a Book for Young Readers

From Hilda Simon, "Nests, Eggs, and Young."
In *Wonders of Hummingbirds.* NY: Dodd Mead, 1964

Hummingbird nests come in a variety of shapes and forms, and may be found in almost any location except on the ground. In many cases, the nests are master-pieces of craftsmanship, fashioned with much care and patience. Take for instance the nest of the ruby-throated hummingbird, a species that breeds in the eastern part of North America. The cup-shaped structure, which is not much larger than a big walnut, often is found straddling a branch. It is made of grasses, moss, plant fibers and plant down, lined with spiderwebs, and decorated on the outside with lichens, the dry flowerless plants that grow on tree bark and rocks. The nest is thus well camouflaged and may look like a big bump in the branch.

■ ■ ■ *SAMPLE 22*

Facts about Birds from a Book for Very Young Readers

M. Friskey, "Most Birds Can Fly" and "Perching Birds."
In *Birds We Know.* Chicago: Childrens Press, 1981

All birds have feathers. All birds have wings. Most birds can fly. Most of them are at home in the air.

Birds are alike in many ways.

But birds have different ways of doing things. Each kind of bird has the tools it needs for the way it lives.

Most of the birds we see are "perching" birds. They can lock their toes around a tree branch.

Perching birds have four toes. The one in back is about as long as the middle one in front.

Sparrows are perching birds. They have strong bills for cracking seeds.

Many birds eat seeds.

Birds that can get the kind of seeds they need in winter do not need to fly away when snow comes.

Some perching birds eat insects, bugs, and worms.

Birds that eat insects must fly away when snow comes.

This bird screams its own name. Jay! Jay! Jay!

A blue jay eats seeds.

A cardinal eats weed seeds and nuts and grain.

As these samples show, informational writing is characterized by use of:

☐ long, complicated noun phrases
☐ the frequent use of generic noun phrases such as "a blue jay" and "birds" in sample 22 to refer to categories rather than to individuals
☐ passive verbs
☐ a limited set of verbs
☐ present tense.

Long, complex noun phrases are often used—as is specialized terminology. The complexity of the noun phrases involves (1) strings of adjectives and nouns in front of the core noun, (2) relative clauses attached to the noun (and often reduced to participle phrases), and/or (3) strings of prepositional phrases after the noun. These features are found in both the writing for mature readers and the writing for newer, younger readers:

☐ a very accurate **tool** for measuring and laying out work
☐ the main **component** of the oscilloscope
☐ a **hole** in its center that allows the electrons to pass thorough without striking the anode
☐ a bright **sphere** of hydrogen and helium gases
☐ the cup-shaped **structure**, which is not much larger than a big walnut
☐ **birds** that can get the kind of seeds they need in winter.

Because the emphasis is on theory, facts, and concepts rather than on human beings, *it* is the most commonly used personal pronoun. On the other hand, this type of material often repeats the same noun phrase rather than using a pronoun to refer to it—possibly because of the importance of using exactly the correct terminology.

Because of the focus on processes, passives are often used not just in the main verb but also in relative clauses and in reduced relative clauses such as the following:

☐ The electron beam is produced by an assembly **called** an electron gun. . . .
☐ In many cases, the nests are masterpieces of craftsmanship, **fashioned** with much care and patience.

These samples also show the use of past participles as complements of *be*—in phrases that are not easy to differentiate from passive verbs:

☐ The rules will usually be **graduated** on two edges. . . .
☐ The screen at the front of the tube is **coated** with a fluorescent material. . . .
☐ . . . they are positively **charged**. . . .

Notice, too, that the number of different verbs used is relatively low, with present tense forms of *be* and *have* used repeatedly. That is, the range of lexical verbs and of verb tenses is narrow in comparison with conversational or narrative uses of English.

CONCLUSION

As these samples show, the same features of grammar are used repeatedly and predictably in clusters that are characteristic of particular types of communication. Even materials written for very young readers share grammatical features with textbooks written for use in college and university courses. Narrative, "oral" communication, and informational communication all have their own "look and feel" that exist almost completely intact across a wide variety of proficiency levels and in many different communication settings. The texture of each comes from its characteristic use of particular grammatical forms that cluster together in that type of communication.

NOTES

1. Britton, Gulgoz, and Glynn are interested in ways to improve the quality of textbooks used in U.S. public schools. Their concerns are with the presentation of content in ways that make that content more accessible for students. That is, they are not at all interested in the issues of authenticity in language that are so important in second-language instruction. They do, however, make an important point for us—not all "expert" writing is good writing; not all "authentic" text is clear and accessible to readers. Using their principles in the selection process can help us to provide materials that are authentic and accessible. Using their principles in the teaching process can help our students learn to deal with authentic text that might be required by their courses but that might have some of the accessibility problems suggested by the three principles.

2. Materials for new and/or young readers often differ from materials for adult or more experienced readers in format rather than in content or grammar. The "simpler" materials might use larger print, more illustrative support, and/or more white space around the text.

3. Or as many levels as there are classrooms available for the courses. Or any of a number of administrative and financial restrictions that have nothing to do with language proficiency levels of the students.

4. Teachers and curriculum coordinators should also be aware that Krashen's theories do not have universal acceptance among reputable second-language-acquisition specialists. For information about other points of view, see Barasch and James (1994).

4. Teachers and curriculum coordinators should also be aware that Krashen's theories do not have universal acceptance among reputable second-language-acquisition specialists. For information about other points of view, see Barasch and James (1994).

5. As is seen in Chapters 3 and 4, passages in textbooks (and other large collections of written material) are seldom made up of just one type of communication or one type of grammar. One paragraph can be a statement of theory, using primarily informational grammar, with the next paragraph a short narrative used to illustrate that theory. These categories are not meant as absolutes but as continua.

6. A chart is provided in Appendix A if you would like to use one in your analysis of the reading passages (samples 1–12).

7. Notice that sample 7, a discussion of famous cases of accounting fraud, makes heavy use of passive sentences. Narratives that focus on a topic such as fraud (or soccer or anything other than an animate subject) can be expected to include the passive along with the other features of past time narratives. Sample 7 is also unlike the others in its lack of personal pronouns. In comparing history textbook materials to accounting textbook materials, I found that the history materials seldom used *it* and frequently used the various forms of *he, she,* and *they*. Accounting, on the other hand, seldom used *he, she,* or *they*, but often used *it* to refer to concepts and business entities. Thus, the narratives in accounting are like other narratives in their use of past tense verbs and chronological vocabulary such as adverbs of time, but they differ when the "story" that is being told is about corporations and accounting principles rather than individuals or groups of individuals.

8. Appendix B provides a chart that can be used to analyze these passages (samples 13–15).

9. However, the "logic" of these samples is not for the most part signaled through grammatical devices but depends on culturally embedded notions about organization that can be quite difficult for ESL learners to understand and to use in their own writing.

10. Appendix C has a chart that you can use to analyze samples 16–22.

11. Generic nouns are noun phrases used to refer to groups or classes rather than to individuals. All of the articles can be used to create different types of generic nouns:

Teachers work hard.
A teacher works hard.
The teacher works hard.
In most societies, the teachers have been respected and underpaid.

Appendix A: Chart to Analyze Narrative Reading Passages

READING PASSAGE	VERB TENSES	NOUN TYPES (COMMON, PROPER, COUNT, NONCOUNT)	PERSONAL PRONOUNS (*HE, SHE, IT*; *I, WE, YOU*)	ADVERBIALS AND LOGICAL CONNECTORS (TIME ORDER OR LOGICAL ORGANIZATION)	ALIKE? DIFFERENT?
1 Fiction*					
2 History					
3 Personal History as Example					
4 Case Study					
5 Political History as Example					
6 Personal History to Support a Theory					
7 Economic & Criminal History as Example					
8 Fiction for Young Readers					
9 History of Science for Young Readers					

			Appendix A	(continued)		
READING PASSAGE	VERB TENSES	NOUN TYPES (COMMON, PROPER, COUNT, NONCOUNT)	PERSONAL PRONOUNS (HE, SHE, IT; I, WE, YOU)	ADVERBIALS AND LOGICAL CONNECTORS (TIME ORDER OR LOGICAL ORGANIZATION)	ALIKE? DIFFERENT?
10 History of Greeks in the U.S. for Young Readers					
11 Biography for Young Readers					
12 Biography for Young Readers					

*My notes on this paragraph from The Yearling: [The dialogue in the novel has quite different grammar, of course, from this section.]

☐ Verbs: *rose, was, left, trailed, was, watched, was dying, was hanging, was, would sweep, were, would scrub, scrubbed, would miss, had reached, stood* [nice combination of past tense possibilities]

☐ Nouns: common (*column, smoke, chimney*, etc., = common; *Jody* = proper. Note the lack of abstraction—a description of a specific place and of specific people.)

☐ Pronouns: *it, she, he*

☐ Adverbs: *after the noon dinner, after that,* and the *if* clauses

☐ Sentences: all complete, a combination of simple, complex, compound

☐ Participles: *The boy Jody watched it, <u>speculating</u>. He stood a minute, <u>balancing the hoe on his shoulder</u>.* [There's a tendency for present participles to be used more in narratives with their descriptions of actions and past participles to be used more in informational writing with its passives. Compare the *-ing* participles here with the past participles in sample 16 with its <u>used</u> in *making electrical measurements, <u>shown</u> in Figure 16.24a,* and others.]

☐ The paragraph has a chronological sequence that includes a logical set within the actions. Bardovi-Harlig (1996) provides a discussion of the "foreground" and "background" of narratives. Her observation is that the narrative foreground uses simple past tense to tell the events of the narrative while other verb forms are used in the "background" to comment on the story and to provide interpretations of the action. The foreground is chronological; the background is not. She notes that simple past can be used in the background as it is here in the description of the smoke and the sky. Her point is that the other verb tenses generally tend to be used for background descriptions and elaboration. The events in this scene from the beginning of The Yearling are told with simple past tense—Jody watched the smoke and stood thinking about his options. Interestingly, the use of the past progressive in the description of his mother underscores the differences between Jody and his mother—his love of daydreaming and her realistic sense that without hard and constant work they will not survive in the Florida wilderness. When the author turns away from the events to Jody's speculation about possible future events, the verbs change to the subjunctive use of *would* and *were*.

	Appendix B: Chart to Analyze Reading Passages with Features of Conversational English			
READING PASSAGE	VERB PHRASES (TENSES, CONTRACTIONS, ACTIVE, PASSIVE)	NOUN AND PRONOUNS	SENTENCE TYPES (FRAGMENTS AND QUESTIONS)	ORGANIZATIONAL LANGUAGE (HOW ARE THE PASSAGES TIED TOGETHER— TIME, LOGIC?)
13 Murder Mystery				
14 Newspaper Column				
15 Psychology Textbook				

Appendix C: Chart to Analyze the Grammar of the Informational Passages

READING PASSAGE	VERBS (ACTIVE, PASSIVE, COMMON, PROPER, PAST PARTICIPLES IN PHRASES AND AS ADJECTIVES)	NOUNS (GENERIC, SPECIFIC)	NOUN PHRASE STRUCTURE (ARTICLES USED OR NOT USED?) & NOUN PHRASE LENGTH	ORGANIZATIONAL LANGUAGE (TIME ORDER, LOGICAL ORDER)	SENTENCES— HOW LIKE OR UNLIKE THOSE IN THE "CON- VERSATIONAL" SAMPLES? IN THE NARRA- TIVE SAMPLES?
16 Description of an Instrument from a Physics Textbook					
17 Description of a Tool					
18 Definitions from a Physics Textbook					
19 Description of the Sun from a Book for Young Readers					
20 Information about Bird Songs for Mature Readers					
21 Description of Hummingbird Nests for Young Readers					
22 Facts about Birds from a Book for Very Young Readers					

Section III

Teaching Grammar in the ESL Writing Class

Planning for the grammar element in the writing program requires that we think creatively and break through ideas and approaches that have limited our effectiveness in the past. Knowing who the students are and what they need is certainly the first step; looking at grammar in context is the second. While there are many issues for teachers to work through in developing effective teaching strategies, here we focus on topics that we've discussed repeatedly over the past few years: What makes writing "persuasive" and how is "persuasion" different from the traditional "argumentative essay"? How can teachers recognize and deal with "errors"? What changes are occurring in teaching grammar and writing as a result of new technologies?

Chapter 6

Writing to Persuade and the Language of Persuasion

Joy Reid and Patricia Byrd

Undergraduate Natural Resource Course
IN-CLASS EXAMINATION

Describe the differences between the wild cat, the mountain lion, the bobcat, and the lynx. Use characteristics such as size, coloring, habitat, and hunting ranges.

Senior-Level Nutrition Course
TERM PAPER

Choose a food production or processing technique. Discuss the effects of the technique on food quality, quantity, and safety.

Graduate Seminar in Philosophy
SEMINAR PAPER TOPIC

To what extent do considerations from physics, especially the insistence of relativity on frameworks, affect the status of metaphysical theories which take places and times as basic and nonderivative?

THE PERSUASIVE NATURE OF WRITING

On a rhetorical level, all writing is "persuasive": The science-fiction author asks the reader to suspend disbelief; the explanatory writer expects the reader to accept the writer's authority and evidence; the joke writer assumes that the reader will use cultural background information in order to recognize and respond to the humor; the student writer wants the teacher to believe that she or he knows the material covered by examination questions and project topics such as those given at the beginning of this chapter.

While all writing tries to persuade the reader for some purpose, the methods that are used to persuade change in different settings to fit what is expected by readers in each particular context. Subtle rhetorical conventions, structures, word forms, and vocabulary items are combined in academic writing to persuade:

- □ the teacher that the student writer understands the material in a course
- □ the reader that the material is valid and worth reading
- □ the audience that the author is reliable
- □ the members of the academic discipline that the writer is ready to join that discourse community.

This chapter explains the basis for our assumption that all writing is persuasive. We describe rhetorical and linguistic differences in the ways that other languages and cultures present written material, and then concentrate on the rhetorical and language techniques necessary to write effective, persuasive U.S. academic prose.

BUILDING TRUST AS ACADEMIC WRITERS

Persuasion is based on trust. If a reader trusts and believes the writer, persuasion follows easily. In contrast, a hostile reader who mistrusts the writer may never be persuaded—and may never finish reading the essay or article. Whether the audience is a leisure reader starting a novel, a discipline expert beginning to evaluate a grant proposal, or a teacher grading a student essay, the writer's basic responsibility is to connect with the reader. Therefore, audience analysis is essential for any successful academic writer. Writers must learn to initiate and build the trust of their audience—reaching across the "distance" of time and space to connect with readers in ways that the readers think are appropriate and, as a result, persuasive.

Our assumption, then, is that academic writing is nonthreatening, that it seeks to persuade by opening lines of communication with the reader and fulfilling the expectations of that reader. To achieve their ultimate goal of convincing their readers to accept their ideas and information, academic writers must:

- □ understand the needs and expectations of academic readers
- □ avoid a confrontational stance
- □ rely on establishing common ground with the audience
- □ establish the author's reliability and good will
- □ acknowledge that other views exist (when arguing for acceptance of a particular point of view)
- □ exhibit flexibility and compromise (when dealing with argumentation).

In general, the rhetoric of U.S. academic prose persuades its audience in several ways, each of which contributes to the comfort level of that U.S. audience and thus builds trust by:

- □ immediately establishing context for the reader through
  - directness of the introductory material (and appropriateness for that writing context)
  - brevity of the introduction
  - clarity of focus through the thesis statement
- □ providing adequate objective background material that
  - establishes the ability and authority of the writer
  - acts as a foundation for the reader for the rest of the text
  - "connects" the reader to the material
- □ fulfilling the expectations of the reader by using such supporting material as required in that type of writing, possibly including
  - facts and statistics that validate the material
  - examples that increase the perceived reliability of the material
  - experiences that culturally, intellectually, or emotionally connect the reader to the writer
- □ refusing to overgeneralize, overextend, or overstate when drawing conclusions from the facts, the verified detail, and the examples in the piece of writing.

ARGUMENTATIVE WRITING COMPARED TO PERSUASIVE WRITING

In contrast, argumentative writing, in which the writer "argues" for one side of a controversy, "defeating" the counterarguments of opponents of the view, is constructed with a different purpose from most academic prose. That is, the writer "persuades" by confrontation, polarization, and adversarial language, and the expected outcome is a change in the behavior, thought, or theory of the opposition. However, in sensitive, belief-based issues, (e.g., assisted suicide of terminally ill patients, parental rights), even argumentative writers are often taught to take a persuasive approach, called "Rogerian argument." Crucial to Rogerian argument is

the building of a bridge of trust between the writer and reader by (1) accommo-
dating the views of the audience, (2) not taking the opposite side of the issue, and
(3) fostering common ground and compromise. Writers using Rogerian argument
realize that "convictions and beliefs are not abstract but reside in people. If people
are to agree, they must be sensitive to each other's beliefs" (S. Reid, 1992, p. 330).

THE LANGUAGE OF "OVERTLY PERSUASIVE COMMUNICATION" IN ENGLISH

Chapter 4, "Grammar FROM Context," has a list of the features that Biber (1988)
found in materials that he calls "overtly persuasive communication." The materials
that had these features were either expressions of the speaker/writer's point of
view or "argumentative discourse designed to persuade the addressee" (p. 111).
The characteristic grammar of "overt persuasion" involves the use of:

- ☐ modal auxiliary verbs to express values and opinions,
- ☐ *if* and *unless* clauses to give conditions that the writer argues will lead
  to certain results
- ☐ "suasive verbs" such as *agree, arrange, ask, beg, command, decide,
  demand, grant, insist, instruct, ordain, pledge, pronounce, propose,
  recommend, request, stipulate, suggest, urge*.

This set of grammar offers special challenges to ESL/EFL learners and to ESL/EFL
teachers. It will be considered here in reverse order, starting with suasive verbs,
moving to conditional and hypothetical sentences, and concluding with modality.

☐ VOCABULARY IN CONTEXT: SUASIVE VERBS AS A SPECIAL CASE OF A GENERAL PROBLEM

ESL/EFL programs, lessons, and materials have never come to grips with the teaching of vocabulary—at least not in any generally agreed upon or sustained way. The
core problem has been that English has a huge vocabulary with the result that making reasonable decisions about what to teach remains a matter of educated guesses and random selections. Word lists based on frequency counts are not much
help because they reflect a truth about English—the most commonly used words
are the articles (*the, a/an*), certain prepositions (especially *of*), various forms of *be*,
and other function words rather than the content vocabulary. For example, Table
6.1 lists the ten most frequently used words in the chapters from the accounting
and history textbooks cited in Chapter 3, "Grammar in the Composition Syllabus."

Table 6.1: Most Frequent Words in Textbook Samples

10 MOST COMMON WORDS IN ACCOUNTING TEXTBOOK SAMPLE OF 8,695 WORDS (NUMBER OF USES, PERCENTAGE OF THE TOTAL, WORD)			10 MOST COMMON WORDS IN U.S. HISTORY TEXTBOOK SAMPLE OF 7,648 WORDS (NUMBER OF USES, PERCENTAGE OF THE TOTAL, WORD)		
548	6.6088%	the	532	6.9561%	the
362	4.3657%	of	284	3.7134%	of
264	3.1838%	and	230	3.0073%	to
217	2.6170%	to	215	2.8112%	and
216	2.6049%	in	189	2.4712%	in
173	2.0863%	a	182	2.3797%	a
161	1.9416%	is	127	1.6606%	was
125	1.5075%	information	80	1.0460%	were
115	1.3869%	be	78	1.0199%	that
112	1.3507%	that	75	0.9806%	for

These two samples from textbook chapters reflect another problem in vocabulary learning and teaching—the large number of words that students encounter while reading for their degree courses.[1] While the accounting textbook uses fewer new words and repeats vocabulary more often than the history textbook, the sample chapter still has 1,613 individual words. Table 6.2 compares the amount of vocabulary in the two textbook chapters that provide samples for our study.[2] In sum, a reader of the history chapter has to handle many more different words over a space of approximately the same length of reading as in the accounting chapter, and the student has to make decisions about which of all of these new words are worth learning (that is, which ones will be used on tests or will recur as basic terminology in other related courses). Thus, ESL/EFL learners who enter academic programs face real problems in learning new vocabulary, and those problems can differ in complexity in different environments.

Table 6.2: Amount of Vocabulary in History Text Compared to Accounting Text

	TOTAL # OF WORDS	TOTAL # OF INDIVIDUAL WORDS	TYPE/TOKEN RATIO FOR THE COMPLETE CHAPTER	TYPE/TOKEN RATIO FOR 1ST 1,000 WORDS IN EACH CHAPTER
History Textbook Chapter	7,648	2,374	31.0	47.9
Accounting Textbook Chapter	8,695	1,613	18.5	39.1

Although deciding on the particular words to be learned has remained an unresolved problem for ESL/EFL teachers, we have another very useful alternative approach to vocabulary teaching—helping students with strategies to improve their skill at selecting and learning new vocabulary that fits their particular communication situation. In a particularly thorough and helpful article on a topic not often covered in the literature on second-language teaching, Oxford and Crookall (1990) evaluate techniques that can be used by teachers and students to select and learn new words. Dividing their analysis into techniques that are "decontextualizing," "semi-contextualizing," "fully contextualizing," and "adaptable," they give practical examples of techniques that can be modified or used to help students learn how to expand their store of usable words. For example, a "decontexualized" technique such as the use of flashcards, which are highly popular with many language learners, can be enriched beyond simply being pairs of words:

> Learners can sort flashcards into piles representing different groups of words (e.g., nouns, adjectives, adverbs, verbs, prepositions; words that are already learned vs. words still needing to be learned; past tense forms vs. present tense forms). Learners can tape flashcards to particular objects like lamp, table, and chair signified by the words on the cards, thus providing a visual (and to a degree tactile) context. Visual context might also be added by taping relevant pictures to the cards. Learners can arrange flashcards on the floor in a type of semantic map, with related words closer together and unrelated words farther apart. Finally, students can add context by writing the new words in complete, meaningful sentences on the cards. (p. 12)

In addition to covering other techniques, Oxford and Crookall discuss ways that vocabulary instruction can be integrated in second-language classes and can be built around students' various learning styles.

This emphasis on technique still leaves unsolved the basic issue of deciding which words to teach. Discourse studies might provide another route to effective selection of vocabulary to be taught in ESL/EFL courses—at least in EAP programs. Biber's list of suasive verbs is one example of the kind of information that might be used in EAP vocabulary lessons. Students can observe these verbs in reading passages selected from authentic texts used in courses the students are likely to be required to take, and they can learn to use them appropriately in their own writing. Work on more general academic vocabulary should be of help, too—for example, lists of the commands that are used in textbook activities and on examinations across several academic disciplinary areas should be very useful in EAP courses. (See sample 7 on pages 48–49 for illustrations of this type of vocabulary.)

Vocabulary lists of academic terminology imply grammatical issues since the words are not used just as single items (except perhaps as short answers on quizzes) but also must be used in complete sentences. What kinds of subjects are appropriate for these verbs—who can *agree, arrange, ask, beg, command, decide, demand, grant, insist, instruct, ordain, pledge, pronounce, propose, recommend, request, stipulate, suggest, urge*? Depending upon the writing task, the recommendation could be from the point of view of the student writer ("I recommend that. . .") or some quoted authority ("Plato recommended that. . ."). What kinds of objects do they require? Most of these verbs require (or often require) noun clauses as their objects—as in "I agree **that English vocabulary presents ESL/EFL learners with substantial challenges**."

□ *IF*-CLAUSES: AVOIDING THE "FOCUS ON FORM" TRAP

The second feature listed by Biber for communication focused on overt persuasion is the conditional clause with either *unless* or *if*. Instruction in the grammar of conditional and hypothetical clauses has all too often focused entirely on form issues—which verbs have to be in the *if*-clause and which verbs have to be in the main clause. Traditionally, practice with conditional sentences involves forming sentences in response to prompts such as "what would you do if you won the lottery" or "what will you do if you make 600 on TOEFL." EAP materials and lessons need to pull conditional sentences into academic context and to focus instruction on meaning and use in context rather than simply on getting the verb tenses right. Students need to see how conditional and hypothetical sentences are integrated into larger arguments and are used for content a bit more academic than winning the lottery.

□ MODAL AUXILIARIES AS A REFLECTION OF VALUE SYSTEMS

Eli Hinkel (1995) studied differences in the ways that native speaker undergraduates and ESL students used modals in argumentative writing. She analyzed the ways that the modals *must, have to, ought to, should,* and *need to* were used to express values in essays on assigned topics that she labeled "Academics, Politics, Family, Friendships, Traditions, Patriotism, and Racism." She found that native and nonnative speakers of English use *must, have to,* and *should* in different contexts. In her conclusion, she provides the following interpretation of her observations:

> The results of this study indicate that the usage of root[3] modals *must, have to, should, ought to,* and *need to* in NS and NNS writing appears to be culture and context dependent. NNSs who operate within domains of Confucian, Taoist, and Buddhist sociocultural constructs and presupposed values employed root modals *must, have to,* and *should* significantly differently from NSs on topics of Family, Friendships, and Traditions. The fundamental social values and presuppositions associated with the notions of harmony maintenance, family and group responsibility, and extrinsically

imposed obligation and necessity are often expressed through root modality in NNS writing. On the other hand, NS essays on similar topics showed a preponderance of *need to* to convey intrinsically imposed responsibility and necessity. The reason for the divergence may lie in the NS and NNS culturally bound understandings of the nature of obligation and necessity and adherence to sociocultural norms and codes fundamental to Anglo-American, and Confucian, Taoist, and Buddhist cultures. The achievement of advanced L2 linguistic proficiency and exposure to L2 sociocultural constructs for a period of approximately 2 years does not necessarily lead to NNSs assuming nativelike beliefs and presuppositions. (p. 337)

As Hinkel suggests, this result has numerous implications for the teaching of ESL/EFL grammar and writing—especially for teaching students about persuasive writing.[4]

□ Hinkel mentions the limited usefulness of working on the forms of modal auxiliaries and the importance of having ESL/EFL students learn about the use of these forms in context.

□ She also suggests that students can observe how these modals are used by native speakers as one method for learning more about the value system that lies behind the materials that they are studying in their academic programs.[5]

It seems likely from Hinkel's results that ESL/EFL students could be misunderstanding the reading materials that are required for their degree courses. Since academic textbooks are products of the value system of U.S. mainstream society, they will certainly reflect the values and the linguistic expression of those values. How are students prepared to recognize and deal with these values? How do they learn to use the language of a value system in which they do not fully participate? If ESL/EFL students are going to be judged by native-speaker teachers for the quality of their persuasion, and if ESL/EFL students are likely to provide arguments that do not fit the expectations of these teachers, should the ESL/EFL students be taught to mimic the persuasive language of native speakers? Should ESL/EFL students at least learn to recognize the sociocultural differences that lie behind argumentation—and the selection of modals to express arguments? Should—and can—the ESL faculty have any communication with faculty from other programs about the ways that value differences can lead to linguistic differences?

DIFFERENCES IN THE "LANGUAGES" OF ACADEMIC DISCIPLINES IN THE U.S.

While the grammar clusters discussed earlier in this book are found in all of the academic disciplines, they are used for different purposes, in different combinations, and in differing amounts in the different disciplinary areas. MacDonald's

(1994) study of the nature of academic writing in the humanities, social sciences, and sciences shows how members of these disciplinary subcommunities create texts that are admired and persuasive in each context—using writing styles that differ from those in the other disciplines. In addition, she finds that members of the different disciplines consider the writing styles of the other disciplines unconvincing and even stylistically ludicrous. While they are all using English and using the clusters of grammar identified by Biber, members of the different academic disciplines are convinced by quite different ways of organizing written materials and by quite different kinds of content. Thus, students in the undergraduate general education curriculum must learn to recognize the communication patterns appropriate for the different courses that they are required to take—a task made all the more difficult for students who come to the U.S. academic world from cultures with different approaches to presentation of ideas and information.

CONTRASTIVE RHETORIC AND PERSUASIVE PROSE

In a recent article, Milton Bennett (1996) narrates the story of a student from Nigeria in a U.S. university class. The student is answering a question elaborately, and the U.S. students eventually grow irritated with the "deviations" and "irrelevancies." They break into his storytelling, asking him why he's telling them all of "that stuff," and wanting to know the "point." The Nigerian student is surprised: "I'm telling you everything you need to understand the point." He denies their request to state "the point," indicating that only *children* would need to have it explicitly stated. This example points out one basic difference in (1) the pres-entation of material and (2) the expectations of audiences from different cultural backgrounds. In this case, it may be that greater understanding of surrounding detail is a form of evidence in persuading an audience; it is certainly true that in the Nigerian student's culture, baldly stating a point is seen as insulting to the audience.

Fortunately, the Nigerian student was immediately available to explain and bridge the differences, even though he did not offer his classmates their proposed solution. Unfortunately, ESL students who write U.S. academic prose seldom have that opportunity to explain themselves when they have confused their U.S. readers. Often they import cultural and linguistic techniques from their native languages and cultures into their presentation of written material in English. Even if their English language skills are excellent, they may not have the pragmatic competence to use those skills to compose effective U.S. academic prose. As R.B. Kaplan, the father of contrastive rhetoric studies, states, "The nonnative speaker does not possess as complete an inventory of the possible alternatives, and does not recognize what sorts of constraints a choice imposes on the text that follows" (1987, p. 11).

Kaplan began his seminal work in the rhetorical differences among cultures and languages (1966/1987) because of his interest in teaching ESL students appropriate strategies and frameworks for English academic prose. Today, research in contrastive rhetoric investigates "written language use in different cultures in order to compare and contrast the devices that writers use to present information, establish coherent ideas, unify the text, and present information in an appropriate way that is in accordance with the convention of that culture" (Indrasuta, 1988, p. 1). Investigators peruse U.S. academic prose written in English by native speakers of other languages, as well as prose written in the native languages of the authors, and analyze the rhetorical and linguistic characteristics of the discourse. They also analyze the characteristics of English speaking and writing in various contexts to use as a baseline for comparisons with speaking and writing in other linguistic and cultural contexts (e.g., Connor, 1996; Grabe, 1987; Grabe & Kaplan, 1996).

Only limited contrastive rhetoric discourse analysis research has been done on the persuasive rhetoric and language techniques used by other cultures. Among these limited research results are that, in **Arabic**, for example:

- ☐ like English prose, there is concern with direct introductions and clearly establishing the topic (Ostler, 1987, 1996; Sa'Adeddin, 1989)
- ☐ writers do not seek to persuade their audience overtly because their prose "elegantly present[s] universally accepted truths" (Koch, 1983, p. 55)
- ☐ repetition has: "a special discoursal role" and is not merely an ornamental device. Reiteration of general statements "tend[s] to create an immediate emotional impact" (Al-Jubouri, 1984, pp. 106–107).
- ☐ there is much coordination, repetition, and parallelism in persuasive writing (Hatim, 1991; Moros, 1986; Zellermeyer, 1988)
- ☐ alliteration, elaborate balance, rhythm, and repetition are used for emphasis (Ostler, 1987)
- ☐ there are few statistics or emotional appeals, even in written argument (Koch, 1983).

In **Chinese** persuasive writing, authors:

- ☐ value history and historical references, not statistics; they use quotations and allusions that have cultural and persuasive impact on the reader (Li, 1996; Tsao, 1983)
- ☐ value ancient authorities over recent empiricism (Li, 1996; Osbourne & Down, 1987)
- ☐ often conclude with a proverb or formulaic statement that taps into cultural persuasion (Chen-yu, 1981; Ostler, 1987)
- ☐ use set phrases that may also employ cohesive devices effectively within the text (Wong, 1992)

- □ are not taught and do not present acknowledgment of other points of view in persuasive writing; there is not even a "cursory awareness of alternative points of view" (O'Brian & Krause, 1996)
- □ practice "reader responsible" prose in which readers are "expected to supply some significant portion of the propositional structure," resulting in a more elliptical, referential, and allusional prose (Connor & Kramer, 1995; Fu, 1995; Hinds, 1987; Li, 1996; Ricento, 1987).

In contrast, conventions of **Spanish** persuasive writing include:

- □ more subjective and digressive strategies (than does English) that appeal strongly to the reader through "connective" or "associative" prose (J. Reid, 1988; Ostler, 1987)
- □ conscious deviations from the topic, then a return to it with a cohesion (signaling) device (Montaño-Harmon, 1991).
- □ employment of more reiteration and restatement than English includes, with more modification per clause (Montaño-Harmon, 1991; Ricento, 1987)
- □ like Arabic prose, presentation of material in long sentences with loose, elaborated patterns of information (Ostler, 1987, 1996).

Finally, because many ESL students have never studied writing in their own languages (Leki, 1991a), they may not be able to describe the conventions that result in effective written communication in their cultures. However, raising student awareness about the different rhetorics available, and about U.S. academic prose, can assist the ESL students in looking carefully at their writing strategies and techniques.

PEDAGOGICAL IMPLICATIONS OF CONTRASTIVE RHETORIC

In the early days of contrastive rhetoric, researchers concluded that only English prose was "linear" and "direct" and therefore "effective." Such cultural ethnocentricity has disappeared; clearly, all cultures have rhetorical conventions that, when followed, result in effective prose. More important, current research looks at specific differences in the conventions in presenting written materials, so that teachers can help students identify those conventions and then make choices about how best to communicate in the U.S. academic environment (Becker, 1995; Brock & Walters, 1994; Grabe & Kaplan, 1996; Li, 1996; Ostler, 1996).[6]

In U.S. academic prose, for example, authors write to present an individual point of view for an audience whose background and viewpoints may differ from theirs. Presenting this "individual point of view" can be especially difficult for students from academic cultures in which harmony and collective beliefs are highly valued; for these students, stating a personal opinion is considered remarkably self-involved and disrespectful. Another way in which native English writers persuade their readers is to follow the U.S. culture of facts and statistics: "Prove it or cut it!" is the attitude of the academic reader. Indeed, native English-speaking students and teachers are so immersed in academic culture of up-to-date evidence that it may be hard for them to believe that their use of such "facts" is culturally bound.

Effective native English authors also practice "writer-responsible" prose (Hinds, 1987). That is, the person primarily responsible for effective communication is the writer rather than the reader. Because U.S. academic readers are so diverse (ethnically, geographically, religiously, politically), the writer cannot assume a common framework. As a consequence, in order to reach the heterogeneous U.S. audience, the writer must provide a direct statement of purpose, transitional signposts that lead the reader through the piece of writing, and other conventions (e.g., introductory techniques, reference to outside authorities) that build comfort and trust between the writer and reader. When these conventions are ignored, the audience struggles.

In contrast, writers from "reader-responsible" cultures (e.g., Japan, China, Korea) assume that in their more homogeneous populations, the reader relies heavily on her or his parallel knowledge of the world to arrive at meaning in prose. Some ESL students from these reader-responsible cultures use references to cultural beliefs for persuasive impact, proverbs to "prove" and conclude their presentation of written ideas, and even surprises to interest the reader; moreover, they do not have to consider differing views. As a result, the use of detailed evidence in U.S. academic prose may well seem like insulting overkill.

It is therefore essential that ESL writing teachers discover the rhetorical conventions of their students' cultures and present the expected conventions of U.S. academic prose, not because academic prose in U.S. schools is more linear, more direct, and more effective, but because students can communicate more effectively with their audience of U.S. teachers if they understand and practice those conventions. Because students take undergraduate courses in so many different academic disciplines, they need to learn not just one way of dealing with U.S. academic prose. Rather, ESL writers need to learn how to analyze the reading and writing required by the different courses that they must take in their undergraduate program. Teaching students to be savvy learners seems a more reasonable and more effective strategy for ESL teachers and programs than trying to prepare students for all of the disciplinary writing communities that they will encounter in their general education courses.

U.S. UNDERGRADUATE WRITING

While the information that we have presented from contrastive rhetoric and discourse analysis has many uses in teaching ESL, some care must be exercised in deciding exactly what such studies tell us and exactly where to apply that information. In their first years in U.S. undergraduate courses, students seldom write anything that could even remotely be termed "argumentative essays," except in their introductory courses in composition in the English department and perhaps in public speaking courses. Certainly all students in all courses are trying to persuade their teachers that they know the materials for the courses, but the writing done to provide such evidence is often limited to test taking and project work rather than to writing "argumentative essays." In addition, students generally are required to write products that are strictly defined, in the syllabus for a course, in terms of content and organization. Writing assignments are likely to be in response to prompts like those given at the beginning of this chapter rather than the "argumentative" topics traditional in freshman composition courses.

We are only starting to understand the nature of undergraduate communication through studies such as those by Carson (1992), Carson and Leki (1993), and Ferris and Tagg (1996). Other studies such as Byrd (1995) and Conrad (1996a and 1996b) are providing descriptions of the language of the textbooks that students use in their undergraduate courses. While more information is needed about the kinds of writing that instructors in these undergraduate courses find persuasive, we already have indirect evidence such as that presented by Johns (1991): The biology teacher in this study is clearly more interested in the accuracy of the information given by ESL students on tests than in their use of correct English to display that information. What we do not know, of course, is how the teacher expects that information to be presented and what makes the difference between a "good" answer and a "bad" answer on a biology examination or in a biology lab report.

WRITING IN GRADUATE PROGRAMS IN THE U.S.

Like undergraduates, many graduate students in the U.S. write on topics selected and structured by the instructors for their courses (Canseco & Byrd, 1989; Horowitz, 1986). However, undergraduate programs in the U.S. aim generally at the preparation of the educated citizenry while graduate programs take as a major function the preparation of new members of their academic disciplines.[7] That is, undergraduate and graduate writing are similar in that purposes and formats are selected by the instructor but seem to differ in their ultimate goals. Just as a teacher education program in TESL/TEFL is preparing new members of our profession, so too are graduate programs in biology preparing the next generation of biologists; psychology programs, psychologists; and so on. Some of the new members of the profession will become academics, teaching and doing research in the college and university setting; others will find work in other settings. All are given training that is designed not just to have them learn about the knowledge base that characterizes that field but also to have them learn to communicate in the manner appropriate to members of that discipline—to talk and write like ESL/EFL teachers, biologists, psychologists, and so on through the disciplines.

These graduate programs also expect that their students will have received their undergraduate education in the U.S., having a uniform experience of the information and written texts that make up the foundation materials for that discipline. This assumption can lead to difficulties for international students who have done their undergraduate work in another country and then enter graduate study in the U.S. Here contrastive rhetoric comes into play even more strongly than for undergraduates who are from other countries or minority cultures in the U.S. As we argued earlier, ESL students who are preparing to take graduate programs in the U.S. need to understand the discourse community they are entering. On one hand, their task is easier than that of the undergraduate student because graduate students need to learn only one major community (although they will generally learn about subgroups within that major group). However, they will be expected to perform at high levels of proficiency and with close congruence to the communication patterns of their discourse community—and they are likely to be given less help with their writing than undergraduate students. Evidence for this last point can be seen in the ESL publication market with its dozens of composition textbooks aimed at general and undergraduate writers, whereas texts aimed at graduate writers can be counted on one hand.

Our rapidly developing knowledge of "academic literacy" in graduate education includes information about the use of appropriately persuasive language in various types of writing (i.e., MacDonald, 1994). Hyland (1994) gives an overview of other studies of the language of "hedging" in professional academic writing in the sciences. As he comments:

> Rather than being factual and impersonal, effective academic writing [in the sciences] actually depends on interactional elements which supplement propositional information in the text and alert readers to the writer's opinion. Significant amounts of this interactive element are hedges. (p. 240)

Hyland's list of hedging devices includes (1) modal auxiliaries; (2) "modal verbs" such as *believe, assume*; (3) *if*-clauses; (4) questions; (5) passivisation; (6) impersonal phrases; and (7) time reference. His comment on this list of forms explains the purposes that he finds in the group as a whole:

> These forms imply that statements contain personal beliefs based on plausible reasoning, for without them the implication is that the writer has knowledge, deduced from logical reasoning or empirical data, that the proposition conveyed is true. Such tentativeness avoids personal accountability for statements, reducing the author's "degree of liability." (p. 240).

An additional point for EAP grammar-writing about this list of hedging devices is that writers need to learn to use all of these grammatical features in context and in relation to each other in order to present their writing in a manner that persuades their readers.

At the same time, EAP courses for graduate students must deal with the fundamental differences detailed in MacDonald (1994) between persuasive writing in the humanities and such writing in the social sciences and the laboratory sciences. Using passive voice to distance the author from the statement is a valued tactic in the sciences and social sciences. In the humanities, critics deride the passive and call not just for the active voice but also for dramatic and individual choices in verbs. Thus, the creation of materials and courses that fit the precise needs of particular ESL/EFL learners remains a challenge to the flexibility of EAP programs.

CONCLUSION

Our current state of knowledge about persuasive writing in U.S. academic settings has the following implications for EAP programs designed to prepare ESL writers for success in their degree studies:

1. Because different disciplines use English in different ways, students must be prepared to recognize that different discourse communities exist within the university. Students need to learn about the cultural organization of the university into disciplinary fields and subfields, and they need to learn about the different writing styles used in those fields.

2. Students need to learn about the core writing types that are used throughout academic writing—informational writing, narrative writing, interactive writing, and persuasive writing. However, they need to learn to use the grammar and writing formats of English in flexible ways—knowing the basic patterns and recognizing how those basics are used in different settings.

3. Students need to recognize different cultural traditions and cultural value systems without denigrating their own backgrounds.

4. Teachers need to be careful not to imply that there is one universal standard for persuasion in the U.S. academic world. Students must be persuasive in their biology classes as well as in their composition courses.

5. Authentic materials are absolutely necessary for students to learn about the ways that language will be used in different settings. Moreover, authentic materials must be used from a variety of academic disciplines so that students have experience with the humanities, the social sciences, and the laboratory sciences. Just as we must be careful not to teach just to our own preferred learning styles, so too we must be careful not to teach just to our own academic backgrounds and to our own disciplinary interests and experience.

6. Teachers need to provide instruction in how to analyze and recognize the differences in language for different audiences in different settings. We cannot assume that being in the presence of the samples will lead students to recognize differences in the ways that language is used.

Finally, we must be aware that while they might appear to be stable and settled, the academic disciplines and their communication styles are in considerable flux and under pressure from critics (for example, feminists and minority representatives) who see the current disciplinary standards as exclusionary. Like our students, we must be careful observers of a complex environment. On behalf of our students, we must be careful about our roles as change agents—seeking to help students achieve their own goals and providing support during the often painful changes that occur during the educational process.

NOTES

1. I decided to use the entire chapter for these counts to emphasize for teachers the large number of words that students must handle when reading for their academic programs. In other settings, I would use samples of exactly the same number of words.

2. The relationship between the total number of different individual words and the total number of words used in a passage is called the "type/token ratio" (see next to last column in Table 6.2). The relationship is reported using a percentage figured by dividing the number of individual words by the number of total words and multiplying by 100. For example: If a sample of 100 words used 100 different words, the ratio would be 100. At the other extreme, if a sample of 100 words used only 1 word, the ratio would be 1. That is, the more individual words used, the higher the number in the type/token ratio.

History Chapter: 2,374 divided by 7,648 = .3104 multiplied by 100 = 31.0
Accounting Chapter: 1,613 divided by 8,695 = .1855 multiplied by 100 = 18.5

Thus, the type/token ratio for the accounting chapter is much lower than that for the history chapter—another way of saying that the reader has more words to deal with in the history textbook than in the accounting textbook.

In the final column of Table 6.2, I have included the total word counts for the two chapters for the type/token ratio—even though the samples are of different sizes—to illustrate the effect over whole chapters for student readers. However, 1,000-word samples from these same chapters show the same type/token pattern of the history chapter using more words, many of them only one time: accounting (39) and history (47.9). Notice that type/token figures will rarely remain the same over expanding samples—the more words in a sample the more opportunities for words either to be repeated or to be used just one time. It is, however, revealing to see how the ratio drops for the accounting text as words are recycled in the chapter—dropping from the ratio of 39.1 in the first 1,000 words to 18.5 by the end of the chapter, whereas the ratio for the history text remains relatively high. In the first 1,000 words, the accounting text uses 260 words just one time; the history text has 344 words used just one time in its first 1,000 words.

3. "Root" modals are those that are used to give advice and talk about values. In contrast are "epistemic" modals—the use of modal auxiliaries to talk about guesses and explanations—the use often termed "logical conclusion" in ESL/EFL materials.

4. Hinkel's project also has implications for composition teachers both in the evaluation of student writing and in the selection of topics for student writing assignments. A native speaker of English could find a student's choice of modals strangely off-key, overly emphatic in some contexts and not very strongly felt in others. That is, the student writer might not have chosen the "wrong" modal but might be stating a meaning that is new to the NS teacher. Care must be taken in making suggestions for changes to other modal auxiliaries since the teacher might be imposing her/his values on the student writer rather than correcting a true "error" in modal selection.

Teachers generally try to select topics for compositions that they think students will find interesting and about which they will have something to say. However, topic selection based on NS interests and emotions might not fit the interests and emotions of NNS writers. The most extreme examples of this problem come when a NNS takes a composition course designed for and dominated by NS students. I remember a Japanese student coming back to me for advice on how to handle a topic required for her freshman composition course: How to Solve the U.S. Drug Problem. She knew nothing about our drug problems and, although politely, did not much care about them either. A more common version of the problem is the ESL writing teacher who assigns topics on politics or family relationships for teaching of argumentative writing—and gets back papers that do not fit her or his expectations for strength of feeling.

5. As discussed in Chapter 9, "Technological Innovations and the Teaching of English Grammar and Composition," concordancing software is a highly dramatic and effective way of having students seek out and observe the use of particular words in context. Grammar Safari, a Web site for ESL/EFL learners, uses similar techniques to have students search text on the Web to see how words and phrases are used in authentic writing.

6. For more specific detail on teaching ESL students about contrastive rhetoric, see J. Reid, 1989.

7. MacDonald (1994) explores the tensions in undergraduate education between the desire on the part of the institution (and society) for courses to prepare educated citizens and the inclination of faculty in the various disciplines to see those courses as preparing new members for their field of study.

Chapter 7

Responding to ESL Student Language Problems: Error Analysis and Revision Plans

Joy Reid

Settling down to grade a set of ESL papers can be—actually, should be—an unsettling experience for teachers. Besides the assignment questions (Did the students follow directions? Did they fulfill the assignment?) and the content questions (Are the purpose and audience clear and integrated? Are the ideas and evidence appropriate, sufficient, and persuasive?), we are also faced with developing a process for identifying, analyzing, and evaluating language errors that will help us:

- □ send the students back into the writing process (through revision)
- □ increase the students' language knowledge and writing skills
- □ identify curriculum strengths and weaknesses
- □ evaluate the writing.

Moreover, simply marking (and even correcting) every error present may not be the most effective and efficient approach to improving the language of second-language writers. The primary purpose for identifying errors is not simply to require student revision of that particular bit of writing, but to determine what language knowledge remains to be developed. Errors are signs of a student's underlying system; the teacher should be looking for patterns of language use that can be analyzed and presented to the student, and perhaps to the whole class. Therefore, although this chapter begins with overall issues of response, its focus is the development of teacher processes for responding to language error in ESL student writing.

Again, a caveat: It is important to point out that I value fluency in ESL writing and self-confidence in ESL student writers as much as I value accuracy. The deficit model of teaching writing—searching for and penalizing students for errors as an approach to teaching composition—has no value in my teaching philosophy. I firmly believe that writing is essentially a social act; that is, writing takes place in a context, with the author's purpose(s) and the needs and expectations of the intended audience considered. Thus, the integration of communicative and linguistic competence in ESL writing classes is equally necessary. However, ESL writing teachers have multiple resources to consult about incorporating fluency and confidence into their classrooms (see Brookes & Grundy, 1990; Grabe & Kaplan, 1996; Hedge, 1988; Kutz, Groden & Zamel, 1993; Leki & Carson, 1997; Peyton & Staton, 1993; Reid, 1993; White & Arndt, 1991). In contrast, real-world teaching and evaluation of student writing involves recognition of student error and the development of strategies to encourage students to return to their writing and have the confidence and knowledge to revise. As language specialists, ESL teachers work with student error as we seek to understand what language skills/knowledge remain to be developed.

RESPONSE ISSUES

The issues of responding to student writing have plagued teachers for decades; research in this area has had, at best, mixed results (cf. Leki's 1990 review), perhaps because of the complexity and number of variables involved. Included in these variables are the following:

1. **Who** responds?
   - teachers
   - tutors
   - classmates
   - writing centers
   - other peers
   - self
2. **What** kinds of response?
   - positive as well as corrective
   - just to content and ideas
   - prescriptive vs. nonprescriptive
   - just to language errors
   - make full corrections and rewrite suggested changes
   - give clues for revision (e.g., underline error, ask questions about content)
   - overall reactions vs. specifically detailed comments
3. **When** to respond?
   - to each draft
   - to the final draft
   - during drafting
   - to a beginning draft
   - before drafting
   - not at all
   - to content errors only on early drafts
   - to language errors only on final drafts
4. **Where** to respond?
   - writing in the margins
   - mini-conferencing during class
   - audiotaped comments
   - writing an end comment
   - office-based detailed conferencing
   - on-line comments/conversations

5. **Why** respond?
   - to teach
   - to grade
   - to negotiate change
   - to build trust
   - to send student back to the writing
   - to stimulate student revision
   - to collaborate with the student
   - to build classroom communication/community

6. **How to**
   - identify response needs of individual students
   - teach through responding
   - evaluate the effectiveness of the response
   - find the time to appropriately respond.

In short, responding to student writing is hard, usually time-consuming work, and it reflects a teacher's philosophy of teaching and attitudes toward students. Some teachers prefer to mark each error; others mark only errors that they have been teaching. Many teachers have elaborate marking systems and notational lists; some do not believe in the efficacy of marking errors at all.

In a more student-centered classroom, however, student needs and preferences must hold as much weight as teacher preferences in the response and marking processes. The newer research has focused not so much on teacher preferences as on what motivates students to revise their writing effectively (Cohen & Cavalcanti, 1990; Ferris, 1995a; Hacker, 1996; Hedgcock and Lefkowitz, 1994; Leki, 1991; Peitzman and Gadda, 1994; J. Reid, 1994). However, much of this research is concerned with what students do with teacher feedback, how they react to teacher response to their writing. I believe that the next step is to ask students what kinds of response they find most motivating and helpful; students may have as many different revision strategies as they do composing strategies. Indeed, teachers should probably spend as much time teaching students multiple revision strategies as they do teaching students to compose, stressing the value and potential processes of "re-vision-ing," and the coping skills needed to revise effectively.

Researchers and teachers do agree about the objectives of response: long-term improvement in linguistic and writing skills and cognitive change (Grabe & Kaplan, 1996; Leki, 1992). And most agree on the following basics of response to student writing:

   □ responding need not be evaluative, although it is often seen in that light

   □ responding is not a single act; the teacher may mini-conference with students about their topics in class, write responses on student drafts, conference with students throughout their writing processes, and write an evaluative response on their final drafts

   □ teacher response is not the only kind a student should receive: others include classmates, writing center tutors, friends, and self-evaluation

   □ teachers must live up to their role as "reader" first, without getting bogged down in their multiple roles of editor, coach, grader, etc.

   □ one major purpose of response is to motivate and encourage students

   □ ESL students generally take teacher response very seriously.

In addition to the eventual expertise that ESL writing teachers gain through their responding experiences, several sources provide information and illumination about teacher response processes. Arndt (1993)[1] discusses the mismatches between students' and teachers' perspectives concerning teacher response; Li (1996) reports detailed interviews of teachers concerning their responses to students' writing; Reid (1994) argues for more teaching of rhetoric and language through teacher responses. Detailed presentation of response processes and advice in ways to prevent teacher burnout are demonstrated in Reid (1993);[1] Fox (1994) and Connor (1996) demonstrate rhetorical and cultural differences in student writing that help the teacher to individualize responses; and Hamp-Lyons' (1991) anthology focuses on the assessment component involved in teacher response. Richard Straub (1996) describes teacher response in terms of teaching style and philosophy but stresses that while there are many ways to respond successfully, almost certainly there are ways to respond unsuccessfully: on the one hand, being overly harsh or disrespectful, and/or usurping control of the students' writing by dictating precisely what and how the student should write; on the other hand, responding minimally or generically, being detached and unhelpful (p. 247). Finally, Bates, Lane, and Lange's text, *Writing Clearly: Responding to ESL Compositions* (1993), "offers instructors an overall system for responding to their ESL students' writing" (p. v).

Because these sources provide substantial information about teacher response, and because this book focuses on grammar in the composition classroom, the remainder of this chapter describes ways in which teachers may respond to language errors in their students' writing. Controversy also exists in this more constrained area of language error; for example,

1. Should teachers
   - mark every error
   - mark no errors
   - mark just what they're teaching or have taught
2. As teachers identify errors, should they
   - correct errors or simply indicate them (by underlining, X-ing, etc.)
   - prioritize errors based on
     —egregiousness (how much they interfere with communication)
     —commonness of occurrence
     —reason(s) for occurrence
3. How might teachers incorporate student language error into their overall evaluation of a student's paper?
4. How can teachers analyze patterns of error that will help their students learn correct language structures? And which of these patterns needs to be presented to the whole class or to groups of students in the class?

Depending on the student's level of ESL/EFL writing proficiency, as well as on such variables as level of motivation and learning style, the teacher must finally decide which errors to mark, change, and/or discuss with the student. In pedagogical terms, identifying errors for ESL writing students must be based in rational decision-making, and should lead the teacher and the ESL student writer to work together to develop revision plans that are knowledge-based.

IDENTIFYING ESL LANGUAGE ERRORS

ESL student writers make second-language errors for four basic reasons that evolve from linguistic factors:[2]

1. First-language interference: Transfer of first-language structures to ESL writing may help or hinder an ESL writer, depending on the similarities or differences between the student's first and second languages (see Chapter 1 in this volume for a detailed discussion of first-language transfer). For example, like English, Arabic uses some relative clauses. Arabic ESL students therefore use more relative clauses in their written English and use them more confidently than do Chinese ESL writers, whose language does not include relative clauses. Instead, Chinese writers have been shown to avoid the use of relative clauses when they write in English (Gass, 1988; Schachter, 1974).

2. Overgeneralization of English language rules: ESL students (like native English speakers) may extend a rule past its parameters in English. For example, a student whose first language is not inflected may practice the third person singular -s on English verbs ("he walk_s_"), then incorrectly use that -s on second-person "singular" English verbs ("you walk_s_"). A student whose first language has overwhelmingly regular verb tenses may easily generalize to "he com_ed_" and "she go_ed_." For the immigrant students who have acquired much of their English without formal study of the language (see Chapter 1 in this text), incorrect rules gleaned from both their first- and their second-language oral/aural experiences may exist and be generalized, because language acquisition, as well as language study, encourages cognitive rule-formation processes.

3. High level of difficulty of the language structure: This category is more complex than meets the eye (or the ear). There are, of course, no absolutes of ease and difficulty in language structure. So although curriculum designers believe that we should begin with "easy grammar" and progress to more difficult structures, in practice what is "easy" and "difficult" will differ for students from different language backgrounds (although not necessarily systematically). "Modifications due to L1 influence may delay initiation of a [language] sequence, delay or speed up passage through it, or even add sub-stages to it" (Larsen-Freeman & Long, 1992, p. 96). For example, for the Arabic and Chinese students described above, acquisition of relative-clause use may differ in time and level of accuracy because Arabic speakers are familiar with the structure in their first language and Chinese students are not. However, it is necessary to note that within the group of Arabic students, some students may be more conscious of relative-clause use than others, and the latter may have more difficulty than the former.

Moreover, teachers must not confuse "difficult to explain" with "difficult to learn." Some language structures may be easy to teach but difficult to learn (e.g., subject-verb agreement, for some learners); others may be the opposite. Still others may be difficult both to teach and to learn (e.g., articles, for some learners). And for learners, both length of time and consistency of use can vary.[3]

4. Production errors: Called "mistakes" (as opposed to "errors") by some ESL researchers, these are random blunders that the writers can recognize and repair if the errors are pointed out to them. That is, the writer knows or has acquired the structure rule and can usually produce it correctly. Production errors occur for native English speakers (NES) as well as ESL writers because they are writing too fast, they are fatigued, they are not paying attention, and/or they do not monitor for errors effectively.

BEFORE MARKING ESL LANGUAGE ERRORS

Before teachers mark ESL student language errors in their writing, we must develop a rational marking process. It is essential, for example, to consider which student errors are:

□ related to what we are teaching (and therefore able to be corrected by the student)

□ production errors (and so both monitorable and able to be corrected by the student)

□ important for reader comprehension (and therefore necessary to correct, by either the student or the teacher)

□ probably not able to be corrected by the student (e.g., a difficult structure attempted by the student). Should the teacher be responsible for making the correction or not? Should the error be ignored?

First, it is probably not necessary to say that students should not be asked to make corrections for structures they have not been taught. Perhaps just as important, teachers need to decide (1) whether marking a correction for each error would benefit the student; (2) which errors she/he should correct in order to extend the student's learning experience; (3) and which errors should remain unmarked because the student is not yet ready to be confronted by the error. Finally, we must know what we want students to do in response to our comments and marks. That is, in what ways can the students' revision processes benefit from our responses to their texts?

Moreover, we must understand which language errors occur in a *pattern* and are "frequent, global, and stigmatizing" (Ferris, 1995b, p. 19). That is, just looking at and marking (even correcting) discrete errors may not help students improve their writing; sentence-level errors need to be discussed and revised in light of the discourse rather than just the sentence. Errors made in the predominant grammar of the writing genre (e.g., informational writing or narrative) are errors that should be corrected with the text-type involved. We might define genre as social constructivists do: "communicative events" that are characterized by their "communicative purposes" and by various patterns of "structure, styles, content and intended audience" (Swales, 1990a, p. 58). As teachers examine a student's writing, we might ask:

- □ What grammar predominates in this genre?
- □ In what way(s) has the student violated the dominant grammar of the genre (that is, what cluster of grammar errors is worth working with)?

For further discussion of text-types and grammar "clusters," see Byrd's Chapter 5 in this volume.

Next, teachers should consider precisely what we expect students to do in response to our comments: merely correct that discrete error, immerse themselves in further language development, record the error and the reason for the error? The answer to that question will help us decide which language errors:

- □ should merely be indicated because students should be able to recognize and correct the error without additional teacher intervention (student-responsible errors),
- □ require additional language work by the student writer, and what materials or activities are available to assist the student in this language development work,
- □ are part of a "cluster" of grammatical errors that occur within a genre and should therefore be dealt within the context of that genre (Dykstra, 1997; Hyon, 1996; Meyer, 1996),
- □ should be flagged by the teacher for a fuller discussion with the student (in a conference or with the whole class).

In addition, before marking a student's writing, the teacher should be aware of the student's preferences for teacher response:

- □ **Quantity:** Does the student want every error marked, the better to trust the teacher's abilities and to demonstrate the student's abilities to correct every mistake, or does the student prefer to have just the most important errors marked?
- □ **Affect:** Does the student react well to encouraging notes from the teacher, or does she/he believe that such notes are "fluff" and therefore prefer "just the facts" about errors without elaboration?
- □ **Interaction:** Does the student learn better by answering questions written in the margins (or at the end) of the student writing, or might she/he prefer an audiotape made by the teacher, or might she/he depend on teacher response in the form of a conference?

Table 7.1: Teacher-Response Process for Language Problems in ESL Student Writing

- □ Reflect on the assignment, the purpose, and the audience for the assignment, as well as your expectations about the language in this piece of writing.

- □ Read the writing quickly, without making any marks, gathering information about the overall topic, focus, language, and comprehensibility. If you have a set of student papers, read through all of them quickly, looking for patterns of successful and unsuccessful responses to the assignment. Teachers can only live up to their role as reader if we first read the texts without a pen in hand.

- □ Determine which student papers have been written by U.S. resident students and which have been written by international students (see "Analyzing ESL Language Errors," p. 128).

- □ Reconsider (and perhaps modify) your language expectations and your marking criteria.

- □ Consider your individual students' preferences about teacher response.

- □ Decide on the marking criteria you will use for your response to language problems: Will you mark each and every error equally? If not, which will you mark, which will you focus on for the students to correct, and which will you correct yourself without comment? Which will you ignore?

- □ Read each student's writing again, slowly, considering each individual student and that student's probable response to your marks.

- □ Mark those language problems that you believe the student is ready to correct and integrate into his/her monitoring knowledge.

- □ Comment (in writing or orally) on those language problems that you believe the student needs to learn how to correct.

- □ Correct those errors that interfere with reader comprehensibility but that the student probably has not yet confronted.

- □ Recheck your marks and comments: Are they clear, accurate, and relevant? Will they draw the student back into the writing process to revise?

Table 7.1 summarizes one process for reading and responding to ESL student errors. Teachers can discover student preferences by trying (and even experimenting with) many forms of response and having the students decide which they prefer; students can also make their discoveries through simple informal surveys, class discussion, and/or a writing assignment early in the ESL writing course, asking students to reflect on their preferences.

ERROR GRAVITY

Teachers must also learn to prioritize student mistakes because some grammatical and syntactic errors are more serious than others. Research in error gravity has found that mistakes that interfere with reader comprehension are more substantial than those that do not (Janopolous, 1992; Johnson, 1985; Santos, 1988; Vann, Meyer, & Lorenz, 1984; Vann, Lorenz, & Meyer, 1991).[4] For example, errors in word order, verb tense, and word choice can prevent the reader from making sense of the message. Of these, word order is often the most serious error, yet for students from some language backgrounds, word order in English, which is relatively fixed, is particularly difficult. The following English sentence has been translated into correct Korean and then back-translated directly, word-for-word, into English. The problem of word order is evident:

> **English:** *Even though I told John not to take the Chemistry class, he took it.*
>
> **Korean:** *Even though I John Chemistry class not to take told John it took.*

See the Norwegian student sample on p. 141 of Chapter 8 for a classic problem with word order that is based on first-language transfer.

Word order errors might also include multiple adjective or adjective phrase placement and adverbial phrase placement (see Appendix A on p. 133). Notice the phrases in "He is going to Japan by ship twice a day during December," and try to decide what the rules for such placement might be.

Verb tense (e.g., past and present) and verb form (e.g., *reading* vs. *to read*), errors often interfere with reading comprehension. English is a moderately (some would say highly) inflected language, and the concept of time is important in U.S. culture, so correct verb use is important. The paragraph below demonstrates some of those errors considered most serious by error gravity research. Verb errors are <u>underlined</u>; word order errors are in *italics*, and incorrect word choices are **boldfaced**.

> First I <u>use</u> library when I <u>been</u> high school in past several years in america, I am still using library now and I <u>realized</u> that *visits library* are on the increase at every **goes** on higher education. The pupose that I visit library is such as for research, assignment, and study for myself; therefore, i think this library <u>gave</u> us good *benefit* **influence**. However, using library is **anxiety** with the fact that many students have <u>complin</u> about library research skills. I can easy <u>to see</u> that happen in high school and college library: although I am going to compare with high school librairies and college libraies.

Error gravity research lists the following as less serious errors: article mistakes, incorrect preposition choice, lack of pronoun agreement, comma splices, and spelling mistakes. While these errors are visible to the NES reader, and while they often differ from NES error (and therefore seem even more "visible" and strange to the reader), they do not usually interfere with direct communication of ideas. The writing may sound "foreign," but the meaning is clear. The ESL student-generated paragraph below (written by a Venezuelan undergraduate) contains several of these less important errors. Article errors are indicated by parentheses; spelling errors are italicized; incorrect preposition use is underlined; comma splices are marked with brackets. I have corrected verb tense and word choice errors.

> Calculus is also *esential* on military purposes. For instance, on what angle should a soldier adjust a *canon* to hit (X) target precisely? A skillful *artillary* soldier who knows calculus very well can easily predict the angle in which (X) cannon should be adjusted, [__] if he knows the equation which shows the path of the pellet, he can plot a graph. Once he plots the equation, he can tell where the pellet will hit (a) ground, [__] that does not sound too weird, right? The U.S. army would be (X) strongest army on the world if every soldier in the army knew calculus very well.

While some academic readers may be irritated and report such errors to ESL teachers ("This student can't even use articles!"), I view such a report as an opportunity to educate. The fact is that article and preposition errors are the most difficult for many ESL writers to remediate—for several possible reasons: (1) articles may not occur in their first language; (2) English article rules are very complex; (3) prepositions may not occur, or may not occur in such numbers, in their first language; and (4) preposition rules in English are particularly arbitrary. I often send the offended faculty member demonstrations of these facts. See Appendices B and C (pp. 134–135) for article exercises and a preposition chart, respectively, which I have found useful in educating other members of the faculty.

To summarize:

1. ESL errors must be seen in the context of communicative purpose (genre).
2. They often occur in "patterns," and so should be approached as "clusters" that predominate in that genre.
3. They need to be prioritized if ESL writers are to benefit from correction.
4. Some errors are almost never 100% remediable. Fortunately, these errors do not usually interfere with reader comprehension.
5. For such errors (in particular, articles and prepositions), ESL writers should spend their time more wisely on other, more serious errors, and ask a NES for assistance in correcting the articles and prepositions in their writing.

ANALYZING ESL LANGUAGE ERRORS

Analyzing student errors can provide valuable data. By identifying errors and by asking student writers about their errors, the teacher can suggest resources for student assistance, direct the student back into the writing/revision process, plan language development activities to help with the major grammar issues, and determine what changes need to be made in lesson planning and assignment development in the ESL writing course.

While each student writer is unique, we can generally divide ESL student writers into two categories: those who are U.S. residents, students who have lived and attended school in the U.S., and international students, those who have studied English in their own countries before coming to the U.S. to study.[5] Typically, U.S. resident student writing will contain phonetic spelling, incorrect or missing verb endings, and often a sprinkle of inappropriately informal idioms and language. Sometimes these ESL students have learned about thesis statements and/or topic sentences during their prior U.S. schooling, so their rhetoric may be easily accessible to the reader. However, the language problems may interfere substantially with comprehension. In contrast, typical international student writing will contain easily identifiable grammatical errors: article and preposition use, verb tense use within the framework of a paragraph, word order and word choice errors, and sentence boundary errors. Often the vocabulary and syntax will be relatively sophisticated, and few idioms will be present, and often international student writing will not demonstrate knowledge of U.S. academic rhetorical conventions. Furthermore, for all students (native English speakers included), the "discourse community" for whom they write during their academic careers may well be strangers, and the appropriate styles and conventions for those discourse communities foreign.

The initial process of error analysis is not difficult. Once teachers have formed their philosophies of marking, they can mark the language errors in whatever way seems most efficient (underlining, checking, circling, etc.). They might mark prioritized errors in a different color, or circle the errors they choose to discuss with the student or the class. If opportunities for detailed conferences are limited, teachers might try to mini-conference with the students during class or, in their end-comments on the written drafts, refer students to viable sources of assistance: the writing center, tapes in a language laboratory, ESL handbooks, or peer tutors.

During a full-class discussion (using overhead transparencies of information and, perhaps, student papers from previous classes or the current class), teachers might also introduce their students to error analysis. Initially, teachers might ascertain whether the students understand the abbreviated marks the teacher has made by asking whether students recognize and can correct each of the selected errors. In addition, teachers might ask their students to record their errors on an error chart (see the sample error chart in Appendix D, p. 135). Teachers and students may decide to list just the major errors (e.g., verb tenses and forms, word choice, agreement, word order, and sentence boundaries), or just the errors the students should concentrate on correcting, or perhaps all the errors. The error chart can be used to prioritize errors as well, and students can see their progress through a semester of writing. For students who do not find this process effective (and eventually for each student), the teacher might hold small-group conferences that the students themselves organize—either during or outside of class—in which the students ask questions about errors they didn't understand or had trouble correcting.[6]

REVISION PLANS

We can define revision as adding, deleting, or substituting words, sentences, and paragraphs (S. Reid, 1995). As teachers introduce the concept of revision—how essential it is (even for professional writers) and how it is a golden opportunity for students to learn—they can explain that language correction is only one part of the revision process. Correcting language errors is sometimes called "editing," to distinguish it from the more global "revisions." In fact, some teachers call language correction "merely editing" and insist that "editing" should be the very last step in preparing a final draft, well after the "revision" process.

Indeed, for some students, "editing" their language errors is most effective and efficient when they focus on it only after they complete their drafts; for others, however, language correction takes place as they compose and draft. For these ongoing editors, waiting to "edit" is like waiting to exhale. Again, teachers should be asking their students about their revision/editing strategies: What works best for each student? What does each student prefer?

The question, of course, is when the *teacher* should mark student drafts for editing language. The answer varies, depending on the teacher's response philosophy and the students' learning styles and strategies.[7] Many teachers prefer to comment more globally on initial student drafts, speaking primarily to content and organization; if students can postpone editing their language errors, these teachers argue, they can concentrate more effectively on the content and context of their writing. Some students, however, may object; again, individual preferences of students as well as teachers must play a part.

However, whenever teachers decide to mark language problems, they should also be able to give suggestions. Students should understand the reasons for "looking again" and making changes to the language of the drafts (e.g., easier for audience comprehension, more relevant to the purpose, accuracy for author credibility). As an integral part of the revision process, student writers should be active participants; they should learn to articulate useful intentions for revision in the same way they articulate and plan for their initial writing (Wallace, 1996). In fact, the student author should learn how to write a revision *plan*. It need not be long or detailed; rather, it should be focused, and the student should be able to accomplish the plan.

The following Sample Student Revision Plans are written by students as a result of classroom discussion about revision and editing.

■ ■ ■ SAMPLE STUDENT REVISION PLANS

I

I plan to expand the essay by explaining more about how women failed the first time and continued to struggle and finally managed to get equal rights with men. I will include a map with the paper to show the geographical position of Tanzania. And I will be careful to use the spell-checker on my computer so that I won't have so many errors.

II

I know my audience is frustrated, so I have to give a very good solution to the problem of parking. I have to include the amount of money and time to build a new parking garage. I need to correct the verb tense errors so that I won't make my audience even more frustrated.

III

The last argument in this essay was the most persuasive, but the lack of accuracy made it not tell if we can or cannot stop whaling. So I will ask my peer tutor for help.

IV

1. reorganize some sentences (esp. the thesis and the very long sentences about autism I will break into smaller sentences)

2. add connection words to help my reader get easily from one sentence to the next sentence

3. add some articles and correct some word forms

One note of caution: Teachers must remember that revision strategies develop slowly. Even with carefully laid revision plans, students will almost certainly struggle with the processes and skills. Moreover, much to the students' frustration, when they take necessary risks to revise, they may well discover that their writing deteriorates before it improves. Consequently, both teachers and students must be willing to be patient as well as innovative.

CONCLUSION

Simply put, successful student revision/editing requires that a student:

☐ recognize that something is wrong

☐ be able to articulate what that "something" is (perhaps in a metacognitive journal entry or on a personal error chart)

☐ know what to do with the "something" that is wrong, and

☐ have a reason to make that change.

Actually, both teachers and students need to be able to do the first two, and teachers have to make the reason(s) for revision clear to the students: A separate grade for revisions? Reading by a different audience outside of class? In other words, students must be fully aware of the social nature of revision and the benefits thereof.

The student's individual ability to recognize errors as errors, to understand the process(es) for correction, and to integrate the correction into her or his repertoire of writing skills are all necessary for optimal learning. If, instead, a student corrects an error but neither understands nor integrates that correction, then remediation does not take place. Mindless correction does not lead to learning; time is wasted (for both the teacher and the student), and frustration levels may rise. Ideally, revision should lead to a true "re-vision-ing" of language and writing (revising as re-visualizing). More practically, students should see that the benefits accrue as they improve their language and cognitive skills. In that way, we can encourage our students to return to their writing, to make a revision plan, and to learn from their re-vision-ing.

Therefore, teachers must consider each individual as they respond to student writing.[8] For example, some students will be invigorated by discovering each error and will trust the expertise of the teacher; others will be overwhelmed by the marks and sink into despair. So learning to prioritize individually—which errors to mark, which to correct, which to ignore, and which to discuss with the writer or with the whole class—takes experience, focus, and trial and error. But the results are worthwhile: The purpose of the revising process goes well beyond making a piece of *writing better*. It can make a student a *better writer* by expanding her knowledge and skills with written English.

NOTES

1. Teachers can reduce the amount of time they spend grading by, for example, assigning some collaborative writing assignments in which the natural cycle of feedback among cooperating writers occurs and is valued (Arndt, 1993), and the teacher responds to one draft instead of several; by persuading students to use multiple

audiences for feedback, including classmates, peer tutors, and the writing center; by responding only to what students ask the teacher to respond to in their drafts; and by not responding to every draft.

2. Of course, other nonlanguage-based causes of error include the age of the student writer, motivation, student learning styles and strategies, and many external context factors.

3. For more information concerning ease and difficulty of acquisition of English language structures, access the following Website:

www.gsu.edu/~eslhpb/grammar/difmatx.ht

4. Without question, more research is needed in the area of error gravity; however, teachers can use the limited results as they begin to prioritize errors. See Rifkin and Roberts (1995) for a review article on error gravity research.

5. For more information about the differences between these two categories of students, see Chapter 1 in this volume.

6. For valuable insights on how to prepare ESL students for writing conferences, see Goldstein & Conrad (1990).

7. See Chapter 2 in this volume for a discussion of student learning styles.

8. See Appendix E (pp. 136–137) for sample student paragraphs.

APPENDIX A

□ POSITION OF ADJECTIVE AND ADVERBIAL MODIFIERS

Generally, English adjectives precede nouns in the following order:

Ordinals	*Cardinals*	*Opinion*	*Size*	*Measurement*	*Condition*
Age	*Temperature*	*Shape*	*Color*	*Origin*	*Season/Time*
Material	*Power*		*Location*	*Purpose*	***NOUN***

Examples of Adjective Placement

	cardinal	***opinion***	***origin***	***material***	***purpose***	***NOUN***
	cardinal	*opinion*	*origin*	*material*	*purpose*	*NOUN*
An	One	ugly	French	silk	cocktail	dress
	opinion	*color*	*material*	*power*	*purpose*	*NOUN*
An	elegant	black	steel	electric	coffee	pot
	measurement	*condition*	*age*	*season*	*NOUN*	
The	long	heavy	old	winter	coat	
	ordinal	*size*	*temperature*	*shape*	*color*	*NOUN*
The	first	tiny	cold	round	blue	ball
	color	*season/time*	*location (general)*	*location (specific)*	*NOUN*	
A	red	spring/early	Colorado	garden	tulip	

(Adapted from Firsten & Killian, 1994.)

□ POSITION OF ADVERBIALS (ADJECTIVE MODIFIERS)

When more than one adverbial modifier occurs in a sentence, the regular order after the verb, is Place + Manner + Frequency + Time.

Examples of Adverbial Placement

	PLACE	**MANNER**	**FREQUENCY**	**TIME**
John went	to the library	by bus	every night	last week.
The King	left here	secretly		on Sunday.
He is going	to Japan	on the Concorde	twice a week	during December.

(Hayden, Pilgrim, & Haggard, 1956.)

APPENDIX B

□ CONSCIOUSNESS–RAISING ARTICLE EXERCISES

Directions: In Exercise A and Exercise C below, write an article in each blank (*a, an, the*). If more than one article could be appropriate, write both. If no article is needed, write *X*. Then discuss the examples in Exercise B.

Finally, begin to write rules for article use (and nonuse) in English, using the sentences in the exercises as examples. Each sentence is numbered for ease of reference.

Exercise A

(1) In _____ United States, we make health _____ end in itself. (2) We have forgotten that _____ health is really _____ means to enable _____ person to do his work and do it well. (3) A lot of people—and this includes many _____ patients as well as many physicians—pay little attention to _____ health but much attention to those who imagine they are ill. (4) Our great concern with health is shown by _____ medical columns in _____ newspapers, _____ health articles in _____ popular magazines, and _____ popularity of _____ television programs and all those books on _____ medicine. (5) We talk about health all _____ time. (6) Yet, for _____ most part, _____ only result is more people with _____ imaginary illnesses. (7) _____ healthy man should not be wasting time talking bout health. (8) He should be using _____ health for _____ work: _____ work he does and the work that good health makes possible.

Exercise B

9. He has (X) pneumonia.	BUT	10. She has a cold.
11. He went to the grocery store.	BUT	12. She went to (X) bed.
13. He participated in the contest.	BUT	14. She won (X) first prize.
15. He hiked to (X) church.	BUT	16. She hiked to a/the church.
17. They are going on a/the journey.	BUT	18. She is going to (X) work.

Exercise C

19. We're going to _____ movie.	20. We're going to _____ movies.
21. She packed _____ suitcase.	22. She packed _____ luggage.
23. He took a bus to _____ library.	24. He took a bus _____ home.
25. The wallet contained _____ dollar.	26. The wallet contained ___ money.

APPENDIX C

Complexity of Preposition Use in English

to	a point of arrival or completion	I traveled **to** Bombay.
	in the direction of, toward	The lake lies **to** the north.
	in comparison	It's nothing compared **to** mine.
	as far as	I went **to** the foot of the mountain.
	until	He'll be busy from two **to** four.
	before (time)	It's five **to** nine.
	a ratio	I'll bet you 6 **to** 10 he loses.
	expressing closeness	We were meeting face **to** face.
	before nouns, expressing emotion	**To** my horror, he died.
	introduce an indirect object	Give it **to** him.
	becomes a particle marking the infinitive	She began **to** sing.

APPENDIX D

Sample Error Chart

NAME _____   Class_____

ESSAY _____   Date _____

ERROR TYPE	*ERROR*	*CORRECTION*
F (word form)		
Sp (spelling)		
Ref (referent)		
Agr (subject-verb)		
Agr (other)		
WW (wrong word)		
VT (verb tense)		
R-O (run-on)		
Frag. (fragment)		

NOTE: The categories on this error chart can be modified for each student essay, or they can remain the same throughout the course.

APPENDIX E

□   SAMPLE STUDENT PARAGRAPHS

Following are three paragraphs from ESL writing students of different language backgrounds and English language proficiency. The paragraphs can be used for practice in responding. Although you do not know these students personally, you can invent a background for each.

I

Undergraduate U.S. Resident Student, Korean-American,
First-Year Composition Class, Midsemester In-class Writing

(1) I agreement of the spirit of competition is not ennobeling. (2) When winning is the "only thing," the spirit of competition is degrading, envy, ager, viciousness and hatred are the only emotions. (3) I watched a movie five years ago in Korea. (4) I didn't remember what's the name of the movie. (5) It was very nice movie; Kim and Han are very friendly each other. (6) They are reserching about solar system together in the Korean university. (7) That research is very important and when they finish of that, they will getting very famous people in my country. (8) Kim doesn't like Han gets a famous people. (9) One day they have to go some where. (10) That time Kim killed Han in the forest. (11) After that Kim talk about his reserch to the newspapers and tv. (12) Then he get famous person in my contry. (13) Kim's wins the that reserch, but it was not win. (14) It was lose, because he killed him friend.

II

Graduate International Student, Costa Rica,
First-Year Composition Course, Draft Paragraph

(1) I am agree that in last twenty years the environmental issue has grown. (2) More and more people discover that if the world shall exist we have to take care for it, we have to protect it from being polluted and ruined of people that do not care. (3) There are many ways to do this, but one of the most popular ones are direct action. (4) Some of this action are ilegal, but still some break the law to show what their meanings are. (5) After action like this there often are discussions about if the law breakers should be punished for what they have done but is this the right question to ask? (6) Why should not environmental terrorists be punished even though they are fighting for a good cause.

III

Mixed Educational Background

For ESL student writers whose prior English language educational experiences include both classroom ESL learning and immersion in U.S. culture, the problems may be more difficult to analyze. The paragraph below demonstrates both resident and international errors:

The recent accusation from People's Republic of China of Clinton Administration's political betryal had just slapped the face of America. The visit of the first leader of Taiwan to the University of Cornell on June 1995 had brought the China–U.S. diplomatic relationship to a era of gap. Although granting the visa to Taiwan's first leader to come to visit United States might bring some positive priviledges for United States, but by considering the effects that may storm the whole Eastern Asia and some troubles that might brought to united States, the Clinton Administration had just not made a wise decision at this time. Instead, the Clinton Administration should refused to allow the Taiwan's President to visit United States.

Chapter 8

Using Contrastive Analysis to Analyze ESL/EFL Student Error

Joy Reid

Learning a second language assumes that the learner has already learned a first (a native language, a mother tongue). While grammatical and structural errors in speaking a second language are sometimes overlooked or easily forgiven so long as the content of the communication is clear, native English readers sometimes expect accuracy as well as fluency from students writing in a second (or third or fourth) language. ESL teachers responding to student writing therefore have a responsibility to identify student errors, to increase student knowledge of appropriate second-language structures, and to expect students to learn to monitor for and correct their language errors. For the ESL writing teacher, this is a complex responsibility. While some second-language errors are contained, easily recognizable, and quickly corrected, others are complicated, dependent on context, and difficult to analyze. This chapter focuses on one aspect of error identification and analysis: students' use of first language grammar and structures in their second-language writing.

As students learn a second language, some of their errors come from "interference" or "transfer" of language components from their first language (**L1**). The term "interference" is usually used to mean that the use of the L1 yields a negative result, whereas "transfer" is used to mean that use of the L1 for L2 output yields a positive result (Odlin, 1989; Robinette & Schacther, 1983). In this chapter I use the term "transfer" exclusively because (1) whether the first-language use results in positive or negative second-language use is not the focus here and (2) the term "interference" implies deviance. In contrast, I suggest that the use of a first language in learning a second language demonstrates the learner's creativity and progress.

ESL/EFL writing teachers can approach L1 transfer problems in their students' writing by:

- identifying L1 transfer errors (e.g., verb tense, spelling, word order, word choice, agreement, etc.)
- analyzing L1 transfer errors (i.e., cause[s], effect[s], level of difficulty, etc.)
- conferencing with ESL student writers about L1 transfer errors.

My objective in this chapter is to integrate L1 transfer error into writing pedagogy by filling a niche about which teachers may know little: the similarities and differences between English and other languages that can hinder ESL student writing. Knowledge of these similarities and differences will help teachers understand their students' errors; moreover, the differences between immigrant student and international student errors demand different teacher interventions.

BACKGROUND

Research in second-language acquisition has demonstrated that:

1. Second-language (**L2**) learners do not acquire that language in the same way they did their native languages (Brown, 1973, 1994; Hatch, 1978; Krashen, 1982; Pica, 1983).
2. In the process of learning a second language, learners go through periods in which they develop an "interlanguage" that combines rules and language use of both the L1 and L2, and that is often systematic and rule-governed (Kellermann, 1984; Meisel, 1983; Richards, 1971; Selinker, 1969, 1972).
3. This "transference" of first-language sounds, words, and structures often results in L2 errors (Selinker, 1992; Swan & Smith, 1987).
4. Error is often a positive indication that a student is progressing in learning the second language; it can serve as an impetus for development (Dakin, 1973; Sharwood-Smith, 1983; Zobl, 1980).

Interest in the transfer and use of L1 skills into a second-language learning experience drove structural linguists in the 1960s and 1970s to research the area of contrastive analysis (**CA**): the description of phonological, lexical, and structural similarities and differences between languages (see Danesi, 1993, for an excellent historical overview).[1] A contrastive analysis researcher might, for example, study the differences between English and a number of languages by assessing their different approaches to asking one's name. When English uses the question, "What is his name?", the following three languages use a construction that more closely parallels the English question "What do they call him?":

	QUESTION	LITERAL TRANSLATION
Spanish:	Como se llama?	("How himself he calls?")
Russian:	Kak evo zovut?	("How him they call?")
German:	Wie heisst er?	("How calls he?")

(Adapted from James, 1980, p. 24.)

The objective of these contrastive analysis investigations is to provide second-language teachers and learners with *predictive* information concerning the areas and the levels of difficulty in learning a second language. If, for instance, a teacher knew the ways in which the sound system of Portuguese differed from the sound system of English, she could *predict* which sounds her Portuguese ESL students would mispronounce, and she could plan her lessons accordingly. According to this "strong" hypothesis of contrastive analysis, ESL learners from different language backgrounds would have different problems, different errors, and different levels of "tenacity" in eliminating those errors, and that by *predicting* the differences, ESL teachers could teach more efficiently.

This strong contrastive analysis hypothesis has faded, as did the Audio–Lingual Method to which it was originally linked. As contrastive analysis researchers encountered more and more complex questions, controversy grew about which learners found what language aspects "difficult." Moreover, developing a complete contrastive analysis between two languages, even for students with the same first language, proved impossible (cf. McLaughlin, 1987; Schachter & Celce-Murcia, 1977). However, the alternative "weak" contrastive analysis hypothesis can be very helpful for ESL writing teachers. It does not claim to *predict* difficulty levels, but it does assume first-language transfer as one cause for ESL writing errors, and it does assume that teachers can identify errors and recognize them as first-language transfer errors.

For example, the Norwegian student author of the following paragraph was a very advanced ESL writer. In this draft, however, the L1 transfer error is immediately visible:

I found out that Laramie do have a great problem concerning drunk drivers. In 1995 **were** then 312 arrests for driving under the influence of alcohol. Altogether **were** 383 arrests made, which is an average of more than one drunk driver every single day of the year. In my opinion **are** these numbers higher than they should be in a little town like Laramie. According to my survey, I **had** 8 out of 10 people been driving under the influence of alcohol.

In a conference with his teacher, the student recognized the consistent verb placement error only when his teacher pointed it out. Initially surprised, he then identified the error as a "carry-over" from Norwegian, and he was fascinated by the discussion that followed about L1 transfer. Indeed, in Norwegian and other Scandanavian languages, it is easy to begin a sentence with something other than the subject—and the subject is then placed after the verb, resulting in a sentence such as "That **have** I not seen" (Swan & Smith, 1987, p. 21).

Similar to this Norwegian student, when other ESL students encounter a language form in a second language, they often infer rules from knowledge of their native language. By consciously borrowing or unconsciously utilizing prior L1 information, they "transfer" that knowledge into a hypothesis about the L2.[2] At the simpler lexical level, ESL students whose L1 is a cognate (that is, the two languages have similarities in vocabulary and structure), "false cognates" can be tricky. Table 8.1 shows some Spanish–English false cognates that can easily be transferred from a student's L1 (Spanish) and used incorrectly in English.

Table 8.1: Spanish–English False Cognates		
SPANISH	SPANISH TRANSLATION	ENGLISH TRANSLATION
libería	bookstore	library
asistir	to attend (a class, a meeting)	to help (assist)
lectura	reading	lecture
sanidad	health	sanity
desgraciado	unfortunate	disgraced

(Killiam & Watson, 1983, p. 98.)

Because students from the same native language background have many of the same language assumptions, they may make similar types of L2 errors, although their hypotheses (and therefore the resulting language) may not be exactly the same. Table 8.2 demonstrates a few areas of L1 structures that may be transferred into ESL student writing.

Table 8.2: Contrastive Analysis Examples

□ In **French** and **Spanish**, adjectives tend to follow the noun, not precede it.
  • "The barn <u>red</u>"

□ **Punjabi** usually has no articles.
  • "He is [ ] teacher."

□ **German** and **French** have grammatical gender markers and use pronouns that agree with the gender.
  • Le livre → "The book" (masculine) → "He"

□ **Indonesian** has no auxiliary verb like the *do* of English used in questions and negatives.
  • "[ ] You like pizza?"

□ In **Farsi**, personal pronouns are seldom used, and if a personal pronoun is the subject of a sentence, it is implicit in the verb unless it is being specifically emphasized.
  • "The girl went home. [ ] was hungry."

□ **Chinese** (both Mandarin and Cantonese) does not distinguish between male and female pronouns; moreover, in Chinese, yes/no questions are formed by using the statement and adding a final particle (*me, ma, a*).
  • "<u>He</u> iron dress [<u>particle</u>]?"

□ In **Serbo-Croatian**, the negative word *ne* usually precedes the auxiliary verb.
  • "They <u>no</u> are walking."

□ In **Japanese**, the basic word order for the typical sentence is Subject-Object-Verb (SOV) rather than the SVO of English.
  • Big boy small boy <u>hit</u>.

□ Because **Polish** is so highly inflected (including endings for nouns, adjectives and pronouns), Polish word order is much less restricted than word order in English.
  • "The book gave John quickly to his mother always" is one of several correct ways of structuring this sentence.

(Killiam & Watson, 1983.) This valuable, informally bound and reasonably priced book, *Thirteen Language Profiles: Practical Application of Contrastive Analysis for Teachers of English as a Second Language,* was written by teachers and students at Vancouver Community College English Language Training Night School (King Edward Campus). It contains a brief history of each language as well as phonetic, syntactic, and cultural information, and it is remarkably accessible and informative. For a copy, write 1155 E. Broadway, Vancouver, BC V5T 1Y8.

In its current use, contrastive analysis is closely linked to L1 transfer error analysis. For example, a teacher who encounters errors in a paper written by a native speaker of Arabic (see Table 8.3) could identify and understand the reasons for the errors, and could thus discuss the problem and the solution with the student.

Table 8.3: Contrastive Analysis, Arabic and English	
ARABIC DIFFERENCES FROM ENGLISH	**RESULTING ENGLISH ERRORS**
□ no verb *to be* (*is, are, was, were*)	□ "The book [ ] old."
□ redundant definite article	□ "I like the book <u>the</u> old."
□ superlative made by adding a definite article to the comparative	□ Not "Ahmed is the tallest." but "Ahmed he <u>the taller</u>."

IDENTIFYING L1 TRANSFER ERRORS

Teachers need not be multilingual in order to analyze L1 transfer errors. From close observation, intuition, and inductive guessing, teachers begin to learn about the fundamentals of the student's native language. Studying a second (or third or fourth) language will certainly broaden and deepen a teacher's perspective about language structure in general and the language studied in particular. However, given the number of languages most ESL teachers encounter in the writing classroom, a simpler approach might be to investigate the literature in contrastive analysis, or to study a summary of many different languages (e.g., Killiam & Watson, 1983; Swan & Smith, 1987).

One excellent way to become better informed is to **ask**; a contrastive analysis conversation with a student can be revealing. After all, second-language writers have considerable knowledge about their native language, although they may not consciously realize it. Even if the student does not know the answers to the questions, he might ask a friend, a parent, or a grandparent. An added advantage: Having the teacher interested in a student's language may well make the student more approachable about his writing. Moreover, students are often unaware of their L1 transfer, but simply recognizing that specific transfer problems exist can enable students to monitor more effectively for those errors.

The observation and interview processes can be helpful, especially if students know that the teacher is respectful, honestly curious, and trustworthy. Phrase the questions in ways that will elicit information about the student's knowledge without accusation:

not	"This is wrong."	*but*	"Do you see the error here?"
not	"Fix this."	*but*	"How might you fix this?"
not	"Why did you write this?"	*but*	"Do you know about ____?"
not	"You made a mistake here."	*but*	"Did you learn about ____?"

If the level of trust is high enough—that is, if the student is sure that the conference is being held to help, not to judge him—he will be more able to identify what he doesn't know (or what he "knows" incorrectly) and more accepting of the suggestions for remediation and assistance.

Table 8.4: Basic Questions About Students' First Languages
☐ Is the language written in Roman letters, right to left? If not, what are the differences from English?
☐ Is the word order of the language SVO (Subject-Verb-Object) as in English, or is the basic word order different (e.g., SOV, VSO)?
☐ Does the language have definite/indefinite articles? If so, are they as widely used as in English? Does the language have prepositions (or perhaps postpositions)? If so, are there as many as there are in English?
☐ Is the language inflected (with plural and verb endings) as English is? If so, are there more inflections (e.g., nouns, adjectives) or fewer inflections than in English?
☐ Does the language have auxiliary verbs? The verb "to be"? If so, are they used in the same way that English uses them?

Table 8.4 lists basic linguistic questions that students should be able to answer, especially if the teacher explains the grammatical terms by demonstrating them in English and/or pointing them out in the student's writing. After these basic questions, teachers can progress to issues about written language such as:

- ☐ capitalization and abbreviation
- ☐ the structure of questions and negatives
- ☐ punctuation and sentence boundaries
- ☐ verb use: passive voice, modals, gerunds, and infinitives
- ☐ other parts of speech: use of gender, classifiers, and particles.

ANALYZING L1 TRANSFER ERRORS

Even after careful investigation and observation, teachers will probably not be able to determine definitely whether some errors are a result of L1 transfer. However, educated guesses followed by a conference with the student author are a powerful combination. Teachers might mark (circle, underline, highlight, etc.) possible L1 transfer errors differently from other errors in a student's writing, and then discuss the L1 errors separately with the writer.

Figure 8.1 shows a typical example of a student paragraph at the advanced level of ESL writing proficiency, with possible L1 errors identified by the teacher and marked with circles. The author is a Chinese speaker from Taiwan who had spent much time in the U.S.; many of his L1 transfer errors represent a form of habituated error (sometimes called "fossilization"). Errors that are probably not caused by L1 transfer are indicated as follows:

Figure 8.1

---

(1) During these 37 year, Taiwan [had changed] from ∧ agriculture country to ∧ technology country. (2) With the progress of technology our people [had lost] our morality. (3) (Due to) the hurry life and work, seldom people have time to (care other) people's life. (4) So people become *sophisticate*. (5) Gradually people had lost their morality. (6) Sometime, ∧ inclination to disobey that law [is increasing.] (7) Many driver didn't (care to) pay ∧ traffic fine, (due to) the traffic fine is not expensive. (8) Drivers again and again *violated*. (9) Although Taipei has been a development city, the traffic problems still is a major problem *in everytime*.

- □ Word choice errors are in *italics.*
- □ Errors that interfere with sentence comprehension are underlined.
- □ Word choice/sentence comprehension are both *italicized and underlined.*
- □ Verb tense errors are [bracketed].

The sentences have been numbered for ease of discussion.

Notice in Figure 8.2 that the teacher marked the L1 transfer errors in this student's paragraph, but did not correct them or plan to discuss them in the conference because she believed that the student should be able to recognize and

---

Figure 8.2

⤳ = adjective-noun agreement (1, 3)

— = word form (1, 9)

⤳ = subject-verb agreement (9)

∧ = article insertion (1, 6, 7)

correct those errors without her assistance (the number of the sentence in which the error occurred is listed in parentheses).

From teaching experience, reading about languages, and conversations with the student, the teacher knew the following about written Chinese (Mandarin):

1. Like English, written Chinese (Mandarin) is SVO, and adjectives precede the nouns.

2. There are no pure articles in written Chinese (the demonstrative "that" is sometimes used).

3. There are no verb conjugations in written Chinese; only the root form of the verb is used, making the choice of verb tenses in English difficult.

4. There are no inflections (-*s* for plurals, –*al* for adjectives, etc.); for the plural noun, the number is referred to in the sentence, and a complex system of "classifiers" are used, which are determined by the characteristics of the noun: "There are four [<u>particle</u> indicating shape] <u>book</u>."

5. Chinese has just a few prepositions; they are sometimes used after the noun (then they are called "postpositions").

6. Time adverbials in Chinese immediately precede the verb or come at the beginning of the sentence: "He <u>yesterday</u> go movies."

The teacher then planned the writing conference with the student. First, she realized that the student was struggling with a difficult task—writing about the past in the present and connecting the past to the present—because of the variety of verb tenses that are needed in such a narrative. As Biber (1988) and Stockton (1995) have described in their discourse analysis research, the genre[3] of past narrative tends to have a specific "cluster" of verb forms: simple past tense, past perfect, and past progressive forms. In addition, Bardovi-Harlig (1996) has demonstrated that the "foreground" of historical narrative (that is, the actual "story" being told) usually occurs in simple past tense, while the "background" of narrative (such as descriptions of character and setting) is often described in past perfect and past progressive tenses. The teacher therefore began by discussing the task itself with the student, looking at the topic demands in terms of the verbs that were needed, and reviewing verb use with the student:

□ VERB TENSE: probable L1 transfer errors
  • "had changed" → have (1)   • "had lost" → have (2)
  • "is increasing" → has been increasing (6)

In addition, the conference focused on the following L1 and non-L1 errors:

L1 transfer errors

□ teach/review GRAMMAR STRUCTURES: possible L1 transfer errors: preposition use
- "because/because of" vs. "due to the fact that/due to" (3, 7)
- "to care for/to care about" vs. "to care" (3, 7)

Non–L1 errors

□ SENTENCE COMPREHENSION: the teacher asked the student what he meant and then helped him to reconstruct the sentences to be comprehensible
- "the hurry life" (3)
- "violated" (8)
- "in everytime" (9)

□ WORD CHOICE: (in *italics*)
- "sophisticate" → ? (4)
- "that" → the (6)
- "Sometime" → Moreover (?) (6)

CONFERENCING WITH ESL WRITERS ABOUT L1 TRANSFER ERRORS

Because both the writing errors and the remediation of such errors differ for ESL students educated in U.S. schools (called "residents" in this chapter) and those students who have studied English as a foreign language in their home countries (called "international students" in this chapter), I discuss each separately here. For more information about these differences, see Chapter 1 in this text.

□ RESIDENT STUDENT WRITERS

U.S. residents may have more difficulty than international students identifying L1 transfer errors in their writing because they may not have studied their mother tongue, and may indeed be orally fluent but nonliterate in their L1. Moreover, their "study" of English as a second language may have been fragmented and incomplete; they may therefore not have adequate understanding of grammatical terms (e.g., auxiliary verbs, noun clauses) and structures. Consequently, the writing conference must begin by ascertaining how much language information, for both L1 and L2, the student author can access and understand.

Figure 8.3 shows a paragraph typical of an in-class diagnostic paragraph written by an immigrant student from Vietnam whose English-language formal schooling had been limited and fragmented, but whose oral skills and listening abilities were high. Possible L1 transfer errors are circled. Errors that are not

Figure 8.3

(1) My room is (con͟fortable) than any place. (2) I have a͟ old brown desk in my room. (3) I broug͟h that desk *for* years ago when I (come) to the United States. (4) It ∧*is* 20 X 40 inches and h͟a͟v͟e͟ t͟h͟r͟e͟e͟ d͟r͟a͟w͟e͟r͟. (5) Two drawers are big and one is [a] small so I can put on anything I want *likes* papers, a dictionary, a pen and textbooks. (6) If I need [a] e͟r͟a͟s͟e͟ d͟u͟r͟i͟n͟g͟ m͟y͟ w͟r͟i͟t͟e͟ t͟o͟ e͟s͟s͟a͟y͟, then I can *bring* it e͟s͟a͟i͟l͟y. (7) Because its o͟n͟ m͟y͟ t͟o͟p͟ o͟f͟ d͟r͟a͟w͟e͟r͟ left hand side. (8) And ∧*if* I need dict:onary to *check up* the spelling, then I open the *buttom* of drawer and used it. (9) I (didn't) have to stand up and f͟o͟u͟n͟d͟ a͟l͟l͟ o͟f͟ t͟h͟e͟ p͟l͟a͟c͟e͟, just open drawer everything in *their* and everything is close to me. (10) (Its feel) like [a] my old friend when I (used) it.

caused by L1 transfer are indicated as follows: word choice errors are in italics; errors that interfere with sentence comprehension are underlined. The sentences have been numbered for ease of discussion.

The most obvious errors in the paragraph shown in Figure 8.3 come from the student's lack of understanding of levels of formality in writing. In planning her discussion with the student, the teacher looked carefully at the oral language in the paragraph, probably the result of "ear learning" (see Chapter 1). The fragment (7), the sentence problem (8), and even the more successful sentence (9) seem more oral than written approaches to communication, a stream-of-consciousness approach to writing that sounds like part of a conversation. His "ear-learning" is visible in *confortable* (1), *a erase* (6), and *its* (10). Since knowledge of levels of language formality is one of the most common problems that inexperienced writers face (native English speakers included) (Dykstra, 1997), this teacher might choose to work with this student, or with a larger group of students—perhaps even the whole class—to describe and delineate the problems and solutions of register, both now and throughout the writing course.

This student's teacher marked some of the L1 and non–L1 transfer errors that she believed the student could correct without her assistance, such as incorrect article insertion [bracketed], and corrected several errors that the student was not prepared to correct (e.g., adding *is* in sentence 4, *if* in sentence 8, and some prepositions). Furthermore, she did not mark some errors that were not as important for comprehension: *its* → it's (7).

In terms of L1 transfer problems, the teacher depended on the following information about contrastive analysis between English and Vietnamese:

1. There are no articles or prepositions in Vietnamese; ESL writers usually guess about usage.

2. Vietnamese has few consonants that occur at the end of words, and those that do are unvoiced. Typically, Vietnamese ESL speakers/ writers do not hear (and therefore leave off) final consonants. Different verb endings and plural nouns are therefore a mystery, and students may add a vowel sound to a word that ends in a hard, voiced consonant.

3. There are no verb conjugations or other inflections (no grammatical endings), no verb *to be*, no modal verbs in Vietnamese (just the root form of the verb). Verb endings are therefore doubly difficult for this student, as are irregular verb forms.

Based on this contrastive analysis between English and Vietnamese, and knowing that the student was orally fluent in English, the teacher decided to conference about the following L1 and non–L1 transference errors. The number of the sentence(s) in which each error occurred is listed after each error:

L1 transfer errors

□ teach/review GRAMMAR STRUCTURES: possible L1 transfer errors
  • more X than Y
  • "its feel" → it feels

□ VERB TENSE: probable L1 transfer error; the teacher asked the student about each error in order to distinguish between a lack of knowledge and ineffective monitoring
  • "come" → came
  • "used" → use
  • "didn't" → don't

□ UNNEEDED ARTICLE: possible L1 transfer error; the teacher questioned the student in order to determine if the student is inserting a vowel sound because of Vietnamese final sounds
  • "one is a small"
  • "a erase"
  • "like a my old friend"

□ AGREEMENT: probable L1 transfer error
  subject-verb agreement   *adjective-noun agreement*
  • "have" → has   • "three drawer" → drawers

Non–L1 errors

□ SENTENCE COMPREHENSION: the teacher asked the student what he meant, and then helped him to reconstruct the sentences to be comprehensible
  - "a erase during my write to essay"
  - "on my top of drawer"
  - "and found all of the place"

□ WORD CHOICE (in *italics*): the teacher observed whether (a) the student could hear the sound differences or notice the visual differences between the paired words; (b) the student immediately recognized the differences and so would easily be able to monitor for that error in future writing; or (c) the student has never before noticed that the difference existed and must now learn it.
  - "for" → four
  - "buttom" → bottom (and perhaps button)
  - "check up" → check
  - "likes" → like
  - "their" → there

□ INTERNATIONAL STUDENT WRITERS

In contrast to U.S. resident students, international students will almost invariably have a working model of English grammar available to them. Their errors are typically more "visible" than resident errors because they are not typically errors of native English speakers. The paragraph shown in Figure 8.4 was written by a

---

Figure 8.4

---

(1) The availability of only one open door becomes ∧ much bigger problem for residents during spring and fall *brakes*. (2) This is because at the time of breaks *left* residents are forced to use only that back door all (over) the time, even during a day. (3) In this situation, the statistics looks worse. (4) Now 90 percent of the *left* residents consider this question as a problem. (5) This is about 40 percent of the all residents in Hill Hall. (6) The 30 percent of the surveyed students agree that this is not convenient, even though they do not leave (to) their homes for breaks. (7) The other about 30 percent of residents really do not care because they do not stay in the dormitory. (8) All this information makes this question at least be mentioned and discussed especially during long breaks.

highly skilled Russian undergraduate as part of a problem-solution essay. Possible L1 transfer errors are circled. Errors that are not caused by L1 transfer are indicated as follows: Word choice errors are in *italics*; sentence comprehension errors are underlined. The sentences have been numbered for ease of discussion.

The teacher had learned the following about Russian:

1. Like English, Russian is a SVO language, and adjectives come before nouns.
2. Russian has no definite or indefinite articles.
3. English auxiliaries (e.g., *do, have*) and modals (e.g., *will, may*) are not relied on in Russian, so writers may have difficulty with these verb forms.
4. There are three different forms of the prepositions *to* and *from* in Russian.

In this paragraph, the teacher marked and analyzed the L1 and non–L1 errors and decided to conference with the student about the ways to handle numerical information in English (e.g., how percentages are reported in academic research reports), using the following:

L1 transfer errors

□ teach/review GRAMMAR STRUCTURES: probable L1 transfer errors
  • article use (1, 2) (i.e., how are articles used in report writing?)
  • preposition use (2, 6)

Non–L1 errors

□ AGREEMENT: probably not an L1 transfer error but rather confusion about the word "statistics" used as a singular in English: subject-verb agreement (3)

□ SENTENCE COMPREHENSION: the teacher asked the student what he meant and then helped him to reconstruct the sentence to be comprehensible
  • "makes this question at least be mentioned and discussed" (8)

□ WORD CHOICE (in *italics*):
  • "left" → remaining (2)
  • "brake" vs. break (1)

CONCLUSION

The additional time spent studying ESL students' languages may seem an unacceptable burden to the ESL writing teacher. After all, a majority of ESL writing errors may not be attributable to L1 transfer, perhaps an average of only 30 percent, and "what on the surface looks like the same error can have a multitude of different causes" (James, 1994, p. 185). However, many teachers will find such investigation both interesting professional development and worthwhile pedagogically.

Furthermore, the influence of L1 transfer is "not negligible" (Danesi & Pietro, 1991). Many ESL student authors will find the resulting discussions personally satisfying and pedagogically beneficial. Recognizing a teacher's interest in their L1 may mitigate the widespread resentment that may accrue with ESL writers about English being the "right" language. In addition, monitoring for a relatively small error "type" (i.e., L1 transfer errors) can be less intimidating than facing an entire page or essay of errors, and understanding the theory of transference can add self-confidence to students' monitoring for error. From this perspective, learning about students' L1 structures is time and energy well invested.

NOTES

1.   Much contrastive analysis research concentrates on phonological differences between languages; this chapter does not focus on those differences.

2.   Such first-language transfer occurs not only with grammatical structures but also with first-language writing skills and strategies, and with rhetorical knowledge as well. However, this chapter focuses solely on language problems from first-language interference.

3.   In this chapter, the term *genre* refers both to the form of writing (such as narrative, definition, exposition) and the function of writing (that is, the social context—the audience, the purpose, the situation—for the writing) in which students must master the rules of a particular discourse community (Hyon, 1996; Meyer, 1996).

Chapter 9

Technological Innovations and the Teaching of English Grammar and Composition

Patricia Byrd

INTRODUCTION: WHEN THE PRINTED BOOK WAS "HIGH TECH"

In the late sixteenth century, when the Huguenot refugees fled France for England, they had many of the same needs as modern refugees for help in learning survival English and the English of the workplace. Jacques Bellot, a bilingual Frenchman who went to England as a Huguenot refugee himself, used the relatively new technology of printing to produce what is the oldest extant ESL textbook, *The English Schoolmaster* (Howatt, 1984). Published in 1580, *The English Schoolmaster* is a bilingual manual of information about English, with an emphasis on vocabulary and spelling, provided to help French learners understand the written version of the language they were learning through their ears.[1]

From a technological point of view, Bellot's second book, *Familiar Dialogues* (1586/1969) is a fascinating advance over his first publication. The dialogues are very like such materials today: They emphasize the language of everyday interactions, especially shopping, going out to eat, and dealing with the problems of being refugees. Bellot took advantage of the technology by having his dialogues printed in three columns—in English on the left, French in the middle, and a "semiphonetic" version in the third column, showing how the English is to be pronounced (Howatt, 1984).

While our technological resources have changed greatly since 1586, current interest in technology and language teaching can be put in perspective by remembering that "technology" does not just mean "computers" and the "Internet," but includes all of the tools from books to chalkboards to overhead projectors that teachers have used to make language learning more effective, efficient, and interesting for ourselves as well as our students. As will be seen in the following information from studies of technological innovation, our definition of technology should not be limited to machines or other physical tools but needs to include ideas and information when they are used to solve problems.

TECHNOLOGY DEFINED

Scholars who study change in human societies use the term *diffusion of innovations* to refer to the process by which new ideas and products are created, learned about, accepted or rejected, and then implemented if accepted or forgotten if rejected. In these studies, *technology* is given a much broader definition than in our everyday usage. Everett Rogers is one of the most influential of the communications researchers who have contributed to our understanding of innovation—what it is and how it occurs as people in social groups accept or reject new ways of dealing with problems. His definition of *technology* in the fourth edition of his book *Diffusion of Innovations* (1995) makes it clear that technology must not be thought of simply as "machines" but as some combination of a tool and an idea about how to use that tool—or as simply a new idea or new information:

> A technology usually has two components: (1) a hardware[2] aspect, consisting of the tool that embodies the technology as material or physical objects, and (2) a software aspect, consisting of the information base for the tool. [Sometimes hardware dominates the combination—sometimes software.] But in other cases, a technology may be almost entirely comprised of information; examples are a conservative political philosophy, a religious idea like Transcendental Meditation, a new event, a rumor, assembly-line production, and management by objective (MBO). (pp. 12–13)

For example, Bellot's textbook used the hardware of the printing press and the possibility of putting materials into three columns to give physical body to his idea that a language learner needed to work with bilingual materials and that both reading and speaking could be learned from the written page.

"Social technologies" are powerfully at work in TESL today as we consider changes in the very foundations of our work—what are the most effective ways of teaching and learning a language, what are the most effective relationships between teachers and students, what is a language class like, what are the true purposes for ESL programs? New information and new ideas are surging around us. New information is being provided about the real-world tasks that students perform in English (e.g., Carson, Gibson, & Hargroves, 1992; Bazerman, 1988; Ferris & Tagg, 1996; Long & Crookes, 1992; MacDonald, 1992) and about the characteristics of English itself as shown in computerized analyses (e.g., Biber, 1988; Conrad, 1996a and 1996b; Grabe, 1987; Sinclair, 1987a, 1987b, 1991). New ideas are associated with changes in communication "machines" such as computers with their systems for wordprocessing and electronic communication and networked writing classes. (Computers, of course, are not the only "communication machines" that are being used to change communication; radios, televisions, and telephones are involved in the changes that are occurring in how we conceptualize and carry out communication.) Working from a broader definition of technology helps us to recognize that something more powerful is happening than having new machines on our desks: We have new information and new ideas about the substance of our work as language teachers.

INNOVATION DEFINED

Perhaps as a result of the vast changes that have occurred in the twentieth century and that seem destined to continue to occur in the twenty-first century, the topic of "innovation" has been popular with scholars and researchers in many different academic disciplines—including ESL (Stoller, 1994). In the fourth edition of his *Diffusion of Innovations* (1995), Rogers gives the following definition of *innovation:*

> One kind of uncertainty is generated by an innovation, defined as an idea, practice, or object that is perceived as new by an individual or another unit of adoption. An innovation presents an individual or an organization with a new alternative or alternatives, with new means of solving problems. But the probabilities of the new alternatives being superior to previous practice are not exactly known by the individual problem solvers. Thus, they are motivated to seek further information about the innovation in order to cope with the uncertainty that it·creates. (p. xvii)

PATTERNS OF CHANGE AND ACCEPTANCE OF INNOVATIONS

As teachers and learners we have come to value information about learning styles and strategies (e.g., Bennett, 1995; Oxford, 1990; Reid, 1995). Because I know that I am primarily a "visual" learner who likes to learn by doing things, I can organize new learning experiences that work more effectively for me than if I passively accepted a different learning style. I also recognize that I need to expand my skills as a learner by trying to be a bit more oral/aural, to learn from other people as well as from books, and to take in a little more information before trying out a new skill. On the whole, I tend to want to learn a new software program by loading it and giving it a try. Or, I put together a new bicycle by spreading the parts around the room and figuring how which goes with what. Nevertheless, I've learned over time that reading a little bit in the owner's manual and asking a few questions before I get started of people who already know the software or the bike are probably more effective strategies—as little as I really enjoy them.

Scholars who study diffusion of innovation have likewise developed a system for analyzing the reactions of individuals to new "technology." whether it is a new product, a new idea, or new information. Proposed by Rogers in 1962 in the first edition of *Diffusion of Innovations*, the system is widely recognized in the U.S. to the extent that many of us know the terms without knowing the system in great detail. People are categorized by the rapidity with which they accept an innovation and by the types of evidence that they need to accept and integrate something new into their lives. Table 9.1 is based on Rogers (1983 and 1995) and Gundersen (1996). As with learning style categories, these need to be applied with some caution because our styles can change over time and in different contexts. Generally, however, most of us recognize ourselves in these categories as we deal with innovations in our lives. I myself am not an innovator, but I like to be around them and

Table 9.1: Adopter Categories		
CATEGORY NAME	**PERCENTAGE OF TOTAL**	**PRIMARY CHARACTERISTICS**
Innovators	2.5%	like new ideas, eager to try them out, able to deal with frustration and failure, often not deeply integrated into the social network and thus not entirely trusted by the rest of the group to be a reliable source of change
Early Adopters	13.5%	respected by other in the social group, able to bridge between the innovators and the rest of the society. "The early adopter is considered by many as 'the individual to check with' before using a new idea" (Rogers, 1983, p. 259).
Early Majority	34%	take longer to decide to change, not usually leaders in change, need to see the change tried out by others, generally positive about change but careful
Late Majority	34%	generally negative about change and skeptical, perhaps change because of the growing pressure from peers since at this point 50 % of the members of the group have adopted the change. "The late majority do not adopt until most others in their social system have done so" (Rogers, 1983, p. 250).
Laggards	16%	focused on the past, last to adopt the change, like the innovators in not being fully integrated into the society, change sometimes based on force or on fear of being left behind

Source: From Rogers (1983 & 1995) and Gundersen (1996).

to learn from them. Accordingly, I think of my self as being in the "Early Adopter" category. However, because of the frustrations that can come from early adoption of a new idea or new machine, I have learned that sometimes it is better to move into the next category of "Early Majority" and to let someone else take the lead in working out the details of an innovation.

Knowing ourselves well is an important part of dealing with change. Lasarenko (1996) provides a vivid and entertaining discussion of the difficulties she faced as an early adopter when she first taught a composition course in a net-worked environment. In brief, the students did not have the computer skills she had expected; the system was prone to going down in the middle of class; collab-orative activities that had worked in a conventional class did not work in the net-worked class; some students liked the World Wide Web (WWW) better for its entertainment value than for its research potential. Throughout the process, Lasarenko exhibited many of the characteristics needed by those working at the early stages of an innovation: she was not easily deterred from implementation of the new system; she handled difficulties and even failures with considerable grace; she made adjustments rapidly to meet unexpected difficulties; she wanted the change to occur and made considerable personal and professional investment of energy and time to the process.

The term *laggard* is a troubling one because of its judgmental implications. No one would want to be termed a *laggard.* Diffusion of innovation studies have been pursued with special zeal in the U.S. perhaps because they appeal to the U.S. love of change and lack of deep interest in the past. The lesson is clear: We need to be careful in applying this label in a negative manner. Rogers (1983) tells of a farmer in Iowa in the 1950s who refused to adopt the new system of poisons recommended by the U.S. Department of Agriculture (USDA) as the latest thing in modern farming. The old man had seen that the poisons were killing earth-worms and birds on his farm and he would not use them. At that time, Rogers labeled the farmer as a *laggard* and thought him foolish. By the 1970s, Rogers had grown to understand the dangers of DDT and other poisons on the envi-ronment; by the 1980s, the USDA had recognized that excessive poisoning was dangerous and that organic farming was a reasonable alternative. That is, the "laggard" had been correct in his suspicion that the innovation was not a positive advance even though all around him were getting on the bandwagon. Thus, we need to listen carefully to the "laggards" who are giving thoughtful consideration to the innovation we are suggesting and to consider their concerns about possi-ble harmful results from the innovation if it is adopted.

While *thoughtful laggards* deserve our respect, I would like to suggest a cate-gory that does not. I use the label *Early Rejecter* for a person who instinctively rejects all innovations at the instant of a new idea's birth. These people are espe-cially dangerous when they have administrative positions because their dislike of innovation is then coupled with their control of resources. Unlike the "thoughtful laggard," the Early Rejecter makes decisions based on gatekeeping, power, control, and fear that innovation will lead to a loss of that power and control.

Recognition of our own location on the acceptance-of-innovation continuum can be a valuable tool as we consider the many innovations that are being suggested for our profession. Innovators need to learn to make friends with Early Adopters—to find people who can help to convince the rest of the group to give the innovation a try. Early Adopters need to understand that they are bridges between the Innovators and the great majority of the rest of the members of the society—encouraging the Innovators and helping the rest of the group understand the value of the change and how to live with it. Members of the Early Majority need to find Early Adopters that they trust and respect—who can provide concrete evidence that the change is valuable and practical. People who keep finding themselves as members of the Late Majority on every issue might want to consider the issues in their lives that make them skeptical about all innovations. People who find that they are the last to adopt any change might want to find a system for evaluation of changes based on evidence other than fear of the unknown. The old farmer who rejected DDT had the evidence of dead birds to support his rejection of the innovation. The teacher who, given the opportunity, refuses to use wordprocessing in a composition class or to use e-mail to communicate with colleagues and students might not have as solid evidence for rejecting these innovations.

THE PROCESS OF TECHNOLOGICAL INNOVATION

Like other aspects of human society such as language learning, the spread of a "technological" innovation throughout a group is a process that occurs over time (see Rogers, 1983 & 1995; Stoller, 1994). Awareness of the stages of this process can help us to understand the changes that are happening in TESL and to make decisions about adoption or rejection of innovations. The creation of an innovation does not lead automatically to its adoption—nor does the suggestion of an innovation mean that the change would be a good one. Thus, the birth of an innovation can lead eventually either to its adoption and implementation in a group or to its rejection. Rogers (1983 & 1995) outlines these steps in the innovation process:

1. knowledge
2. persuasion (positive or negative)
3. decision
4. implementation
5. confirmation.

This seems a common-sense process that fits what we know of changes—something is invented; we learn about it; we are persuaded to accept or to reject; an accepted innovation is implemented; if it really works, we confirm it and keep using it. Another important step in the process is the possibility of later rejection if the innovation does not live up to its promise. Think of the high expectations for language laboratories in the 1960s and the gradual process of adoption, disappointment, and modification, if not outright rejection. When we are thinking about an innovation for our ESL programs, planning around these steps in the process can help to produce more rational decision making and less confused implementation.

ISSUES IN THE DIFFUSION OF TECHNOLOGICAL INNOVATIONS IN THE TEACHING OF ESL WRITING AND GRAMMAR

Rather than focusing on the details of ways to implement use of particular machines in ESL classes, the following discussion uses the ideas on "social technology" and "diffusion of innovation" to identify issues that are arising from the current version of technological change in TESL. For teachers of ESL writing and grammar, the following questions have emerged:

1. What technologies have influenced and are now influencing the teaching of and practice of writing?

2. What technologies have influenced and are influencing the teaching of grammar?

3. What is the life cycle of a technology? What have been the reasons that some technologies fail—or at least fail to live up to the initial excitement and expansive claims made for them? Machines and ideas seem to come and go in the language classroom—how are teachers to make judgments about when to add something new and when to drop something old?

4. Where is U.S. higher education going with computers in the language teaching classroom and in the language learning process? What is occurring right now and what is projected for the intersection of computers with the teaching of ESL writing and grammar? Given the usual patterns of innovation that accompany change, what are the implications for us as teachers, for our students as learners, and for our programs and departments as educational institutions?

TECHNOLOGICAL INNOVATION AND (ESL) WRITING

Bolter (1991) reminds us that writing is by its very nature a technology that is dependent on some form of "hardware": a stylus to write on wet clay in ancient Sumeria, ink to brush on papyrus in ancient Egypt, chisels to carve in stone, pencil and ink to mark on paper in more modern times, ink to print on paper for books, chalk to mark on a chalkboard—all are technologies as much as wordprocessing and laser printing with a computer. Thus any teaching of writing involves the use of some technology and the teaching of the use of that technology to writers for whom it is new.

On one level, the relationship between writing and its hardware seems superficial—mere handwriting or typing. Teachers of ESL/EFL who have worked with students coming to English from other writing systems know that handwriting can be a source of tremendous difficulty for some students, whose ability to communicate in written English would progress faster if it weren't for their problems in getting the letters the right shape and in the right order and in the right direction on the page. Programs such as IBM's *Writing to Read 2000*[3] software and machines are designed to help native-speaking children overcome the limits of their handwriting (and "small motor skills" in using their young hands to control pens and pencils); in this case, computer technology is used to build reading and writing skills faster than would be possible when the children are limited to using a different technology. Similarly, ESL students who come from languages that use other writing systems can use the computer keyboard before they have complete control over their ability to produce the letters and other shapes of English by hand. That is, the computer keyboard allows writers to recognize and use letters without having to produce them as is required by handwriting.

From another perspective, the relationship between "composing" and "writing it down using some technology" is a complex one. Bolter (1991) points to the ways that particular technologies have controlled the organization and content of written materials: Papyrus scrolls required an approach that was linear and that could not depend on readers easily moving back and forth through the materials; handwritten and bound books in the early form called a codex were also linear but gave the reader the opportunity to move back and forth in the material and to add comments in margins; a printed book was shaped like a codex but the printed format gave the material a much more authoritative and standardized appearance. Bolter comments that a handwritten note in the margin of a codex blended in with the materials so that the reader was also the writer and had transformed the materials by adding comments. In contrast, a handwritten note in the margin of a printed book does not have the same status as the print and does not blend in to become part of the material. This complex relationship between writing and the technology of writing means that our definition of "writing" changes as a result of technological changes in the equipment used to create "writing." All of which is vitally important for teachers of ESL writing in the late twentieth century as wordprocessing replaces the handwritten or typed product—and as materials written for and read from the Internet (both from e-mail and from the Web) become a regular part of our lives.

ESL writing teachers are involved in innovations that result from the introduction of a range of hardware and software technologies. While the following appear at first to be innovations in machinery, they actually involve substantial innovation at the conceptual level: wordprocessing, e-mail, networked writing classrooms, and the Web all involve changes in both the machines that are used in writing and in ideas about what writing is and who writers are.

□ INTRODUCING ESL STUDENTS TO WORDPROCESSING

Teachers are introducing ESL writers to wordprocessing both to prepare them for their academic studies so that they have skills expected of college/university students in the U.S. and to use that technology to learn language and writing skills. This change requires that schools have adequate equipment and that someone knows how to teach the students how to use it. Ideas about written products and the writing process are also involved. A wordprocessed paper always looks more finished than it is; spell-check software means that some of the spelling was done by the machine, not by the writer (a great advantage for many of us who are not good spellers); revision is no longer a physically demanding task so that asking for revisions no longer troubles teachers as it did when students had to produce handwritten revisions. For many writers, the writing process has been changed remarkably by wordprocessing, with its systems for cutting and pasting—and importing materials from other documents—and the adding of different fonts and graphic elements for desktop publishing. If you are old enough, you might remember as I do turning in handwritten papers in college and the great advance to typing on erasable bond paper and the leap to IBM Selectric typewriters so that papers were no longer covered with little blobs of whiteout and not quite accurate re-typings. Those technological innovations led to a change in what we expected a "paper" to look like, a change that is continuing today as a result of wordprocessing and of the possibilities for attaching images and sound to "papers" on the World Wide Web. What we expect in a paper produced at home or at work by an individual writer has changed—in how it is produced, how it looks, and what it might contain. Students coming to U.S. colleges and universities from parts of the world where computer technology is not yet so accessible need immediate instruction in using wordprocessing, but they also need to understand how attitudes and expectations for written products have changed as a result of wordprocessors. ESL programs need to offer training in wordprocessing that is aimed not just at the technical skill of running a machine but also at reconceptualizing what a student-prepared written product should look like. Student writers need to see and to analyze example papers produced by other students carrying out tasks required in academic programs in U.S. colleges and universities.

□ INTRODUCING ESL STUDENTS TO THE USE OF E-MAIL

Teachers are ensuring that ESL students have access to electronic mail (e-mail) both to involve them in a communication system that will be useful in their lives and to expand their use of English in a written format (e.g., Tella, 1992; Warschauer, 1995a and 1995b). As with wordprocessing, e-mail involves not just hardware but also social technological innovations. Our ideas about what is involved in communication are changing as we learn to use a medium that requires writing but where the writing has many of the features of spoken conversation—even a tolerance for "errors" that would not be so easily overlooked in other written formats. The conceptual changes here also involve who can communicate with whom—and when—and in what styles and tones. Teachers and students communicate outside of the classroom; students can initiate communication with teachers; we even communicate with strangers.

Warschauer (1995a) provides practical applications of e-mail to the teaching of ESL, reviewing the published literature and adding new information on teaching applications. Some of the more interesting applications involve international communication through which students in one country work with students from another country to carry out some research or project. Other uses include having students prepare and submit journals on e-mail. EAP programs are also starting to see e-mail instruction as part of their academic preparation work, since U.S. college and university professors are beginning to expect that students know how to use e-mail. Additionally, numerous discussion groups have been established through which teachers can communicate with each other about teaching issues (such as TESL-L, the discussion group for teachers of ESL/EFL) or through which students can talk with other students (classmates working on projects, pen pals from other places, and other groups focused on particular topics or nationality groups). E-mail provides a communication system that is becoming a basic tool in the teaching of ESL/EFL and in the professional lives of ESL/EFL teachers.

□ DEVELOPING WRITING COURSES FOR NETWORKED ENVIRONMENTS

Many teachers are developing writing courses to be taught in classrooms where each student works at a computer and where all of the computers are networked to each other using software that allows students to read each other's writing, to "talk" about it, and to suggest written revisions (e.g., Barker & Kemp, 1990; Bruce, Peyton, & Batson, 1993; Kemp, 1993; Knox-Quinn, 1996; Lasarenko, 1996; Slatin, 1992). These systems often combine wordprocessing, e-mail (to communicate with the group outside of class meetings), and the ability to have an online "conversation," with everyone contributing to the ongoing flow of a written discussion that takes place during the class meeting—a discussion that is available in a written transcript for later study. Students can communicate with the teacher and with other students during the process of writing. The machines required for these networked classrooms are not nearly as innovative as the conceptual changes that lie behind what occurs in these spaces. The great innovation here is the set of ideas that is referred to as the "social construction of meaning" (for example, see Barker & Kemp, 1990). Students work together on writing projects; students communicate directly with other students rather than going through the teacher; much and sometimes all of the communication in class is done by writing rather than by speaking, so that the whole class is to some extent about the production of written text. Reports about such environments and the classes taught in them show that new ideas are in play about relationships between teachers and students, and among students, as well as about the ways in which writing is carried out and the purposes for which writing is done.

However, for ESL programs working in the EAP paradigm, two major questions need to be asked about networked systems such as the Daedalus Instructional System and CommonSpace (developed by Sixth Floor Media, a division of Houghton Mifflin):

1. What kinds of English are the students encountering in the system—what are they learning about the English of academic writing through their reading and commenting on the writing of other ESL writers?
2. What are students being taught about the relationship of the academic writer to the materials that she or he reads—are they learning to be "editors" or "miners" of text? What are they learning about the purposes for reading and writing in academic settings?

First, these networked systems can be just as much "closed systems" as the traditional classroom—with students and their teacher a closed group with limited (if any) connection to the larger institution or academic disciplines. If the materials that the students read and write are solely the products of this group, the range of language and information encountered by the students is limited to the knowledge and skills of this particular group. While our ESL students often bring considerable intelligence and life experience to their writing classes, EAP teachers and curriculum designers must think about the result of having nonnative speakers of English learning their English from other nonnative speakers of English.[4] One solution offered by modern technology would be to open the system by connecting the network to the Web, a solution found in the system used by Lasarenko (1996). In that network, the students could work with each other (and the teacher) but could also reach out to the Web for information (and models for language and writing). A low-tech but obvious and academically appropriate solution would be to ensure that the students were reading appropriate materials that could be the basis of discussions and writing activities. However it is done, students need to encounter and learn to make use of the kinds of professionally written text that will be the basis of the courses they take in their degree programs. Learning to read and respond to the writing of other students can be a part of this process but not the complete program.

The second problem posed by networked writing systems for EAP programs is a more difficult one to solve: In these systems, the role taken by student writers and the relationship that they are taught to have with other student writers is primarily that of reader-editor. Students read the writing of other students and comment on it in ways that will be helpful to the other writers—that is, the student writer learns to be an editor of the writing of other students. It is true that students learn that other students can be the source of ideas about a topic, but the interactions are designed to help students learn to work together as a community on writing tasks—much like those in more traditional writing environments—as can be seen in this description by Kemp (1993) in a section of the article subtitled "What happens in the computer-based networked classroom":

> The instructor decides upon an issue to write about, say the dress code in public schools. She initiates a synchronous discussion[5] in class concerning dress codes, perhaps with a provocative statement such as "dress codes promote the kind of behavior that helps students learn in school." Very quickly (with this topic especially) the screens are alive with comments about individuality, basic rights, and so forth. (p. 173)

Students eventually write essays on the topic in which they can quote other students; as Kemp says, "This thesis is pursued and supported by citing remarks (direct quotations, of course) by classmates as experts" (p. 174).

As interesting as this type of interaction might be for students, EAP teachers and curriculum coordinators need to think about whether or not learning to handle these interactions is preparing students for their work in courses other than the freshman composition sequence. Degree courses in all disciplines require student writers to read professionally written text (and to take written lecture notes that become another source for language and ideas) and then to use that written material in their own writing (Carson et al., 1992). Other students can provide many kinds of help for their peers, but they are not the source of data, information, and ideas to be quoted directly or indirectly in student writing done in history, biology, psychology, and other degree courses. Thus, the kinds of materials read and the uses to which they are put might need to change in an EAP networked writing system. Instead of the current focus on student-produced writing as the core reading material and on helping other student writers to improve their work, the system should include professional academic writing for students to read and learn to use in their own writing. The writers would also need to learn about techniques for using other people's writing in their own writing—not just quotation marks but the whole range of techniques that academic writers have for pulling other people's materials into our own writing.

In a modern poetry course taught at the University of Texas using a networked writing system, Slatin (1992) brought both modern poetry and professionally written text (criticism and biography) into the system by having his students post summaries of their reading on the network using e-mail. Other students were required to read these summaries, and Slatin's analysis of the transcripts of their class sessions shows that the students were using ideas, information, and vocabulary/wording from the summaries (and their own reading of the poetry) in their networked discussions. However, the current networked systems are not designed to have students read materials other than the writing of other students—and both the network designers and teachers who want to use the networked classroom need to think about the kinds of reading to be done by the students in the system and the kinds of reading to be done in preparation for their work on the system. While the networked system can be refocused on appropriate work for EAP programs, teachers and curriculum designers will need to be careful that these adjustments are made so that ESL writers become proficient in the combination of reading and writing often required of students in degree courses—reading materials from professionally written sources (textbooks, journals, books, Web materials) to find resources to be used in writing tasks assigned by their instructors.

INTRODUCING STUDENTS TO THE WORLD WIDE WEB

E-mail and networked classrooms are text environments. While we "chat" through our e-mail connections, we do so by writing (and reading) printed words in a process that is essentially a version of wordprocessing. In contrast, the World Wide Web (WWW or the Web) is a multimedia environment that allows for the transmission of text, graphics (still photographs and video), and sound. While the ability of the Web to transmit graphics and sound is still only in the early stages of development, improvements are happening rapidly. It is startling to realize that the first version of the Web did not appear until 1993; such feverish rate of change in the development of the multimedia capacity of the system seems unlikely to slow down, and so we can expect high-quality sound and images to be available very soon. (Indeed, we can expect that e-mail and networked communication will be pulled into the Web environment so that they, too, involve more than text and become multimedia tools.)

The Web is built around a hypertext system that allows for easy and quick linking of materials to other materials. While reading a set of materials, we can "click" on underlined words that take us immediately to other information linked to the original site. In addition to its multimedia and linking features, the Web allows for interactivity in various ways: Readers can comment on materials by sending e-mail messages to the author; real-time discussion sessions are popular features of some Web sites; and materials can include "forms" through which readers send information to the author (for example, some universities have application forms on the Web that students fill out and send back to the admissions office).

An exciting feature of this system for teachers is the relative ease with which individuals can publish materials on the Web. Moreover, the popularity of the Web is leading to rapid improvements in the equipment needed to produce, transmit, and receive Web materials. ESL/EFL teachers are experimenting in several different ways with the Web by (1) having their own students produce Web products, (2) putting learning materials on the Web to make them accessible to students around the world, (3) putting resource materials on the Web to share them with other teachers, (4) pulling together lists of useful Web sites in a clearinghouse that makes access easier for teachers and/or students, and (5) creating magazines and journals to publish articles and materials.

As with the other technological innovations discussed in this chapter, the unchecked growth of the Web is a result of fascinating new ideas about communication. The hardware and software that make the Web possible are important because they facilitate these new ideas. The conceptual innovations of the Web include at least the following:

1. Written text can become multimedia by the addition of pictures and sound—any piece of writing has potential to be multimedia. For example, a paper on Tennessee Williams can include links to interviews with Williams or to scenes from movies of his plays.

2. Any set of text can be connected to other sets of text through links provided by the writer. In fact, readers with even a little experience on the Web start to expect links—a new idea about what a text is supposed to contain and what a writer is supposed to do for readers.

3. The reader takes control of the reading process by moving through the links in the order that she or he prefers. In this system, the reader can have more control over the sequencing of the text than the writer.

4. The reader can be given opportunities to communicate with the writer through e-mail links embedded in the text. Consequently, the text can be seen as linking the reader to the writer; the writer becomes more approachable; readers and writers can interact over the text in immediate ways not generally possible for other types of published, written text.

5. Because of the linking feature and because of the convention that no piece of text be more than four to five pages long, texts are made up of linked chunks. This feature of text on the Web means that writers think in terms of linked chunks of material and that readers might choose to read these chunks in an order different from that originally planned by the writer.

For writing teachers, this new text will require innovative ways of teaching students about organization, content, and appropriate methods of delivery and formatting of written products. The new text is interactive, multimedia, linked, chunked, and frequently nonlinear. It is delivered by computer and formattedto fit the conventions now being adopted on the Web. Readers expect different things from this text—including links and interactions but also appearances, since Web text can involve color and images more easily than can wordprocessed text.

The Web is a delivery system for information (and entertainment). One way of imagining the Web is as a huge library full of information that can be accessed by using research tools. Because the system is so large and has so much information, users are learning to expect to have masses of information at their fingertips. To make access to this tremendous system of information possible, software has been developed to do automatic searches through databases. These research tools, called *search engines*, are so efficient and fast that our ideas about the difficulty involved in library research are changing, as are users' ideas about how fast they can expect to get information out of the system. This almost overwhelming pooling of information in a fast, efficient retrieval system is leading to new ideas about how we get information for our research and where we get it from. Additionally, we can do research using the Web from any computer that is hooked to the system—at home and at work as well as in many libraries. For this reason, the location for doing research has started to shift away from the library to the computer. In this model, the library is not a building, but a system that allows access to information through computers; the library is becoming a "virtual library" rather than a physical place. One sign of the rate of change is the speed with which the American Psychological System has had to develop referencing guidelines for materials from the Web. Although the 1994 edition of the *Publication Manual of the American Psychological Association* (4th edition) does not mention the Web, information about Web referencing can be found through the APA's Web site (http://www.nyct.net/~beads/weapas/). Composition teachers in EAP programs need to understand these changes in research methods and resources in order to prepare ESL students for the new world of academic research.

TECHNOLOGICAL INNOVATION AND ESL GRAMMAR

Like the teaching of ESL writing, the teaching of grammar is being impacted powerfully by social and conceptual technologies and by the machines that embody those technologies. Competing ideas and systems abound to provide answers to fundamental questions: What is grammar, anyway? What does it mean to "teach grammar"? What grammar is teachable and in what order to what kinds of students for what real-life purposes? What kinds of materials should be written for what media (printed books, computer software, Web documents)? In short, computers are being used to change the ways that grammar is conceived and studied.

New information is available about the characteristics of English grammar in different types of communication (e.g., Sinclair, 1987a, 1987b; Biber, 1988; Conrad,1996a and 1996b; Grabe, 1987). The innovation that is moving us from "grammar **in** context" to "grammar **from** context" is still in the early stages of the change process for ESL teachers and material writers. While massive collections of millions of words of written and spoken English have been put together for computerized analysis, the information from those studies is only gradually becoming available in usable form for language teachers. In the past, we worked to design the grammar component of a course based on educated guesses and traditions about what to include. Now we are able to make decisions more rationally based on concrete information. Information about corpus linguistics and applications to language teaching can be found at various sites on the Web, including one at the University of Birmingham (U.K.) and one focused on the *Collins Cobuild Dictionary of English*. Both are included in the reference list at the end of this book.

Another conceptual technology has already moved far along in the innovation-acceptance process and is influencing decisions about grammar in ESL programs. However the concept is interpreted, the term *task-based curriculum* has been widely accepted and even implemented. When a curriculum is based on the communication that students actually do after completing the program, decisions about the "grammar" or "language" to be learned become much easier because they can be based on analysis of materials that the learners are expected to be able to read and write or to talk about and listen to.

□ GRAMMAR CHECKERS: CONCERNS OF ESL/EFL TEACHERS ABOUT STUDENT MISUNDERSTANDING OF THE ACCURACY OF CURRENT CHECKERS

No hardware or software has influenced the teaching and learning of grammar as profoundly as wordprocessing has influenced the teaching and practice of writing. Some more-or-less clever grammar games and drills have been written, but these have failed to reach universal knowledge, much less universal acceptance. While spell checkers have influenced the accuracy of written products, grammar checkers have not been as successful in handling the errors typically made by ESL writers. At a session on responding to student writing at the International TESOL Convention in Orlando in 1997, a group of teachers voiced serious concerns about the use of grammar checkers by their ESL/EFL students: Students are getting incorrect information but believing it because they have a naïve faith that the computer must be right—and if the teacher disagrees, she must be wrong. One participant reported that she had used a grammar checker on a piece of writing and that it identified only two out of fourteen errors. Another concern voiced was that the grammar checkers give the students an unwarranted sense that their writing is grammatically perfect—if the grammar checker did not find any problems, there must not be any problems. To give a sense of the strengths and weaknesses of a grammar checker, I used the one that comes with Microsoft Word for Windows95 (version 7.0) to check the sample of student writing from Chapter 8, "Using Contrastive Analysis to Analyze ESL/EFL Student Error." Here is that passage. The four errors found by the grammar checker are marked with bold print; the recommendations made by the grammar checker are listed under the passage.

During **these 37 year**, Taiwan had changed from agriculture country to technology country. With the process of technology our people had lost our morality. Due to the hurry life and work, seldom people have time to care other people's life. So people become sophisticate. Gradually people had lost their morality. Sometime, inclination to disobey that law is increasing. **Many driver** didn't care to pay traffic fine, due to the traffic fine is not expensive. Drivers **again and again** violated. Although Taipei has been a development city, the traffic **problems still is** a major problem in overtime.

ERROR #1: Consider *this* instead of *these* OR consider *years* instead of *year*.
ERROR #2: The word *Many* does not agree with *driver*. Consider *drivers* instead of *driver*.
ERROR #3: Wordy expression. Consider *repeatedly* instead.
ERROR #4: Consider *problem* instead of *problems* OR consider *are* instead of *is*.

Errors 1, 2, and 4 are certainly agreement errors that need to be changed—and that need to become part of the regular editing done by this student until his English moves to a level that will include such agreement automatically; #3 is probably a more sophisticated word choice. However, the grammar checker found neither of the more serious problems for this writer—the lack of understanding of how English verbs work within a passage to signal time relationships and the lack of accuracy in the building of noun phrases (problems with word form and article usage).

Thus, the grammar checker would be misleading if this writer thought that his grammar included only these four errors to correct. More importantly, the system is not helpful for showing the student the areas where his writing needs editing—and areas where he needs to spend time studying to better understand how English grammar works.

While current grammar checkers seem not to offer much to either ESL/EFL writers or their teachers, work is going forward to create grammar checkers that are built around ESL errors. However, such development needs to focus on the use of English in various discourse contexts rather than attempting to check grammar more generically. For example, being told not to use the passive in technical writing is not much help for writers. In addition, rather than just "checking" and "offering corrections," spell checkers and grammar checkers are needed that will record the errors and the corrections made by students so that they and their teachers can see patterns that can be the basis of further study instead of ongoing correction for the same error. There seems to be no way to print the comments of the grammar checker provided with Microsoft Word for Windows95 (7.0); thus, the user can make the corrections suggested but has no easy, automated way to keep a record of the pattern of problems.

□ CONCORDANCING SOFTWARE: A RESEARCH AND TEACHING TOOL

Concordancing software analyzes text and provides various kinds of information about the sample. Concordancers generally provide word lists (all the words in the sample it analyzed), frequency lists (how many times each word is used), and information about the type/token ratio (a comparison of the number of individual words to the total number of words used in the text). In addition to this information about the words in the sample text, the concordancer can show the environment where any word in the text is used.

For example, a concordance of the introduction to this book (done using the software program MonoConc for Windows 1.1) shows that the introduction has 2,829 words, with the ten most frequent words being *the, and, in, to, of, we, that, about, grammar,* and *students.* Various forms of the word *grammar* are used along with the pronoun *it* to refer to "grammar" for a total of 57 times; various forms of the word *student* are used along with the pronoun *they* to refer to "student(s)" for a total of 57 times. So, we talked about students and grammar in equal quantities. Our preference for avoiding sexist language by using plural nouns and *they* lies behind another pattern revealed by the concordance software program: The single form *student* is used only in prenominal positions in phrases such as *student writing* and *student demographics.* A concordance of the word *writing* is given in Figure 9.1 to show the environment in which we used that word in the introduction.

Concordances based on published materials have been used in a number of inventive ways by teachers, with much of the interest in applying concordancing to teaching located in England, continental Europe, and Hong Kong. Flowerdew (1996) provides a useful overview of applications in teaching ESL/EFL, including work that teachers can do to improve our own knowledge of English as well as activities to use with students. The article also reviews useful information from master's degree studies done in Hong Kong that would otherwise probably be difficult to access in the U.S.

My attempts to find out about applications of concordances to teaching reveal the state of flux in information retrieval at this point in our technological history: Searches on the databases for ERIC and Linguistics Abstracts revealed very little published work and suggested a pattern of great interest in the late 1980s and early 1990s (when most of the referenced materials were published). However, a search on the Web using the keyword[6] *concordanc** quickly led to a rich assortment of references and a lively, ongoing discussion of ways to use concordancing software in teaching and research. Admittedly, not as many ESL/EFL professionals are talking about concordancing as are discussing e-mail and the Web, but the conversation continues at a level not indicated by journal publications. While concordancing has not led to the revolution in language teaching envisioned by Owen (1993), concordancing remains a tool with exciting potential if more teachers were to have access to the software—and to the other teachers who have made such interesting

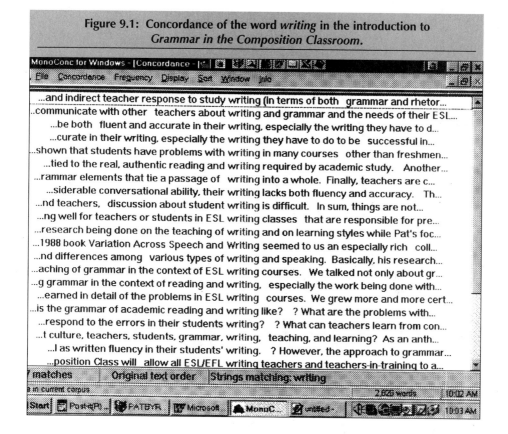

Figure 9.1: Concordance of the word *writing* in the introduction to *Grammar in the Composition Classroom*.

use of it. Perhaps the Web can help to provide that access by connecting newcomers to the experienced users of concordancing. The reference list gives the URLs for Tim Johns Data-Driven Learning Page, Michael Barlow's Corpus Linguistics Site, Sites Related to Concordancing, and a very useful course syllabus provided by Catherine Snow for her LING-468 course at Georgetown University. A clever application of this technology is behind the *LinguaCenter Grammar Safari*, a Web site that teaches learners how to analyze readings on the Web. (The *Grammar Safari's* Web address is given in the reference list.)

Concordances can also be a useful tool for looking closely at various aspects of student writing. For example, Figure 9.2 shows a concordance of the words *a, an,* and *the* from an essay written by an ESL writer on the topic of student evaluation of teachers (*an* was not used in this piece of writing). The essay has 381 words; the ten most commonly used words are *the, of, a, students, to, and, when, his, in, be,* and *about.* The concordancing software system makes it much easier for the teacher and the writer to see how the writer is using the articles in the paper—both what is done accurately and where the writer needs to do some editing (and have a better understanding of how articles are used).

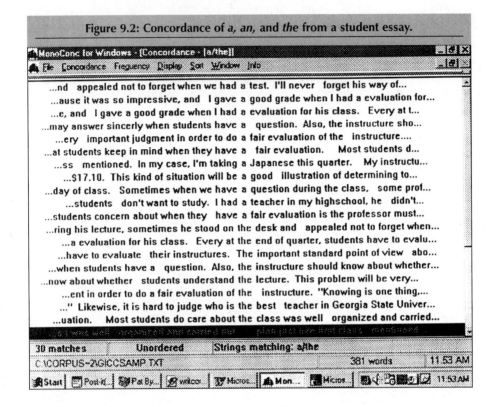

Figure 9.2: Concordance of *a*, *an*, and *the* from a student essay.

□ **PUBLICATION AND ACCURACY**

Perhaps a more immediately useful intersection between computer hardware and conceptual software is seen in the frequent comment by teachers that students who are going to publish their writing (in a student magazine, on the World Wide Web, or other venues) care more about the accuracy of their writing (e.g., Tella, 1992; Warschauer, 1995a and 1995b). Accuracy becomes a student concern rather than a teacher mandate and, as has often been pointed out, internal motivation for change is a more powerful force than external motivation (e.g., Brown, 1994).

THE LIFE CYCLE OF TECHNOLOGIES AND COMPUTERS AND THE CURRENT INNOVATION PROCESS IN U.S. HIGHER EDUCATION

Hardware and software technologies clearly have life cycles from creation to abandonment (or at least to relegation to the sidelines). For example, "new" ideas about learning and languages become "old" ideas and are replaced by updates and even radical changes. Audio-lingual is in, is modified, is out. One "hot" methodology after another arrives, is tried, has some usefulness, isn't perfect, and is modified or dropped except, perhaps, for a few determined proponents. As for changes in hardware innovations, think about how "music players" have changed—from machines that played 45 RPM records, then long-play record albums, then cassettes, then CDs—with changes not just in the delivery systems but also in our expectations for quality of sound, for length of "performance" in the delivery package, and for control of the listener over not just quality and loudness but also order of play. While some audio-historians and audiophiles still own and use the earlier technologies, those machines are no longer the mainstream approach to reproduction of music (and other sounds).

Hardware technologies involved in language learning and teaching can be analyzed in terms of the sets of features in Table 9.2. These are not divided into "positive" vs. "negative" sets but are descriptive categories.

Take, for example, television in the U.S. and outside the U.S. While many individual students studying English in the U.S. say that they have learned quite a lot of English by watching television, few courses in U.S. ESL programs make use of television in a regular, consistent fashion that has integrated television into the course and program syllabus. In the U.S., television is widely available, used mostly by individuals without textbook support, develops mostly listening skills (but also vocabulary and cultural knowledge), and while important to many students is not a "hot" topic with TESL/TEFL teachers in the U.S. Television delivery of EFL seems, however, to be quite a different technology in countries like the People's Republic of China, with its highly developed system for delivery of education by way of television. Thus, the "diffusion" of a technology (both its hardware and software systems) can proceed in divergent ways in different social, cultural, political, and even geographic locations.

Table 9.2	
Used in-class with groups of students	Used outside of class by individual students
Used to support printed textbook materials	Used without textbook support
Used in support of particular language skills	Used in support of an integrated selection of language skills
Not student controlled (teacher controlled, machine controlled, system controlled)	Student controlled
Widely available	In limited but growing use / In limited and declining use
"Hot"	"Not"

Another example of a technology applied to teaching ESL is the language laboratory with its collection of different types of machines (audio, video, tape copiers, CD-players, computers, and other machines in various combinations using many different types of software). As they were originally conceived, language labs were to provide support for the development of listening and speaking (or at least pronunciation) through activities that were generally connected to printed textbook materials. Students were supposed to come to the lab in class groups to work under the supervision of a teacher (or another qualified teacher-like person). At this point in the history of language labs, the facilities are used by either class groups or individuals (in the "library mode"). While the labs provide work that is still primarily focused on listening/speaking/vocabulary development, materials are used to work on reading, writing, and grammar—and on integrated sets of skills. Materials are still usually in support of printed textbooks. In the U.S., labs of some sort are widely available, although widely variable in their equipment and function within the program. However, in spite of the tremendous efforts of many talented lab directors, labs are not "hot." They have seldom become central to the work of the ESL program in the U.S.; teachers still are not convinced of their value, and most students would not go to the language lab voluntarily. Consider the difference at most universities between their language labs and their computer labs. Are students willing to stand in line for hours to get into the language lab? Are they willing to come at strange hours—late at night or early in the morning—to have a chance to use the language lab?

In contrast, computers and their use in language teaching are "hot" with teachers and with learners. At TESOL conferences, teachers crowd into already overcrowded rooms to see demonstrations and to share their latest CALL (Computer Assisted Language Learning) materials and ideas. Computers are used both for group work (in networked and un-networked settings) and for individual study. While most materials and activities are still aimed at grammar, reading, vocabulary, and writing, use of sound is developing rapidly and many activities integrate two or more skills (reading and writing being the most frequent combination). Because computer use and ownership is spreading rapidly in the U.S., students are also using computers at home (or work) for individual learning activities from wordprocessing to looking for information on the Web. Networked classrooms are still not commonly available, but growth in that area can be expected in most college and university settings.

Unlike the traditional language laboratory, the bulk of the work being done with computers at this point does not grow out of activities done in support of a printed textbook. For example, wordprocessing by students seems to be the most widely used application of computers in ESL, and the "typing" being done is not to carry out activities that come from a printed textbook. The other major use of computers is communication with e-mail; students communicate with their teachers and with other students (sometimes with "pen pals" from places far away). Again, e-mail is not carrying out activities that supplement a particular textbook—students are not doing grammar drills in their e-mail messages. Even in the networked setting, students and teachers are interacting over student-produced writing rather than over activities done to expand on work in a particular textbook. Although some textbooks have been written to be used along with accompanying software, these do not seem to be widely adopted, compared to the quite general expectation that ESL students will use wordprocessing to prepare papers and other assignments, especially in ESL composition courses—and compared to the expanding use of e-mail by students for class-related activities and for individual communication. The relationship between CALL materials, activities, and systems can be expected to change over time and to lead to many innovations in the ways that "textbooks" are conceived and delivered by publishers.

While many language labs have added computers to their equipment, keeping up-to-date with a rapidly changing technology is an enormous financial burden for a program or a college/university. Universities are moving rapidly away from their earlier commitment to providing computer labs for students because of the high costs of purchase, maintenance, and upgrades. This trend can be seen in two innovations: (1) requiring students to purchase or lease their own computers and providing financial systems to make such acquisition possible; and (2) requiring students (and faculty) to purchase access to the Internet through providers such as CampusMCI rather than having free access through telephones to the university's own system. Access to programs and materials on the university's mainframe computers will still be available but not through the university's own telephone lines. As a result, growing numbers of students will have their own computers and their own individual access to the Internet and to materials on the university's mainframe. The language lab is starting to migrate to the student's home or dorm room. In this scenario, one aspect of language learning on the computer is individual, outside of class study. Group work remains in the networked classroom setting rather than in the language lab. Thus, innovations in hardware (caused both by changes in the capacity of computers and by financial pressures on educational institutions) are driving conceptual and pedagogical innovations about who is studying what, with whom, and where.

For language teachers, another aspect of the shift from traditional language labs to computerized approaches to language teaching is vital. Language labs emphasized work on the spoken language. Although sound is being added and many computers are now equipped to play CD-ROM multimedia materials, computers are essentially systems for the manipulation of written text. Computers at this point in their development are about reading and writing. Even when we use them to communicate with other people using e-mail, they require that we write and read written text. Networked classrooms focus on the development of written text and on the use of e-mail–like systems for interpersonal communication. For those teachers primarily interested in the development of students' reading and writing skills, the innovations associated with computer technology are opening new possibilities. For those teachers primarily interested in the development of students' oral/aural skills, computerization of language teaching instruction is more problematic.

CONCLUSION

In ESL programs, colleges, and universities in the U.S. in the late twentieth century, remarkable innovations in teaching and learning are flowing from the computer and from the Internet and the Web. These changes are extraordinary in the rapidity with which they are being proposed and adopted in all types of institutions and programs throughout the U.S. They are powerful for the magnetic attraction that they have for many teachers and students—not just the Innovators and Early Adopters but the Early Majority have joined in the search for applications and understanding of the implications of computers and the Internet for language learning.

For students, the way they do their learning is changing both in what happens in class and in the expectation that they will enter the university with particular technical skills (and leave the university with even higher levels of technical skills when they enter the work force). Both how students learn written English (and grammar) and how they use what they have learned are going to be deeply influenced by multimedia, interactive approaches to written communication.

For teachers, the way we do our work is changing both in the classroom and in the preparation we do before class, as well as in the connections we have with students outside of the classroom. The whole definition of "contact hours" undergoes reconsideration when teachers and students are meeting by e-mail or other Internet systems rather than gathering in person in a single location. For ESL teachers, three aspects of the changes in teacher-student interaction must be considered: First, we need to know more about how language learning occurs when it takes place in a "virtual classroom." Second, we need to know how such "teaching" is going to be recognized, evaluated, and rewarded by our programs and educational institutions. Third, we take on new ESL teaching responsibilities in this setting because we must prepare ESL students in EAP programs to participate in educational activities far different from those that we currently focus on. ESL composition courses in EAP programs will need to prepare students to use writing for a new range of communication activities such as participating in e-mail discussions or interactive computerized discussion groups—as well as teach them how to prepare wordprocessed papers that have the formatting and physical appearance now expected by most U.S. professors.

The application of computer technologies to educational activities in U.S. colleges and universities is also leading to concerns about access: How will our poorer students afford computers? Are we creating a nation of the "technologically adept" and the "technologically illiterate"—another version of "haves" and "have nots"? If a college or university requires that all students have individual computers, then tuition and fees will go up—who will be cut off from college education because of these higher costs? If colleges and universities do not require all students to become effective users of computers and the Internet, which of its graduates will be left behind in a job market that expects computer skills? If a college or university requires all students to have computers, how is this requirement applied to short-term students in the institution's ESL program? How can a self-supporting ESL program keep up financially with technological change? How will international students who have not before had access to typewriters learn quickly to use wordprocessing (since their university teachers will expect that all papers and written assignments will be prepared in wordprocessed format)? What are the responsibilities of TESL/TEFL teacher education programs to prepare teachers for applications of technology to teaching ESL/EFL? Discussion of the many problems and some solutions can be found in the popular press as well as in special academic publications such as *TESOL Matters* (e.g., Lohr, 1996; Murray, 1996; "The Widening Gap," 1996). Discussion of these issues is also taking place on-line in discussion groups such as TESL-L and various groups focused on CALL—a use of new communication systems that gives more of us opportunities to participate in the discussion than ever possible in the past.

These are not simple issues; they will be with us for a long time. Whatever the ultimate solutions, computer technology is changing education and communication not just in the U.S. but throughout much of the rest of the world. Thus, we cannot refuse to grapple with equality-of-access issues, curriculum changes, changes in what "materials" are and how they are accessed, changes in teacher-student relationships, and other results of computerization. By listening carefully to our Innovators and seeing how their ideas work in the teaching and materials of our First Adopters, and by being supportive of the efforts of those First Adopters, we can avoid just being swept along by technological innovation and can take active roles to influence the changes in our professional lives as curriculum coordinators, materials developers, and teachers.

NOTES

1. In Chapter A, the learning styles and problems of modern "ear" learners are presented in contrast to the learning styles and problems of modern "eye" learners.

2. *Hardware* is generally used to refer to the machinery aspect of technology; in contrast *software* is the program that runs the machine or runs on the machine. So, my computer consists of the hardware (machinery—central processing unit, keyboard, monitor, and so forth) and the software programs that run the machine (Windows95, DOS, and such) and the software programs that are run on the machine (Microsoft Word, WordPerfect, and many others).

3. See the References for a Web address to get information about the *Writing to Read 2000* system from IBM. A search on ERIC showed no recent research on the system.

4. ESL students studying in the U.S. have complained for years about doing group work with other ESL students—and about their limited opportunities for encounters with native speakers of English—but we have generally ignored those complaints. In a student-focused environment, we should perhaps listen a bit more to the ideas our students have about what they want to learn—and with whom.

Providing the solutions might be beyond our abilities and resources but we do need to pay more attention to the learners' ideas about their needs.

5. "Synchronous discussions" are those that take place with everyone writing and "talking" at the same time. "Asynchronous" communication is like that in the usual use of e-mail—or old-fashioned letters—when the participants are not together at the same time.

6. The * is used in keyword searches to tell the system to look for all words that begin with the first part of the word and all other possible endings: *concordances, concordancing, concordance,* etc.

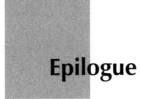

Epilogue

Joy Reid and Patricia Byrd

We come to the end of *Grammar in the Composition Classroom* as we were at the beginning—talking, reading, and thinking about ways to help ESL students become better academic readers and writers. When we began teaching ESL back in the 1960s, our profession was still a new one without a very clear sense of its purposes and methods. Over the years, TESL has matured into a true profession based on a substantial and ever-expanding body of knowledge about language learning and language teaching. We have realized that ESL is a cover term for many different types of learning and uses of English by nonnative speakers. We have discovered that English changes in different contexts as it is used to achieve differing goals. In addition, we have investigated differences in students' approaches to successful language learning. We have come to see that learners need programs to prepare them for their particular goals: that English for the job skills development of adult refugees has important differences in purpose and language from English for academic purposes.

An unfortunate reality about our profession is that we still have with us residues of past practices that were based on ideas that are no longer generally supported but are so ingrained that we have trouble even seeing them anymore. The way that we deal with grammar in ESL programs is the prime example of this disconnection between our current knowledge and our current practice. We know that students need to work with authentic materials and authentic activities that prepare them for their real-life uses of English. We know that grammar not only should be but can be taught in context. We know that students need to be both accurate and fluent in their writing, as well as their listening and speaking. Yet many teachers act as if all students were learning the materials in the same ways.

Many textbooks and teachers give little apparent thought to the ultimate uses for which the students are learning the grammar of written English. In short, we continue to work from curricular designs that make effective teaching and learning almost impossible. Throughout the U.S., teachers and curriculum coordinators are struggling with designs that are not working for them or their students.

Rather than patching up the old pattern by trying yet another shift of grammar from this place to that place, we hope that teachers and administrators will join us in our belief that fundamental changes are needed. We hope that the ideas and information provided in *Grammar in the Composition Classroom*—in our essays, in the reference list, and ultimately on our Web site—will help us to take our profession to the next stage in which we have more congruence between our ideals and our performance in the classroom. Finally, there can be no "finally" for the conversations that we have been having; we must continue to talk together, to carry out research, to think about the implications of that research, and to implement required changes in curriculum, materials, and teaching methods. To this end, we invite teachers, curriculum coordinators, and materials writers to join us in the work that lies ahead.

REFERENCES

Al-Jabouri, A. (1984). The role of repetition in Arabic argumentative discourse. In J. Swales & H. Mustafa (Eds.), *English for specific purposes in the Arabic world* (pp. 99–117). Birmingham: University of Aston, Language Studies Unit.

Arndt, V. (1993). Response to writing: Using feedback to inform the writing process. In M. Brock & L. Walters (Eds.), *Teaching composition around the Pacific Rim: Politics and pedagogy* (pp. 90–116). Clevedon, UK: Multicultural Matters.

Barasch, R., & James, C. (1994). *Beyond the monitor model: Comments on current theory and practice in second language acquisition.* Boston: Heinle & Heinle Publishers.

Bardovi-Harlig, K. (1996). Tense and aspect in (con)text. In T. Miller (Ed.), *Grammar and discourse. The Journal of TESOL France, 3,* 19-33.

Barker, T., & Kemp, F. (1990). Network theory: A postmodern pedagogy for the writing classroom. In Carolyn Handa (Ed.), *Computers & community: Teaching composition in the 21st century.* Port Smith, NH: Boynton-Cook Publishers.

Bank of English. (March 24, 1997). URL:
   <http://titania.cobuild.collins.co.uk/boe_info.html>

Barlow, M. (March 24, 1997). *Corpus Linguistics.* URL:
   <http://www.ruf.rice.edu/~barlow/corpus.html>

Bates, L., Lane, J., & Lange, E. (1993). *Writing clearly: Responding to ESL compositions.* Boston: Heinle & Heinle Publishers.

Bazerman, C. (1988). *Shaping written knowledge: The genre and activity of the experimental article in science.* Madison: University of Wisconsin Press.

Becker, R. (1995). The second language writing of Chinese ESL students: Transfer and writing development. *Dissertation Abstracts International 56*(9), 3485A.

Belcher, D., & Braine, G. (Eds.) (1995). *Academic writing in a second language: Essays on research and pedagogy.* Norwood, NJ: Ablex.

Bellot, J. (1580/1967). *The Englishe Scholemaister. Conteynjng many profitable preceptes for the naturall borne french men, and other straungers that have their French tongue, to attayne the true pronouncing of the Englishe tongue.* Made, and sette forth, by I. B. Gen. Ca. London: Thomas Purfotte (Scolar Press 51, 1967).

Bellot, J. (1586/1969). *Familiar Dialogves, for the Instruction of them, that be desirous to learne to speake English, and perfectlye to pronounce the same.* Set forth by James Bellot Gentleman of Caen. London: Thomas Vautrollier (Scolar Press 141, 1969).

Bennett, J. (1995). *Applications of Kolb's learning styles inventory to the training of trainers. A Workshop.* Washington, DC: NAFSA, Association of International Educators.

Bennett, M. (1996, June/July). Intercultural communication in a multicultural society. *TESOL Matters 6,* p. 3.

Biber, D. (1988). *Variation across speech and writing.* Cambridge: Cambridge University Press.

Biber, D., Conrad, S., & Reppen, R. (1994). Corpus-based approaches to issues in applied linguistics. *Applied Linguistics 15*(2), 169–189.

Bolter, J. (1991). *Writing space: The computer, hypertext, and the history of writing.* Hillsdale, NJ: Lawrence Erlbaum Associates, Publishers.

Britton, B. K., Gulgoz, S., & Glynn, S. (1993). Impact of good and poor writing on learners: Research and theory. In B. K. Britton, A. Woodward, & M. Binkley (Eds.), *Learning from textbooks: Theory and practice* (pp. 1–46). Hillsdale, NJ: Lawrence Erlbaum Associates, Publishers.

Brock, M., & Walters, L. (Eds.) (1994). *Teaching composition around the Pacific Rim.* Clevedon, UK: Multilingual Matters.

Brookes, A., & Grundy, P. (1990). *Writing for study purposes: A teacher's guide to developing individual writing skills.* Cambridge: Cambridge University Press.

Brown, H. D. (1973). Affective variables in second language acquisition. *Language Learning 23*, 231–244.

Brown, H. D. (1994). *Principles of language learning and teaching* (3rd ed.). Englewood Cliffs, NJ: Prentice Hall Regents.

Brown, J. (1994). *Teaching by principles: An interactive approach to language pedagogy.* Englewood Cliffs, NJ: Prentice Hall Regents.

Bruce, B., Peyton, J., & Batson, T. (1993). *Network-based classrooms: Promises and realities.* Cambridge: Cambridge University Press.

Byleen, E. (1986). *Advanced writing for Vietnamese ESL students.* Unpublished manuscript, University of Kansas. Available on URL:
<http://www.gsu.edu/~wwwesl/jegw/byleen.htm>

Byrd, P., & Benson, B. (1992). *Applied English grammar.* Boston: Heinle & Heinle Publishers.

Byrd, P. (1995). Issues in the writing and publication of grammar textbooks. In P. Byrd (Ed.), *Material writer's guide* (pp. 45–63). Boston: Heinle & Heinle Publishers.

Byrd, P. (1995, March). *Nouns without articles.* Paper presented at the convention of International TESOL, Long Beach, CA.

Byrd, P. (1994). Writing grammar textbooks: Theory and practice. *System 22*(2), 243–255.

Canseco, G., & Byrd, P. (1989). The writing required of graduate students in business administration. *TESOL Quarterly 23*(2), 305–316.

Carrell, P. (1987). Content and formal schemata in ESL reading. *TESOL Quarterly 21*(3), 461–481.

Carrell, P., & Carson, J. (1997). Extensive and intensive reading in an EAP setting. *English for Specific Purposes 16*(1), 47–60.

Carson, J. (1992). Literacy demands of the undergraduate curriculum. *Reading Research and Instruction 31*(4), 25–50.

Carson, J., Chase, N., Gibson, S., & Hargrove, M. (1992). Literacy demands of the undergraduate curriculum. *Reading Research and Instruction 31*(4), 25–50.

Carson, J., & Leki, I. (1993). *Reading in the composition classroom: Second language perspectives.* Boston: Heinle & Heinle Publishers.

Celce-Murcia, M. (Ed.). (1991). *Teaching English as a second or foreign language* (2nd ed.). Boston: Newbury House/Heinle & Heinle Publishers.

Chantrill, R. (Ed.) (March 24, 1997). CALLing all EFL/ESL teachers.
<http://www.cltr.uuq.oz.au:8000/~richardc/index.html>
[*Sites Related to Concordancing* is a subset of this site.]

Chen-yu, F. (1981). *Teaching advanced English composition to Chinese college students.* Unpublished master's thesis, California State University, Fresno.

Churcher, P. B., & Lawton, J. H. (1987). Predation by domestic cats in an English village. *The Zoological Record 212*, 439–455.

Cohen, A., & Calvalcanti, M. (1990). Feedback on compositions: Teacher and student verbal reports. In B. Kroll (Ed.), *Second language writing: Research insights for the classroom* (pp. 155–177). Cambridge: Cambridge University Press.

Collins Cobuild Direct. (March 24, 1997). URL: <http://titania.cobuild.collins.co.uk/direct_info.html>

Connor, U. (1996). *Contrastive rhetoric: Cross-cultural aspects of second-language writing.* Cambridge: Cambridge University Press.

Connor, U., & Kramer, M. (1995). Writing from sources: Case studies in graduate students in business management. In D. Belcher & G. Braine (Eds.), *Academic writing in a second language: Essays on research and pedagogy* (pp. 155–182). Norwood, NJ: Ablex.

Conrad, S. (1996a). *Academic discourse in two disciplines: Professional writing and student development in biology and history.* Dissertation. Northern Arizona University. (UMI order no: AAI9625751)

Conrad, S. (1996b). Investigating academic texts with corpus-based techniques: An example from biology. *Linguistics and Education 8,* 299–326.

Crandall, J. (1985). *The language of mathematics: The English barrier.* (Project abstract for the Fund for the Improvement of Postsecondary Education ESL/Math Project). Washington, DC: Center for Applied Linguistics.

Crandall, J. (1995). The why, what, and how of ESL reading instruction: Some guidelines for writers of ESL reading textbooks. In P. Byrd (Ed.), *Material writer's guide* (pp. 79–94). Boston: Heinle & Heinle Publishers.

Currie, C., & Beaubien, R. (1996). Framing the English article: The influence of time frame on article use in academic discourse. *Journal of English Grammar on the Web.* Atlanta: Georgia State University. URL: <http://www.gsu.edu/~wwwesl/jegw/issue1>

Dakin, J. (1973). *The language laboratory and modern language teaching.* New York: Longman.

Danesi, J. (1993). Whither Contrastive Analysis? *Canadian Modern Language Review 51,* 37–46.

Danesi, J., & Di Pietro, R. J. (1991). *Contrastive analysis for the contemporary second language classroom.* Toronto: OISE Press.

Dunn, R., & Griggs, S. A. (1995). *Multiculturalism and learning styles: Teaching and counseling adolescents.* Westport, CT: Praeger.

Ellis, R. (1994). *The study of second language acquisition.* Oxford: Oxford University Press.

Dykstra, P. D. (1997). The patterns of language: Perspectives on teaching writing. *Teaching English in the Two-Year College 24*(2), 136–144.

Fernandez, S. (1995). New malady hits computer users: "Webaholism." *Lawrence Journal-World* (November 28, 3A).

Ferris, D. (1995a). Student reactions to teacher response in multiple-draft composition classrooms. *TESOL Quarterly 29*(1), 33–53.

Ferris, D. (1995b). Teaching students to self-edit. *TESOL Journal 4*(4), 18–22.

Ferris, D. (1997). The influence of teacher commentary on student revision. *TESOL Quarterly 31*(2), 315–339.

Ferris, D., & Tagg, T. (1996). Academic oral communication needs of EAP learners: What subject-matter instructors actually require. *TESOL Quarterly 30*(1), 31–58.

Firsten, R., & Killian, P. (1994). *Troublesome English: A teaching grammar for ESOL instructors.* Englewood Cliffs, NJ: Prentice Hall Regents.

Flowerdew, J. (1996). Concordancing in language learning. In Martha Pennington (Ed.), *The Power of CALL* (pp. 97–113). Houston, TX: Athelstan.

Fox, H. (1994). *Listening to the world: Cultural issues in academic writing.* Urbana, IL: National Council of Teachers of English.

Fu, D. (1995). *"My trouble is English": Asian students and the American dream.* Portsmouth, NH: Boynton & Cook.

Gass, S. (1988). Second language acquisition and linguistic theory: The role of language transfer. In S. Flynn & W. O'Neill (Eds.), *Linguistic theory and second language analysis,* (pp. 384–403). Dordrecht: Kluver.

Goldstein, L., & Conrad, S. (1990). Student input and negotiation of meaning in ESL writing conferences. *TESOL Quarterly 24*(3), 443–460.

Grabe, W. (1987). Contrastive rhetoric and text-type research. In Ulla Connor & Robert Kaplan (Eds.), *Writing across languages: Analysis of L2 text* (pp. 115–137). Reading, MA: Addison-Wesley Publishing Company.

Grabe, W., & Kaplan, R. B. (1996). *Theory and practice of writing.* New York: Longman.

Gregg, K. (1994). Krashen's theory, acquisition theory, and theory. In R. M. Barasch & C. Vaughn James (Eds.), *Beyond the monitor model: Comments on current theory and practice in second language acquisition* (pp. 37–55). Boston: Heinle & Heinle Publishers.

Gundersen, E. (1996). *Publishing and the adoption of innovations.* A presentation to authors and staff at Heinle & Heinle. September 21. Boston: Heinle & Heinle Publishers.

Haas, C. (1994). Learning to read biology: One student's rhetorical development in college. *Written Communication 11*(1), 43–84.

Hacker, T. (1996). The effect of teacher conferences on peer response discourse. *Teaching English in the Two-Year College 23*(2), 112–136.

Hamp-Lyons, L. (Ed.) (1991). *Assessing second language writing in academic contexts.* Norwood, NJ: Ablex.

Hamp-Lyons, L. (1997). More thoughts on academic naming practices. *English for Specific Purposes 16*(1), 72–73.

Hatch, E. (1978). Discourse analysis and second language acquisition. In E. Hatch (Ed.), *Second language acquisition: A book of readings* (pp. 402–435). Rowley, MA: Newbury House.

Hatim, B. (1991). The pragmatics of argumentation in Arabic: The rise and fall of text type. *Text II,* 189–199.

Hayden, R., Pilgrim, D., & Haggard, A. (1956). *Mastering American English.* Englewood Cliffs, NJ: Prentice Hall.

Healy, D., & Bosher, S. (1992). ESL tutoring: Bridging the gap between curriculum-based and writing center models of peer tutoring. *College ESL 2*(2), 25–32.

Hedgcock, J., & Lefkowitz, N. (1994). Feedback on feedback: Assessing learner receptivity to teacher response in L2 composing. *Journal of Second Language Writing 3,* 141–163.

Hedge, T. (1988). *Writing.* Oxford: Oxford University Press.

Hinds, J. (1987). Reader vs. writer responsibility: A new typology. In U. Connor & R. B. Kaplan (Eds.), *Writing across languages: Analysis of L2 text* (pp. 141–152). Reading, MA: Addison-Wesley.

Hinkel, E. (1995). The use of modal verbs as a reflection of cultural values. *TESOL Quarterly 29*(2), 325–341.

Hirsch, L. (1996). Mainstreaming ESL students: A counterintuitive perspective. *College ESL 6*(2), 12–26.

Horowitz, D. (1986). What professors require: Academic tasks for the ESL classroom. *TESOL Quarterly 20*(3), 445–462.

Howatt, A. P. R. (1984). *A history of English language teaching.* Oxford: Oxford University Press.

Hyland, K. (1994). Hedging in academic writing and EAP textbooks. *English for Specific Purposes 13*(3), 239–256.

Hyon, S. (1996). Genre in three traditions: Implications for ESL. *TESOL Quarterly 30*(4), 693–722.

Indrasuta, C. (1988). Narrative styles of writing of Thai and American students. In A. Purves (Ed.), *Writing across languages and cultures: Issues in contrastive rhetoric* (pp. 206–226). Newbury Park, CA: Sage Publications.

Jackson, A., & Day, D. (1978). *Tools and how to use them: An illustrated encyclopedia.* New York: Alfred A. Knopf.

Jacoby, S., Leech, D., & Holten, C. (1995). A genre-based developmental writing course for undergraduate ESL science majors. In D. Belcher & G. Braine (Eds.), *Academic writing in a second language: Essays on research and pedagogy* (pp. 351–373). Norwood, NJ: Ablex.

James, C. (1980). *Contrastive analysis.* Singapore: Longman Singapore Publishers (Pte) Ltd.

James, C. (1994). Don't shoot my dodo: On the resilience of contrastive and error analysis. *IRAL 32*(3), 179–200.

Janopoulos, M. (1992). University faculty tolerance of NS and NNS writing errors. *Journal of Second Language Writing 1*(2), 109–121.

Johns, A. (1991). Interpreting an English competency examination: The frustrations of an ESL science student. *Journal of Written Communication 8*, 379–401.

Johns, T. (March 24, 1997) Tim Johns Data-Driven Learning Page. URL: <http://sun1.bham.ac.uk:80/johnstf/timconc.htm>

Johnson, D. (1985). Error gravity: Communicative effect of language errors in academic writing. *BAAL Newsletter 24*, 46–47.

Johnson, P. (1981). Effects on reading comprehension of language complexity and cultural background of the text. *TESOL Quarterly 15*, 169–181.

Jordan, J. (1997). What's in a name? Consistency! [or, Advice to authors from a bibliographer]. *English for Specific Purposes 16*(1), 71–72.

Kamimoto, F., Shimura, A., & Kellermann, F. (1992). A second–language classic reconsidered: The case of Schachter's avoidance. *Second Language Research 8*(3), 251–277.

Kaplan, R. B. (1966/1987). Cultural thought patterns revisited. In U. Connor & R. B. Kaplan (Eds.), *Writing across languages: Analysis of L2 text* (pp. 9–22). Newbury Park, CA: Sage Publications.

Kaplan, R., & Shaw, P. (1984). *Exploring academic discourse: A textbook for advanced-level ESL reading and writing students.* Rowley, MA: Newbury House Publishers.

Kellermann, E. (1984). The empirical evidence for the influence of the L1 in interlanguage. In A. Davies, C. Criper, & A. Howatt (Eds.), *Interlanguage* (pp. 98–122). Edinburgh, Scotland: Edinburgh University Press.

Kemp, F. (1993). The origins of ENFI, network theory, and computer-based collaborative writing instruction at the University of Texas. In B. Bruce, J. Peyton, & T. Batson (Eds.), *Network-based classrooms: Promises and realities* (pp. 161–180). Cambridge: Cambridge University Press.

Killiam, C., & Watson, B. (1983). *Thirteen language profiles: Practical application of contrastive analysis for teachers of English as a second language.* Vancouver, BC: Vancouver Community College (King Edward Campus).

Knox-Quinn, C. (1996). Authentic classroom experiences: Anonymity, mystery, and improvisation in synchronous writing environment. URL:
<http://www.cwrl.utexas.edu/~cwrl/vln2/article2/aspect1.html>

Koch, B. J. (1983). Presentation as proof: The language of Arabic rhetoric. *Anthropological Linguistics 25*, 46–60.

Krashen, S. D. (1982). *Principles and practice in second language acquisition.* Oxford: Pergamon.

Kroll, B. (1990a). *Second language writing: Research insights for the classroom.* Cambridge: Cambridge University Press.

Kroll, B. (1990b). The rhetoric-syntax split: Designing a curriculum for ESL students. *Journal of Basic Writing 9*(1), 40–55.

Kutz, E., Groden, S.Q., & Zamel, V. (1993). *The discovery of competence: Teaching and learning with diverse student writers.* Portsmouth, NH: Boynton/Cook Heinemann.

Larsen-Freeman, D. (1991). Teaching grammar. In M. Celce-Murcia (Ed.), *Teaching English as a second or foreign language* (pp. 279–296). New York: Newbury House.

Larsen-Freeman, D., & Long, M. (1992). *An introduction to second language acquisition research.* New York: Longman.

Lasarenko, J. (1996). Collaborative learning in a networked classroom. URL:
<http://leahi.kcc.hawaii.edu/org/tcc_conf/lasarenko.html>

Leki, I. (1990). Coaching from the margins: Issues in written response. In B. Kroll (Ed.), *Second language writing: Research insights for the classroom* (pp. 57–68). Cambridge: Cambridge University Press.

Leki, I. (1991a). The preferences of ESL students for error correction in college-level writing classes. *Foreign Language Annals 24*(3), 203–218.

Leki, I. (1991b). Twenty-five years of contrastive rhetoric: Text analysis and writing pedagogies. *TESOL Quarterly 25*(1), 123–143.

Leki, I. (1992). *Understanding ESL writers: A guide for teachers.* New York: St. Martin's Press.

Leki, I., & Carson, J. (1997). "Completely different worlds": EAP and the writing experiences of ESL students in university courses. *TESOL Quarterly 31*(1), 39–70.

Li, X. M. (1996). *"Good writing" in cross-cultural context.* Albany: State University of New York Press.

LinguaCenter Grammar Safari (1996). URL:
<http://deil.lang.uiuc.edu/web.pages/grammarsafari.html>

Lohr, S. (1996, October 21). Weighing costs of net access for every school and library. *New York Times CyberTimes* (URL: <http://www.nytimes.com>)

Long, M., & Crookes, G. (1992). Three approaches to task-based syllabus design. *TESOL Quarterly 26*(1), 27–56.

Lotherington-Woloszyn, H. (1993). *Do simplified texts simplify language comprehension for ESL learners?* (Eric No. ED371583. Clearinghouse No. FL022054)

Love, A. (1993). Lexico-grammatical features of geology textbooks: Process and product revisited. *English for Specific Purposes 12*, 197–218.

MacDonald, S. (1992). *Professional academic writing in the humanities and social sciences.* Carbondale, IL: Southern Illinois University Press.

McCarthy, M. (1991). *Discourse analysis for language teachers.* Cambridge: Cambridge University Press.

McLaughlin, B. (1987). *Theories of second language learning.* London: Edward Arnold.

Master, P. (1987). Generic *the* in *Scientific American. English for Specific Purposes* 6(3), 165–186.

Master, P. (1990). Teaching the English articles as a binary system. *TESOL Quarterly 24*(3), 461–478.

Meisel, J. (1983). Transfer as a second language strategy. *Language and Communication 3*, 11–46.

Meyer, L. (1996). The contribution of genre theory to theme-based EAP: Navigating foreign fiords. *TESL Canada 13*(2), 33–45.

Montaño-Harmon, M. (1991). Discourse features of written Mexican Spanish: Current research in contrastive rhetoric and its implications. *Hispania* (May), 417–425.

Morcos, D. A. (1986). *A linguistic study of coordination and subordination in the writing of Arabic speaking ESL students.* Unpublished master's thesis, University of New Orleans, Louisiana.

Myers, G. (1991). Lexical cohesion and specialized knowledge in science and popular science texts. *Discourse Processes 14*, 1–26.

Myers, G. A. (1992). Textbooks and the sociology of scientific knowledge. *English for Specific Purposes 11*, 3–17.

Murray, D. (1996, August/September). President's message: Technology is driving the future . . . Part II. *TESOL Matters*, p. 3.

O'Brian, D., & Krause, K. (1996). *Argumentative writing in English among students of the Henan Province, China.* Paper presented at the 9th World Congress of Comparative Education (July), Sydney.

Odlin, T. (1989). *Language transfer: Cross-linguistic influence in language learning.* Cambridge: Cambridge University Press.

Osbourne, A., & Dowd, J. (1987). Teaching Chinese students to write essay examinations and papers. *TECFORS 10*(3 and 4), 1–5.

Ostler, S. (1987). English in parallels: A study of Arabic style. In U. Connor & R. B. Kaplan (Eds.), *Writing across languages: Analysis of L2 text* (pp. 169–185).

Ostler, S. (1996). *The contrastive rhetorics of Arabic, English, Japanese, and Spanish.* Unpublished paper, Bowling Green State University, Ohio.

Owen, C. (1993). Corpus-based grammar and the Heineken effect: lexico-grammatical description for language learners. *Applied Linguistics 14*(2), 167–187.

Oxford, R. (1990). *Language learning strategies: What every teacher should know.* New York: Newbury House Publishers.

Oxford, R. (Ed.) (1997). *Language learning strategies around the world.* Manoa: University of Hawaii Press.

Oxford, R., & Crookall, D. (1990). Vocabulary learning: A critical analysis of techniques. *TESL Canada Journal 7*(2), 9–30.

Peitzman, F., & Gadda, G. (Eds.) (1994). *With different eyes: Insights into teaching language minority students across the disciplines.* Reading, MA: Addison-Wesley.

Peyton, J. K., & Staton, J. (1993). *Dialogue journals in the multilingual classroom: Building language fluency and writing skills through written interaction.* Norwood, NJ: Ablex.

Pica, T. (1983a). Adult acquisition of English as a second language under different conditions of exposure. *Language Learning 33*(4), 465–497.

Pica, T. (1983b). The article in American English: What the textbooks don't tell us. In N. Wolfson & E. Judd (Eds.), *Sociolinguistics and language acquisition* (pp. 222–233). Rowley, MA: Newbury House.

Purves, A. (1986). On the nature and formation of interpretive and rhetorical communities. In T. N. Postlethwaite (Ed.), *International educational research: Papers in honor of Torsten Husen* (pp. 45–64). Oxford: Pergamon.

Quirk, R., Greenbaum, S., Leech, G., & Svartvik, J. (1985). *A comprehensive grammar of the English language.* London: Longman.

Reid, J. (1988). *Quantitative differences in English prose written by Arabic, Chinese, Spanish, and English students.* Unpublished doctoral dissertation, Colorado State University.

Reid, J. (1989). ESL expectations in higher education: The expectations of the academic audience. In D. Johnson & D. Roen (Eds.), *Richness in writing: Empowering ESL students* (pp. 220–234). New York: Longman.

Reid, J. (1993). *Teaching ESL writing.* Englewood Cliffs, NJ: Prentice Hall–Regents.

Reid, J. (1994). Responding to ESL students' texts: The myths of appropriation. *TESOL Quarterly 28*(2), 273–292.

Reid, J. (Ed.) (1995). *Learning styles in the ESL/EFL classroom.* Boston: Heinle & Heinle Publishers.

Reid, J. (1996). A learning styles unit for the intermediate ESL/EFL writing classroom. *TESOL Journal 6*(1), 42–47.

Reid, S. (1992). *The Prentice-Hall guide to college writing* (2nd ed.). Englewood Cliffs, NJ: Simon & Schuster.

Reid, S. (1995). *The Prentice–Hall guide for college writers* (3rd ed.). Englewood Cliffs, NJ: Simon and Schuster.

Ricento, T. (1987). *Aspects of coherence in English and Japanese expository prose.* Unpublished doctoral dissertation, University of California, Los Angeles.

Richards, J. (1971). Error analysis and second language strategies. *Sciences 17*, 12–22.

Rifkin, B., & Roberts, F. (1995). Error gravity: A critical review of research design. *Language Learning 45*(3), 511–537.

Robinette, B. W., & Schacther, J. (Eds.). (1983). *Second language learning: Contrastive analysis, error analysis, and related aspects.* Ann Arbor: University of Michigan Press.

Rogers, E. M. (1962). *Diffusion of innovations.* New York: The Free Press of Glencoe.

Rogers, E. M. (1983). *Diffusion of innovations* (3rd ed.). New York: The Free Press, A Division of Macmillan Publishing Co., Inc.

Rogers, E. M. (1995). *Diffusion of innovations* (4th ed.). New York: The Free Press.

Ross, S., & Long, M. (1993). *Modifications that preserve language and content.* (ERIC No. ED371576. Clearinghouse No. FL022047)

Sa'Adeddin, M. (1989). Text development and Arabic–English negative interference. *Applied Linguistics 10*, 36–51.

Santos, T. (1988). Professors' reactions to the academic writing of non-native speaking students. *TESOL Quarterly 18*(4), 671–688.

Schachter, J. (1974). An error in error analysis. *Language Learning 24*(2), 205–214.

Schachter, J., & Celce-Murcia, M. (1977). Some reservations concerning error analysis. *TESOL Quarterly 11*, 441–451.

Schiffrin, D. (1981). Tense variation in narrative. *Language 57*(1), 45–62.

Scott, S., & Stoller, F. (1996). Creating a suitable word processing manual for ESL students. *College ESL 6*(2), 39–49.

Selinker, L. (1969). Language transfer. *General Linguistics 9*, 67–92.

Selinker, L. (1972). Interlanguage. *International Review of Applied Linguistics 10*, 209–231.

Selinker, L. (1992). *Rediscovering interlanguage*. Harlow, England: Longman.

Sharwood-Smith, M. (1983). Cross-linguistic aspects of second language acquisition. *Applied Linguistics 4*, 192–199.

Sinclair, J. (1987a). Introduction. In J. Sinclair (Ed.), *Collins Cobuild English language dictionary*. London: Collins.

Sinclair, J. (Ed.) (1987b). *Looking up*. London: Collins.

Sinclair, J. (1991). *Corpus, concordance, collocation*. Oxford: Oxford University Press.

Sites Related to Concordancing. (March 24, 1997). URL:
    <http://www.cltr.uq.oz.au:8000/~richardc/concord.html>

Slatin, J. (1992). Is there a class in this text? Creating knowledge in the electronic classroom. In Edward Barrett (Ed.), *Sociomedia: Multimedia, hypermedia, and the social construction of knowledge* (pp. 27–51). Cambridge, MA: MIT Press.

Snow, C. (March 24, 1997). *Tutorial: Concordances and corpora*. URL:
    <http://www.georgetown.edu/cball/corpora/tutorial.html>

Stockton, S. (1995). Writing in history: Narrating the subject of time. *Written Communication 12*(1), 47–73.

Stoller, F. (1994). The diffusion of innovations in intensive ESL programs. *Applied Linguistics 15*(3), 300–327.

Straub, R. (1996). The concept of control in teacher response: Defining the variables of "directive" and "facilitative" commentary. *College Composition and Communication 47*(2), 223–251.

Swales, J. (1990a). *Genre analysis: English in academic and research settings*. Cambridge: Cambridge University Press.

Swales, J. (1990b). Nonnative speaker graduate engineering students and their intro ductions: Global coherence and local management. In U. Connor & A. J. Johns (Eds.), *Coherence in writing: Research and pedagogical perspectives* (pp. 189–207). Alexandria, VA: TESOL.

Swales, J., & Feak, C. (1994). *Academic writing for graduate students: A course for nonnative speakers of English*. Ann Arbor: University of Michigan Press.

Swan, M., & Smith, B. (1987). *Learner English: A teacher's guide to interference and other problems*. Cambridge: Cambridge University Press.

Tella, S. (1992). *Talking shop via e-mail: A thematic and linguistic analysis of electronic mail communication*. Research Report 99. Helsinki, Finland: Department of Teacher Education, University of Helsinki.

Tsao, F-F. (1983). Linguistics and written discourse in particular languages: Contrastive studies: English and Chinese (Mandarin). In R. B. Kaplan (Ed.), *Annual review of applied linguistics: Linguistics and written discourse* (pp. 99–117). Rowley, MA: Newbury House.

Vann, R., Lorenz, F. D., & Meyer, D. E. (1991). Error gravity: Faculty response to errors in the written discourse of nonnative speakers of English. In L. Hamp-Lyons (Ed.), *Assessing second language writing in academic contexts* (pp. 181–195). Norwood, NJ: Ablex.

Vann, R., Meyer, D. E., & Lorenz, F. D. (1984). Error gravity: A study of faculty opinion of ESL errors. *TESOL Quarterly 18*(3), 427–440.

Vogt, G. L. (1995). *The solar system: Facts and exploration*. New York: Twenty-First Century Books, A Division of Henry Holt and Company. Scientific American Sourcebooks.

Wallace, D. L. (1996). From intentions to text: Articulating initial intentions for writing. *Research in the Teaching of English 30*(2), 182–219.

Warschauer, M. (Ed.) (1995a). *E-mail for English teaching*. Alexandria, VA: TESOL.

Warschauer, M. (Ed.) (1995b). *Virtual connections*. Honolulu, HI: University of Hawaii Press.

White, R., & Arndt, V. (1991). *Process writing*. London: Longman.

Widening gap in higher education: A special report. (1996, June 14). *Chronicle of Higher Education*, pp. A10–A17.

Wong, S. (1992). Contrastive rhetoric: An exploration of proverbial references in Chinese student L1 and L2 writing. *Journal of Intensive English Studies 6*(Spring/Fall), 71–90.

Writing to Read 2000. IBM Corporation. URL: <http://www.solutions.ibm.com/k12/solutions/tlc/rla/wtr2000.html>

Yano, Y., Long, M., & Ross, S. (1994). The effects of simplified and elaborated texts on foreign language reading comprehension. *Language Learning 44*:2, 189–219.

Young, D. (1991). *Reading strategies and texts: A research study on the question of native and non-native reading strategies and authentic versus edited texts*. (ERIC No. ED338035. Clearinghouse No. FL019651)

Zobl, H. (1980). Developmental and transfer errors: Their common bases and (possibly) differential effects on subsequent learning. *TESOL Quarterly 14*(4), 469–479.

Zydatiss, W. (1986). Grammatical categories and their text functions—Some implications for the content of reference grammars. In G. Leitner (Ed.), *The English reference grammar* (pp. 140–155). Tubingen: Max Niemeyer Verlag.

INDEX